THE THAMES AND HUDSON MANUALS

GENERAL EDITOR: W. S. TAYLOR

Typography

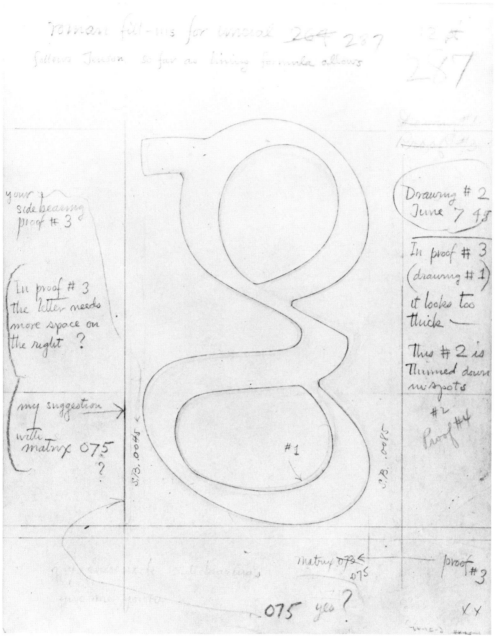

Linotype drawing after a design for
lower-case 'g' by W. A. Dwiggins,
dated 7 June 1945, showing the
designer's comments. Reduced from
the original, made on a scale of
1/156,000 of an inch = 10 inches.
The drawing is 'mirror image'
because the stages are: drawing
'wrong', pattern 'right', punch
'wrong', matrix 'right', type
'wrong'.

Ruari McLean

The Thames and Hudson Manual of

TYPOGRAPHY

With 188 illustrations

Thames and Hudson

For Catriona and Christopher,
my daughter and son-in-law

Half-title page: Ninteenth-century wood engraving.

© 1980 Thames and Hudson Ltd, London

First published in the United States of America in 1980 by
Thames and Hudson, Inc., 500 Fifth Avenue,
New York, New York 10110

First paperback edition 1988
Reprinted 1992 with corrections

Library of Congress Catalog Card Number 80-50803

Printed in Singapore

Contents

Acknowledgments

For reading my manuscript at an early stage and giving me generous advice and encouragement I am grateful to Ian Parsons; and for constant help and constructive criticism I am grateful, first to the editor of this series, Mr W. S. Taylor, and then to my friends on the staff of Thames and Hudson.

For guiding me through some of the mazes of filmsetting and cathode ray tubes, I am indebted to Matthew Carter, Ed Cleary of Filmcomposition Ltd and the experts in HMSO. Various specific typographical or editorial problems have been illuminated for me by Fernand Baudin, John Bell, John Dreyfus, Adrian Frutiger, Sem Hartz, John Lewis, George Mackie, James Mosley, John Saville, Herbert Spencer, Walter Tracy, John Westwood and Hermann Zapf.

Other help and information has also been generously supplied by Professor Michael Twyman of Reading University, Leslie Lonsdale-Cooper of the Open University, Peter Burnhill of Stafford College of Further Education, Ron Costley of the Scolar Press, Günter Lange of Berthold, Douglas Mack of Stirling University Library and K. B. Gardner of the British Library, and Archie Turnbull and John Davidson of Edinburgh University Press.

For help with the chapter on paper I am grateful to J. H. Young, Frank Cook of Book Papers Ltd, Jim Fobbester of the British Paper Industries Federation and F. W. Bray of the National Association of Paper Merchants. For giving me advice and facts on the American paper industry and its terminology I warmly thank Leonard B. Schlosser of New York; and for help on other American matters, I am grateful to Dorothy Abbe and Jack Golden. Harold Hugo, Rocky Stinehour and Steve Harvard have been extremely helpful in reading the whole typescript and commenting on American usages.

Finally, without the patience and unstinted help of both Fianach Lawry and my wife this book would never have been written.

Introduction

'Typography' is the art, or skill, of designing communication by means of the printed word. It thus involves the design of books, magazines, newspapers, pamphlets, leaflets, posters, advertisements, tickets, in fact anything that is printed and communicates to other people by means of *words*. Communicating by means of *images* – i.e. pictures or symbols, as opposed to words – is a different kind of skill, and is not the subject of this book, although a typographer may often have to deal with illustrations, as we shall see.

It must be noted that the difference between communicating by means of words and pictures is not cut and dried. Sometimes both are used together. And books, magazines, newspapers or posters may often depend on images rather than on words. It can be said that images should always be used instead of words, if possible: because they are, or should be, more direct, concise, attractive and easily understood, and can be quickly interpreted by people speaking different languages. However, there are many cases where words (and figures) cannot be dispensed with. This book is about how to make words readable, legible and attractive by means of printing.

The difference between communicating with words and communicating with pictures is fundamental, and requires basically different attitudes and techniques from the designer. Very few designers practise equally successfully as image-makers and typographers.

In order to design for printing, it is necessary to have a knowledge of printing techniques. It is dangerous to know too much: that leads to believing the people who tell you that something 'cannot be done' because it never has been. But some elementary knowledge is essential.

Until recently, the technology of printing was based on metal printing types. Every letter, every figure and every punctuation mark was cast in metal in order to provide a surface which could be inked and then pressed on paper. The invention of lithography in 1798 (see next chapter) did not alter this process: it merely meant that after the letters were cast in metal and composed into pages, the type matter could be transferred on to lithographic plates by various methods, in order to give the same results, when printed, as if it had been impressed on to paper direct from type. The fact that every letter started off as a metal object had an important effect on the way it was designed or drawn, since it had to have a shape that could first be cut on a steel punch with an engraving tool and then be cast in molten lead. If you think about this, you will see that many letter forms which could be drawn with a pencil, a pen, a brush or a crayon could not easily be cut or cast in metal.

But now, in the fourth quarter of the twentieth century, the five-hundred-year-old technology of metal types has been superseded by an entirely different technology, that of computerized typesetting. It is vital for every designer being trained today to understand what the new techniques mean. The old restraints imposed by metal are out of date: the new restraints are utterly different, and are only beginning to be understood. Young designers of today are in the unprecedented position of being able to create a tradition for those who will follow: they must make a tradition that is worth following and preserving.

Since this book was first published, another revolution has taken place: the introduction of personal computers into the designer's office. Now, using machines such as the Apple-Macintosh or IBM PC, typographers have at their command virtually all the resources that were traditionally the preserve of typesetters and printers. The technology is changing rapidly, prices of computers are coming down, and soon no professional book designer will be able to afford *not* to possess his or her own personal computer. There are now numerous magazines and books explaining how to use the new technology. This manual is not one of them: it focuses instead on the *principles* of typography. For the *purpose* of typographic design has not changed. It is to communicate words: without words in the first place, typography does not exist. Typography is the means by which words, conceived in someone's mind and then put down on paper with a pen or pencil, are made available to the world at large.

Beatrice Warde once wrote a book on typography called *The Crystal Goblet*, and the sub-title to her first essay was 'printing should be invisible'. She asked her readers to imagine that they had a flagon of wine before them, and two goblets – one of solid gold, 'wrought in the most exquisite patterns'; the other, of 'crystal-clear glass, thin as a bubble, and as transparent'. If wine meant anything to you, she hoped you would choose the crystal goblet, because 'everything about it is calculated to *reveal* rather than hide the beautiful thing which it was meant to contain'.

As a typographer, you are the servant of the author – colleague, if you like – but your job is to help the author to reach his public. You are not making works of art of your own; you are transmitting, with as much skill, grace and efficiency as may be required, the words of someone else.

'Typography must be clear and good in order to communicate – but that's as far as it goes. The reason why I am interested in typography is because it helps people to communicate with the clarity which an idea deserves. And the reason why I have lost all interest in *avant-garde* typography is because I find it too introspective, too preoccupied with making a picture on the page, instead of being concerned with bringing the idea through the clearly polished window of typography into the mind of the reader.'

Beatrice Warde
Penrose Annual, 63 (1970), p. 76, from an interview recorded and edited by John Dreyfus.

1 Historical outline

The history of typography is important for two main reasons. The first is *enjoyment*: there is an endless treasure of achievement by artists and designers of the past, waiting to be discovered in books and galleries and museums and collections of every kind all over the world. The second reason is *quality*. In music, in wine, in drawing, in typography, words like 'good' or 'very good' or 'superb' do not have meaning until you have some experience of the best that exists – for instance, until you have listened to (say) Beethoven, drunk some Mouton Rothschild, looked at Dürer, handled the printing of Jenson, Whittingham or Bruce Rogers.

> *Now it may be, the flower for me*
> *Is this beneath my nose;*
> *How shall I tell, unless I smell*
> *The Carthaginian rose?*

Comparison is the basis of appreciation, and a study of the work of the past is essential for the purpose of establishing one's own standards of judgment. It also provides the inspiration that all designers need, to be absorbed, digested and then transmuted into achievement.

Designers have more time to study and absorb material when they are young, and learning, than after they have begun to practise; they will draw on what they find in these early years, all their lives.

ORIGINS

The history of typography begins with the invention of writing. The typographer must understand what the alphabet is, and how it differs from other systems of writing like the Chinese and Japanese. The origins of our alphabet are still obscure, but it is now generally accepted that it was probably invented in an eastern corner of the Mediterranean, less than two thousand years before Christ. David Diringer states that all alphabets in use in the world today are descended from this invention, and that 'the inventor or the inventors are to be ranged among the greatest benefactors of mankind . . . only the Syro-Palestinian Semites produced a genius who created the alphabetic writing, from which have descended all past and present alphabets.'[1]

As soon as writing existed, men tried to make it beautiful. The tradition of illuminated, decorated and illustrated manuscripts is highly relevant to typographers, and there are today countless books available on the subject. Old manuscripts often look better when reproduced than in real life, and are certainly more accessible when reproduced in printed books. But there are always delightful surprises when rare manuscripts or prints are gathered together for international exhibitions, such as the Floating World exhibition of Japanese prints at the Victoria and Albert Museum

Previous page: woodcut from Lycosthenes' *Prodigies*, Basel 1557.

in 1973, or the marvellously illustrated borders of Persian Manuscripts in the Islamic Art exhibition at the Hayward Gallery in 1975. The British Museum has a collection of illuminated manuscripts on permanent exhibition, and fine examples are to be found in most other big libraries and museums.

As described in Chapter 7, paper was invented in China, and the knowledge of how to make it passed slowly from the East to the West, via the Arabs and North Africa: the first paper mill in Europe was established in Spain in A D 1150.

Printing from wooden blocks flourished in China, and had become an art by the tenth century A D. The 'Diamond Sutra', in the British Museum, dated 868 and for long rated as the world's oldest extant printed book, has yielded that position to a scroll found in 1967 in South Korea which must be over a hundred years earlier. Then there is an authentic contemporary account of the invention of a method of printing from movable type, made from baked clay and held in an iron forme, by Pi Shêng in China between 1041 and 1048; and the Koreans were casting type from metal, and printing books from it, before 1400. But because the Chinese, Japanese and Koreans did not have the alphabet, movable type in those countries was not an important invention. In T. F. Carter's words: 'The writing of the languages of the Far East is based on some forty thousand separate symbols: for them, until the large wholesale printing of recent years, movable type have seldom been practical or economical. . . . The invention of printing from wooden blocks was therefore *the* invention of printing in China.'[2] In Chinese (and Japanese) books, literature and painting, embodied in woodcut calligraphy and colour printing, become unified on the page in a way that can hardly be paralleled by anything in European art.

Did Chinese wood-block printing, in the form of playing cards, paper money, image prints and books (or even an account of it) percolate to Europe before block-printing began there? No-one knows. We do not know when block-printing from wood began in Europe; it was probably first used for printing textiles, from at least the sixth century onwards.[3] We do know that playing cards were popular in France in the late fourteenth century, and are mentioned, for example, in a Paris decree of 1397, when working men were forbidden to play cards (also tennis, bowls, dice and ninepins) on working days;[4] and the production of playing cards, by printing, 'must have been a thriving industry, especially at Ulm, at the end of the XIVth and beginning of the XVth century'.[5] However, the printing of pictures and text from wood-blocks did not lead to the invention of movable type in Europe: this was essentially an invention that depended on a knowledge of metal, and was in fact made by Johannes Gutenberg (1398–1468), a goldsmith who lived in Mainz. His invention was made, after perhaps ten or more years of trial and error and much expenditure of money, probably before 1440.

A scribe copying a book, from a woodcut (reduced), *c.* 1526.

Gutenberg's 42-line Bible, Mainz
c. 1455.

Above: some of the *c.* 300 alternative
letters and ligatures in his font
which he needed to simulate a handwritten page.

Opposite: part of one of the two
columns (enlarged). The passage
shown is from 2 Samuel V: 17–24.

THE FIRST PRINTED BOOKS IN THE WEST

In the early fifteenth century books were written out entirely
by hand, usually on parchment or vellum (i.e. the prepared
skins of sheep, goats or calves), but also increasingly on
paper, made from linen rags. There was already a trade
in books, whose manufacture was organized on mass-
production lines, in 'scriptoria' where a text was read aloud
and copied down simultaneously by a number of scribes.
There were book fairs; but books were not a normal part of
everyone's daily life as they are today. Only the wealthy could
afford to possess books. Knowledge was still disseminated
among ordinary people by word of mouth; and whereas
many people carried a store of music and literature in their
heads, few could read. But education was spreading,
universities were being founded and some method for
producing books more efficiently than writing every letter
out by hand was clearly needed.

Since Gutenberg was trained as a goldsmith, he knew how
to cast objects in metal, such as coins, and how to cut punches
and stamp letters and images on metal. His idea was to adapt
these techniques to copying the writing of books, in other
words to mechanize book production. We do not know how
or when the concept came to him of casting individual letters
in metal, which could be assembled into words, printed from,
and then re-assembled into different words and printed from
again, but this was in fact what he eventually succeeded in
doing – and in so doing he changed the world.

When he first set to work, he must have realized fairly
quickly that he already had vellum and paper, he had ink, he
had wooden presses (for pressing linen, and grapes, for
example) and, as his model to copy, he had books, written in
gothic handwriting which printers today call 'black letter'
(see below), of great beauty and regularity, and often
decorated and embellished with 'illuminations' – initials and
illustrations drawn on to the pages, in and out of the writing,
finished in colours and gold. A suggestion has been made that
Gutenberg intended to print these as well, and knew how he
could do it: it is one of the most intriguing might-have-
beens of history.[6] Gutenberg knew, in any case, that to be
successful his printing must be indistinguishable from the
highly finished written pages of the scribes. To achieve this,
he had to cast several versions of many letters, and ligatures
for combinations of letters, to simulate all the variations of
the script that he had chosen to copy. His font consisted of over
300 characters; a modern printer's font of upper- and lower-
case roman consists of hardly more than 50 characters.

Gutenberg understood the technique of casting coins and
medals: in order to cast letters, he had to cut a punch, in steel,
for every letter, sign and punctuation mark; he had to strike
it into a softer metal, to make a matrix; he had then to fit the
matrix into a mould, and, to avoid having to make a separate
mould for every letter of different width (the widths vary

Quod cū audisset dauid:descendit in
presidiū.Philistijm autem venientes
diffussi sunt in valle raphaim. Et cō=
suluit dauid dñm dicens.Si ascendā
ad philistijm·et si dabis eos i manu
mea? Et dixit dñs ad dauid. Ascende:
qa tradens dabo philistijm in manu
tua.Venit ergo dauid ad baalphara=
sim:et percussit eos ibi et dixit.Diuisit
dñs inimicos meos corā me:sicut di=
uidunt aque.Propterea vocatū e no=
men loci illi⁹ baalpharasim.Et reliq=
runt ibi sculptilia sua:q tulit dauid et
viri ei⁹. Et addiderunt adhuc philisti=
im ut ascenderent:et diffussi sūt i valle
raphaim.Cōsuluit autē dauid dñm.
Si ascendā cōtra philisteos:⁊ tradas
eos in manus meas?Qui rūdit. Nō
ascendas cōtra eos sed gira post tergū
eorū:⁊ venies ad eos exaduso pirorū.

Seuerine Cuniberte

Phares autez genu
nuit aram. Araz aut g
nadab aut genuit n̄
genuit falmon:falm(
roab. Booz autem g

laomedontea p̄na piur
q̄ Apollo atq̄ Neptunt
dona mercēnariis oper̄
Illis q̄ppe promififfe me(
iuraffe phibe̅t. Miror A

E MIE DEBILE VO
tiofe & diue Nymphe
inconcine alla uoftra b
la terrifica raucitate del

'Black letter' and 'roman' types are based on distinct and different styles of writing. But as printing moved southwards from the Rhineland to Italy, printers had to use types which followed the style of writing used in the places where they set up their presses: these four examples show how the style changed.

1 'Textura' used in Fust and Schoeffer's *Psalter*, Mainz 1457.
2 'Schwabacher' in Fust and Schoeffer's 48-line Bible, Mainz 1462. The type is already more like roman than the textura above.
3 'Fere humanistica' used by Sweynheim and Pannartz at Subiaco, 1467. The sign at the beginning of the second line is an abbreviation for 'quod'.
4 Aldus Manutius' roman type in *Hypnerotomachia Poliphili*, Venice 1499.

from 'i' to 'M' and 'W'), he had to devise a mould of variable width.[8] It seems that this adjustable mould was the one item that did not already exist in one form or another; it was the core of his invention.

He had also to find a metal that would melt easily, that would flow evenly into the matrix, that on cooling would expand slightly so as to make an absolutely exact model of the letter, and that when cool would be hard enough to withstand being printed by pressure on to paper or skin, repeatedly, without wearing out too quickly. The metal he used, which has been the basis of all type metal ever since, was lead, with the addition of antimony for strengthening hairlines and adding hardness, and tin for toughness and to make the lead melt more easily. Modern Monotype casting machines, when casting type, add 6–12 per cent tin and 15–24 per cent antimony to the lead.[9]

When it came to printing, the right kind of ink was found in the mixture of linseed oil and pigments used by painters in oils: it is worth noting that the quality of Gutenberg's ink, in depth of black and permanence, has never been improved on.[10]

No-one knows how many experiments, or small jobs, Gutenberg printed before his first great work, the 42-line Bible. Paper was expensive and not readily thrown away, so spoiled sheets were passed on to the binder, who used them to strengthen bindings or provide end-papers. It is from sheets of this kind, found when old books have been taken apart for repair, that much of our knowledge of the first days of printing is derived.

Gutenberg's 42-line Bible is the earliest book printed in the western world to have survived. It was a mammoth task and the money required to finance it was probably Gutenberg's undoing. It consisted of 1286 pages (the page size of the largest copies in paper is 409 × 290 mm), and was issued in two volumes. It has been estimated that Gutenberg actually printed between 180 and 200 copies, of which probably 30 were on vellum. Of the 48 copies known (36 on paper, 12 on vellum), only 21 are complete.[11] Each copy on vellum required 170 calf skins, so 30 copies would have involved the slaughtering of 5,100 calves. The increased demand for vellum by printers in Germany during the last half of the fifteenth century must have made veal a regular part of the national diet: the extraordinary thing is that the demand seems to have been met without difficulty.[12]

Gutenberg's Bible was printed in a type that simulated the kind of writing then normally used for Bibles and service books in the Church north of the Alps. It was of the family that printers in Britain call 'black letter' and others call 'gothic', although it has nothing to do with the Goths. Its technical name is 'textura'. A. F. Johnson says: 'It is an upright and angular letter characterized by an almost entire absence of curves. It may be described as drawn rather than written.'[13] It had been developed, just like our own 'roman' type, from the Carolingian writing perfected by the Englishman Alcuin at the Abbey of Tours in the reign of Charlemagne (768–814). The name 'roman', incidentally, 'probably originated from the fact that the first roman type used in France, that of the Sorbonne press of 1470, was copied from the fount of Schweynheym and Pannartz used at Rome from 1467.'[14] Textura is a condensed letter and may owe something to the need to get as many letters in a line as possible, and to economize on vellum and paper. It has visual affinities with the pointed architecture of northern Europe. Johnson also mentions that it was deficient in legibility, since 'all the letters are not sufficiently differentiated, for example, the n is merely two i's, and the m three i's, placed in contact, so that a combination such as *imn* is obscure. But legibility was not the chief aim of the medieval scribe. This formal script . . . enabled him to produce a closely packed page with a large proportion of black to white, which had the appearance of a woven texture.' What it lost in legibility, it gained in beauty.

However, although black letter, of varying kinds, remained the type most commonly used in Germany until at least the middle of the twentieth century, the humanist scholars of fifteenth century Italy preferred roman, and as printing spread across Europe from the Rhineland, printers had to copy, in type, the writing their customers preferred. We can watch, as the printers moved south across the Alps, their types changing from black letter to roman.

Printing spread rapidly. It was brought to England in 1476 by William Caxton, born in Kent (probably in 1422). Caxton was a great Englishman and a fascinating character, but was not, from a technical point of view, a great printer. He had learned the art on the Continent, probably in Cologne; in 1475 he printed the first book in English, his own translation of *Receuil des Histoires de Troies*, in Bruges, and then set up his press in Westminster. By 1476, printing had already reached Italy, Switzerland, France, the Netherlands, Belgium, Hungary, Poland and Spain.

The types Caxton used were all varieties of black letter, the earliest ones being Flemish, since his first equipment was bought in the Low Countries. His foreman and successor, Wynkyn de Worde (born in Alsace), first used roman type in 1520, but its first appearance in England was in 1509, in a book printed by Richard Pynson. Gradually roman type ousted black letter for ordinary use in this country. Johnson says: 'The fact that English printers did ultimately adopt roman as their standard type seems to be almost accidental.' He puts it down to the fact that our printers, who in the sixteenth century were much hampered by political and religious censorship, admired and followed the lead of the French printers, who had settled for roman. So when Shakespeare's plays were first printed they appeared in roman type. But black letter survives even today for some newspaper titles and in some legal documents.

William Caxton

Robert Estienne

Geofroy Tory

Three printers' marks.

Johannes Froben

Aldus Manutius

Christopher Plantin

Three printers' marks.

FROM PLANTIN TO BODONI

By the beginning of the sixteenth century printed books were beginning to become objects in their own right, not just copies of manuscripts, but they did not do so without opposition. The advance of printing had been resisted by the scribes, who stood to lose heavily, and indeed did lose. More than one wealthy book collector is on record as having declared that on no account would he admit a printed book into his library. But at first gradually, then quickly, the advent of printing destroyed the scriveners' trade. Only then was printing free to develop its own conventions and characteristics. The title-page, which had hardly ever existed in manuscripts, became normal, usually carrying the name of the printer (who was also the publisher) and his device; italic type was invented in Italy (copying a kind of fast writing known as 'chancery script' that was used for particular kinds of documents) and became an alternative text face to roman which had the advantage of being condensed as well as elegant.[15] Italic continued as a text face in its own right for two centuries, and only gradually came to be used as ancillary to roman, as it is today. From the beginning of the sixteenth century, especially in Italy and France, it was realized that it was no longer necessary to decorate books by hand after they had been printed: and the art of *printed* book design began.

The books printed in France in the sixteenth century, decorated mostly with woodcut borders and illustrations, and typographic ornaments, set standards for decorative book design that have perhaps never been surpassed. This was the period of the Estiennes, Simon de Colines, Geofroy Tory, Claud Garamond, Jean de Tournes, Robert Granjon and many other great names in the history of printing. In Switzerland, Johannes Froben made Basel a famous centre of printing: he was the friend and publisher of Erasmus. Holbein painted a memorable portrait of him and designed woodcut borders for his books.

Perhaps the most famous of all sixteenth-century printer-publishers was Christopher Plantin (c. 1520–80), also a Frenchman, who moved to Antwerp in 1555 and set up a press which continued in business for almost three centuries. When Plantin died in 1589, the Press was carried on by his son-in-law, Jan Moretus, for whom his friend Rubens designed title-pages, engraved on copper. By extraordinary luck and care, the house occupied by the Plantin Press still exists, with much of its original equipment. Known today as the Plantin Moretus Museum, in Antwerp, it is a valuable and fascinating place of pilgrimage for typographers.

The eighteenth century saw the rise of fine printing in Britain. William Caslon (1692–1766) was originally a gunsmith, who moved from engraving gun stocks to cutting punches for lettering on bindings, and was led from this to cut the famous types which are still in use today. His models were the best Dutch types of the seventeenth century. One of

EVVRES
DE
LOVÏZE LABE
LIONNOIZE.
*

*Reuues & corrigees par ladite
Dame.*

A LION
PAR IAN DE TOVRNES.
M. D. LVI.
Auec Priuilege du Roy.

Louise de Labé, *Oeuvres*, printed by
Jean de Tournes, Lyons 1556. A
woodcut title-page characteristic of
French decorative printing in the
sixteenth century.

abcdef

abcdefg

ABCD

Monotype Caslon

e e i n

t x st r

Caslon italic terminal letters from the
Caslon Foundry

By that

GREA

There ar

Monotype Baskerville

Of the documen

Wherever civiliz

ABCDEFGHI

JKLMNOPQR

Monotype Bell, originally cut by
Richard Austin for John Bell
(1745–1831) following after
Baskerville, in the 'modern' style.

Caslon's admirers was John Baskerville (1706–75), who, after being a writing-master and engraver, made a fortune in Birmingham in the japanning trade. He then took up printing: he designed and cut a new typeface (which is still, in various versions, one of the most popular English book faces), he built a new press, made his own ink, had paper made to his own specification, and pressed his sheets, after printing, between hot copper plates to enhance the effect. In 1757 his first book, the *Virgil*, 'went forth to astonish all the librarians of Europe'. He became the first English printer since Caxton whose books are known by their printer's name before their author's. The style of his books is severe and classical: they do not rely on ornament or illustration of any kind, as did most books of his day. Baskerville directed in his will, as a last gesture of rationalism against superstition, that he should be buried upright in non-consecrated ground in his garden at Easy Hill, outside Birmingham.

Whereas Caslon was a tradesman, whose business was to make and sell types, Baskerville was a businessman who took up printing for pleasure, and regarded it as an art. These differences in attitude occur again and again in printing from now on, until they converge at the beginning of the twentieth century in the person of a new professional in the printing trade, the typographer, who tries to earn a commercial living, and be an artist at the same time.

But perhaps today's typographer, applying artistic skills to commercial practice, is someone who has always existed in printing, at least since the seventeenth century. A notable example was Baskerville's contemporary in France, Pierre Simon Fournier le jeune (1712–68). This man, born into a printing family, was taught drawing at the Académie de St Luc in Paris before going to work under his brother in a typefoundry. In 1742 he published his famous specimen-book *Modèles des Caractères de l'imprimerie*,[16] and a smaller *Caractères de l'imprimerie*, which established his reputation. In 1764–66 he published his equally famous *Manuel Typographique*. Fournier's romans were slightly narrower than most earlier faces; his italics, called 'the most legible of all italics',[17] 'carried the idea of conformity with roman further than any earlier designer';[18] and his printer's flowers 'prove their author to have been the supreme master of typographic ornament'.[19] In addition, Fournier was the first to see the need for rationalizing type sizes, and in 1737 introduced the point system (see Chapter 5). He was one of the very few book designers in the history of printing who combined in his own person the skills of punchcutting, typefounding and printing.

In 1925 the Monotype Corporation recut and issued Fournier's roman and italic types, which became, in the 1930s, among the most popular of all book faces. The types and ornaments were brilliantly described and illustrated in a double number of *The Monotype Recorder*, edited, written and designed by Paul Beaujon (Beatrice Warde) in 1926. It was later revealed that before the decision to issue Fournier for Monotype composition was made, two different designs by Fournier were cut, numbered 185 and 178 respectively, and 'owing to some confusion (due to the typographical adviser's absence abroad) series 185 was approved'.[20] It was used for the Nonesuch Press seven-volume Shakespeare, which Francis Meynell considered to be his press's *chef d'œuvre*, and which Morison called 'no less a monument to Fournier le jeune, although the capitals were specially reduced in height'. The better version, named 'Barbou' (series 178), was for long available in only one size: it was used for the last three volumes of Stanley Morison's typographical journal, *The Fleuron*. But in 1967 the full composition range from 8 pt upwards was made available. It can be seen (and compared with 185) in Allen Hutt's excellent *Fournier, the compleat typographer* (London 1972).

The roman types of Caslon and his predecessors, which we classify as 'old face' (but see also Chapter 5), were based on the forms made by a broad-nibbed pen: if you move a pen sideways it makes a thin line; if you draw it downwards it makes a thick one. And a pen in a writer's hand is most easily held at an angle of about 45° to the line of advance. The effect on round letters like 'e' and 'o' is called, in typographical terminology, 'oblique shading' (see illustration, p. 76).

By the eighteenth century, sometimes called the Age of Reason, types were no longer copies of written letters, they were shapes in their own right, subject to intellectual as well as artistic development. Baskerville had made a very slight movement, in his types, away from oblique shading, but the next step, a decisive and long-lasting one, was made in France, and is associated with the name of Firmin Didot. It was the creation of what is known as the 'modern' face, in which the shading is vertical and the serifs are not bracketed, as is natural with a pen or a brush, but become hair-lines drawn with a ruler. This was a logical intellectual and theoretical solution, which has never appealed greatly to Anglo-Saxon typographers; but 'modern' types quickly became, and have remained until this day, the most commonly used types for nearly all French reading matter.

The first 'modern' faces were introduced by Firmin Didot (1764–1836), the second son of François-Ambroise Didot (1730–1804), who in 1775 had improved Fournier's point system and introduced the 'Didot' point (1 point = 0.3759 mm), which is still the standard unit of type measurement everywhere in Europe except Britain (see Chapter 5).

Didot's types seemed, in the eighteenth century, as logical as sans-serif did to the modernists in the 1920s, and were copied all over Europe. They were most conspicuously and successfully taken up by Giambattista Bodoni (1740–1813), who in 1768 was invited to run a private press at the court of Ferdinand, Duke of Parma, where he stayed until his death. At first, Bodoni printed small, delicate books in the style of

BAR
BOU

Monotype Barbou

Wherever civilization
of an expert typograp
Dexterity in the vocat
be acquired by zealous
ABCDEGHIJKLMN
be acquire
ABCDEG

Monotype Fournier

Initials and figures *c.* 1800 by Firmin Didot. Compare the hair-line unbracketed serifs with those of Bodoni on the next page.

Title-page and another page, much reduced, of Bodoni's *Manuale Tipografico*, Parma 1818.

Opposite: a page from Bodoni's *Manuale Tipografico*, Parma 1818.

Fournier le jeune, using Fournier's types, but he then changed his style to large, grand books printed in very black ink, with much white space and little or no ornamentation. His types became 'more and more rigid, their heavy lines thicker, and their light lines thinner and more wiry. Wonderfully perfect as these types were in detail, they contributed to a style of printing that made these later books as official as a coronation, and as cold as the neighbouring Alps!'[21]

Bodoni told Renouard, the French publisher, 'Je ne veux que du magnifique, et je ne travaille pas pour le vulgaire des lecteurs' ('I want only magnificence, and I don't work for the common reader'). He did not really work for readers at all: his texts were carelessly edited. But magnificence he did achieve, not least in his ephemeral broadsides, one of which is reproduced in John Lewis's *Anatomy of Printing* (London 1970), and others are reproduced in Bertieri's *L'Arte de Giambattista Bodoni* (Milan 1913).

Bodoni cut so many variations of his typefaces that when commercial founders started cutting and selling 'Bodoni' type, it is not surprising that all were different. Of the Monotype version, series 135, cut between 1921 and 1928, Stanley Morison wrote: 'The Corporation chose a general rendering, perhaps more rigid than the master's own work. It eschewed his more extreme letters, the pronounced tail to 'R', the 'g' which looked as if it had received a blow in the midriff, and alternative sorts were provided for his favourite highly calligraphic 'v' and 'w'. Series 135 was a true Bodoni in that it looked best well leaded and did not print well on coated paper.'[22] 'Bodoni' variations are available on many modern filmsetting systems; on book pages, Bodoni should always be leaded at least 2 points.

Bodoni's types, and style of typography, could never be called 'lively'; but even before he died in 1813, the thick/thin and vertical shading characteristics were being developed by English typefounders, for the purposes of advertising, into 'Fat Face', which became, especially in its italic form, a positively gay and jovial face. The author of Fat Face seems to have been the distinguished type designer and founder, Robert Thorne (fl. 1794–1820). He may not have taken his inspiration from Bodoni, but the connection is obvious, and was acknowledged by the Monotype Corporation when they cut 'Bodoni Ultra', a Fat Face which (perhaps in deference to its namesake) has lost the jolly curls and blobs that occur in nineteenth-century examples.

THE NINETEENTH CENTURY

The nineteenth century, especially in Britain, was a period of expansion, education, invention, wealth – and poverty. The wealth created a market for fine printing, and the population and education explosions, following on the industrial

MAJUSCOLE

107

ABC
DEF
GHI

Fat face italic letters from the Caslon Foundry, *c.* 1835.

revolution, created a market for cheap printing.

The third Earl Stanhope had made the first iron hand-press towards the end of the eighteenth century; the first power-driven cylinder press was installed to print the London *Times* in 1812. There was an urgent commercial need for newspapers to get the news out on to the streets quickly, which did not apply to books; it was normal for books to be printed on hand-presses – on hand-made paper – throughout the century. Type continued to be cast, and composed, by hand until the American Linn Boyd Benton's invention of the punchcutting machine in 1884 made the Monotype and Linotype composition systems feasible (see Chapter 6). But machine composition did not displace hand composition for books until after the First World War.

The first permanent photographs were made by the Frenchman J. N. Niepce in 1822; the process was developed by the Englishman Fox Talbot, who published *The Pencil of Nature* (the world's first book illustrated with photographs) in 1844; but the process block for printing line and tone subjects was not introduced until after 1880. When the 'block' (photographically made) finally ousted the hand processes for interpreting artist's drawings, a new era began.

At the beginning of the nineteenth century, books, journals, newspapers, posters and all kinds of commercial printing were printed from type by letterpress, i.e. by impression on paper. Illustrations could either be cut on wood (which could be printed along with type), or etched or engraved on copper plates (which had to be printed on separate presses).

In both these processes, the artist's drawing was either made on paper, and then traced on to the printing surface, or drawn direct on to the printing surface: the actual cutting of the wood-block, or etching (with acid) or engraving (with burin) of the copper, was laborious and skilful, and usually carried out by a professional craftsman.

Thomas Bewick engraved his own wood-blocks, but nearly all the famous illustrations on wood of the 1860s and 1870s, by Tenniel, Pinwell, Caldecott, Greenaway and others, were engraved by firms of professional engravers (who signed their work, and whose names, e.g. Edmund Evans, the Dalziels and John Swain, were often better known than those of the artists); George Cruikshank was one of the very few illustrators who etched his own plates, e.g. the illustrations for *Sketches by Boz* (London 1836) and *Oliver Twist* (London 1838). Aubrey Beardsley was the first great illustrator who drew consciously for line-block reproduction.

A third, completely different, printing process, called lithography (literally 'stonewriting') had been discovered in Bavaria in 1798, by Alois Senefelder (1771–1834). He found 'that certain kinds of local stone had an affinity for both grease and water. If the surface of the stone was polished, it could be drawn on in greasy ink, and it held that image. If the surface of the stone was then wetted, and inked with an inking roller, the ink was repelled by the water, but held in those places already drawn on in ink. Senefelder later discovered that certain kinds of zinc plate also have this property. The implications for the printing industry were tremendous, but were only slowly realized.'[23]

Lithography offered an immediate and important advantage to the artist: there was no labour in cutting or etching, it was just a question of drawing (in pen or chalk, with greasy ink) on the prepared smooth surface of stone or zinc, so that much bigger illustrations became practicable. It was even possible to draw on paper (in greasy ink) and transfer the drawing to the stone by pressure. In fact, while lithography was explored and exploited by artists from the beginning, its progress in book illustration was comparatively slow; but it made possible commercial colour printing, and, as a initial result of that, serious books on art or architecture could for the first time be illustrated with reliable colour plates of large size. Previously, the only feasible way to provide illustrations in colour was by the hand-colouring of etched or aquatinted copper plates, which produced results that were charming, but could not be regarded as accurate (if accuracy was required) since each colouring might be different; and there were obvious limitations to what could be painted by hand, as opposed to printed. The first books in which colour printing by lithography (called 'chromolithography') was used for scholarly illustration were probably Wilhelm Zahn's work on the wall paintings of Pompeii (Berlin 1828), and Boetticher's *Die Holz Architectur des Mittelalters* (Wooden architecture of the Middle Ages) (Berlin 1836–42).

In England, the first work of serious chromolithography was Owen Jones' *Alhambra*, of which the first volume began to appear in parts in 1836. It was a very big book, which could never have been produced without lithography, and was the first of a whole series of enormous folios and quartos with superb chromolithographic plates, laying a foundation for the art histories which now flow from the offset-litho printing presses of the world illustrated by colour photography.

The increasing demand for reading matter and the search for cheaper ways to print it led to a gradual deterioration of quality in book design throughout the nineteenth century, but the actual craftsmanship of the period is to our eyes (of the mechanized 1990s) positively awe-inspiring. It is most spectacular in folio pages of complicated hand composition, in pages of colour printing from ten, twenty or even thirty blocks, and in the extraordinary decorated and pictorial cloth bindings (blocked in gold leaf and colours from hand-engraved brass plates and wooden blocks) in small and large gift books.

Very few printing firms in Britain maintained a high standard of typography during the nineteenth century. Of

One of Charles Whittingham's press-marks, designed by Thomas Williams, engraved on wood by Mary Byfield.

abc

THE CENTURY FAMI
L. De Vinne comm
production of the (
appeared over the
face which becam(

Century Schoolbook, cut by Monotype after the face commissioned by T. L. De Vinne for the *Century Magazine*, 1895.

Opposite:
Detail (reduced) of a title-page drawn on stone and published by Charles Knight in 1847–51. Windsor Castle in the background (Wyatville's alterations were completed in 1828) no doubt inspired the exuberant mixture of gothic and rustic lettering, which shows the freedom opened to designers by lithography: no restraints from graver or burin.

those that did, the most notable was the Chiswick Press, founded in 1811 by Charles Whittingham (1767–1840) and carried on by his nephew, also Charles Whittingham (1795–1876). The younger Whittingham was a commercial printer with a large output, but everything he printed had style and can be recognized as soon as it is picked up. After 1828 he had a long and fruitful association with William Pickering (1796–1854), an innovating publisher who was the first to sell books bound in cloth (they had previously been issued in paper, and bound by the customer in leather at his own expense). The books printed by Whittingham for Pickering range from the Diamond Classics (about the size of a Swan Vesta matchbox), via the Aldine Poets (pocket-size volumes of great typographic excellence) to the great series of Prayer Books of 1844, the magnificent illustrated editions of Henry Shaw and folios such as Drummond's *Noble Families*, 1846–52: they are among the greatest achievements of British book design of any period.

It was natural for William Morris to go to the Chiswick Press for his printing, before he set up his own Kelmscott Press; this included his two earliest books of poems, both printed at his own expense, the *Defence of Guinevere* in 1858 and *The Life and Death of Jason* in 1867. The first is a charming example of the Chiswick Press style, with wood-engraved initials and head- and tail-pieces; the second, printed after Charles Whittingham's retirement, when the press was known as 'Whittingham & Wilkins', is still well printed but shows just that small decline in detail that nearly always happens when a master's hand and eye are withdrawn.

When Whittingham died in 1876, the firm continued, and in 1885 came under the able management of Charles Jacobi. Later, it became associated with William Griggs (1832–1911), a pioneer of photolithography and colour collotype printing, who produced some of the best facsimile colour printing, especially of illuminated manuscripts and bookbindings, that has ever been made. The Chiswick Press continued, but was finally closed down in 1962. Many of its archives are preserved in the British Museum and the St Bride Printing Libraries.

The outstanding letterpress printer in the United States during the nineteenth century was Theodore Lowe De Vinne (1828–1914), who originated a famous typeface, 'Century', first used for the *Century Magazine* in 1895 and now, as 'Century Schoolbook', much used for all kinds of information printing by offset-lithography. De Vinne also wrote *The Practice of Typography*, a four-volume work which began with *Plain Printing Types* in 1899, the first modern study of the subject.

There is no doubt that towards the end of the nineteenth century, the quality of ordinary materials and workmanship in many industries, including printing, was declining fast, although if one tries to build up a collection of really bad work produced between, say, 1880 and 1914, it is surprising

The Land we live in

Vol. II.

London, Charles Knight.

Insel Verlag mark designed by Peter Behrens, 1899.

R. Piper mark designed by Emil Preetorius.

Curwen Press mark designed by Percy Smith.

how much easier good work is to find. The Art Workers' Guild, founded by Walter Crane with Lewis F. Day in 1884, and the Arts and Crafts Exhibition Society, founded in 1888, were attempts to improve the situation: so was the Kelmscott Press, founded by William Morris with Emery Walker in 1891. As I once wrote elsewhere:

'The Kelmscott books, all uniform in general style, did not show how books should be designed in 1890 (although some people thought they did). They were in fact quite unsuitable for reading . . . If they did not show how books should be designed, what did they show?

'They showed that books could be magnificent . . . Kelmscott books are rich and satisfying artifacts, to look at, to handle, and to remember. They have an insistent integrity that means much today, and must have meant more in the 1890's. They caused things to happen.'[24]

THE TWENTIETH CENTURY

Kelmscott Press books, first of all, inspired the Private Press Movement, a host of imitators and followers in Europe and America, of whom the most interesting were the Doves, the Ashendene, the Eragny, the Vale and the Essex House Presses in England, and Will Bradley's Wayside Press in USA, all founded before 1900. All these private presses stimulated and affected commercial book production.

Second, Kelmscott books were seen accidentally by young men all over the world and inspired them to become printers: these included Bruce Rogers in America, S. H. de Roos in Holland and Oliver Simon in England, whose account of his conversion is probably typical of many. He had been demobilized in 1919 at the age of twenty-four, and 'spent some months in the North of England attempting to find a job, but without success . . . I had been in London [in search of work] only a fortnight when I happened to pass Sotheran's bookshop, then in Piccadilly, where an astonishing window display of sumptuous, dazzling, richly decorated books caught my eye and arrested my steps. I felt compelled to enter and make enquiries, and was told, for the first time in my life, about William Morris and the Kelmscott Press, and of the Kelmscott *Chaucer* in particular, which held a place of honour in the window. As I left, I knew I could abandon my vague and unenthusiastic plans to enter the cotton trade, forestry or bank: it was plain to me that I *must* become a printer.'[25]

The modern movement in Europe, associated with Walter Gropius's Bauhaus in Weimar, Germany, and, among many others, the typographer Jan Tschichold, will be dealt with in Chapter 5. Typography in Britain and America during the first half of the twentieth century did not explore these new paths, but proceeded along much more traditional lines. In America, the next good printer after De Vinne was Daniel Berkeley Updike (1860–1941), who founded the Merrymount Press in Boston and for many years succeeded in working only for clients who allowed him to print their material the way he wanted to see it. He combined tradition with originality and also made brilliant use of the decorative talents of several rising American illustrators, including Rudolph Ruzicka, T. M. Cleland and William Addison Dwiggins. Updike's great work, *Printing Types*, first published in 1922, had originated as lectures in the Harvard University Graduate School of Business Administration, and proved an inspiration to typographers during the 1920s and 1930s (and is still excellent reading today).

Ginn & Company mark designed by Thomas Cleland.

Updike had spent two years learning about printing at the Riverside Press at Cambridge, Mass.; when he left there in 1895, he was followed by Bruce Rogers (1870–1957), who after sixteen years at the Riverside Press became the first freelance typographer of the twentieth century,* earning his living on both sides of the Atlantic. He designed 'Centaur', a typeface based on Jenson's type used in the Eusebius of 1470 but redrawn with freedom to look like a brand-new face. It was used in three books which are his masterpieces, all designed and printed in England: *The Odyssey of Homer* (T. E. Lawrence's translation) in 1932, *Fra Luca De Pacioli*, by Stanley Morison, in 1933, and the Oxford Lectern Bible of 1935. When Centaur was cut for Monotype composition in 1929, the italic chosen to accompany it was 'Arrighi', designed by Frederic Warde, which had been cut in 1925 in Paris for hand composition. Warde (1894–1939), another gifted American, the husband for a short period of Beatrice Warde, designed a few books of rare distinction, but lived an unhappy life and died by his own hand in New York. Other Americans who made distinguished contributions to printing and typographic history in this century are well described in Joseph Blumenthal's *The Printed Book in America* (Boston 1977).

*The American F. W. Goudy (1865–1947) became a freelance designer in 1899, but in the specialized field of type design.

In England, the most influential figure for the first half of the twentieth century was Stanley Morison (1899–1967), who as typographic adviser to the Monotype Corporation from around 1923 was responsible for the programme of classic typefaces, mostly revived from earlier periods, which were the delight of book typographers all over the world until the filmsetting revolution in the 1960s. Morison himself designed 'Times New Roman', first used for his redesign of the London *Times* newspaper in 1932, which later became one of the most widely used general-purpose typefaces in the world, and has remained so until the present. Morison was only one, but the most powerful and scholarly, of a group who in 1924 formed a dining club in London called the Double Crown Club, which 'acted as a catalyst in the transformation of graphic communication, a matter of no small importance to modern civilization.'[26] Among the other founder members were Oliver Simon of the Curwen Press (who started it), Bernard Newdigate of the Shakespeare Head Press, Gerard Meynell of the Westminster Press, his cousin

Design by Thomas Cleland.

Bruce Rogers' mark designed by himself.

Nonesuch Press mark designed by Stephen Gooden.

*Offset-lithography: instead of printing direct from the stone or zinc plate, the image is transferred onto a rubber surface (usually on a cylinder) and printed from that, which is both faster and does not wear out the original stone or plate.

Westminster Press mark designed by Eric Gill.

Opposite: title-page for a novel, designed by W. A. Dwiggins, 1938. This delightful combination of typography and calligraphy is a technique even more appropriate for book design today when pages are assembled on film.

Francis Meynell who founded the Nonesuch Press, and Wren Howard, Jonathan Cape's partner and designer of the books from that imprint which were among the best of their day.

These men, and some others, were responsible for the best typographic design in Britain in the inter-war period. It was based on a healthy, but not pedantic, respect for tradition, and the Monotype book faces already mentioned, notably Caslon, Baskerville, Bembo, Ehrhardt, Fournier, Garamond, Poliphilus and Walbaum. It was supported by a high standard of letterpress machining in the leading printing houses of the day.

In the second half of the twentieth century, the two most important developments in printing have been the introduction of commercial filmsetting and the advance of offset-lithography.

The first book printed in Britain entirely without metal type is claimed to have been an edition of Eric Linklater's *Private Angelo*, privately printed for Sir Allen and Richard Lane, of Penguin Books, for distribution to their friends at Christmas 1957: it was composed in a version of Garamond on the Intertype Fotosetter and even an experienced eye could hardly tell that it had not been perfectly set in conventional hot metal. However, it was not for at least another ten years that filmsetting became commonplace in even small printing firms up and down the country.

A book set on film does not have to be printed by offset-lithography:* the film can be transferred to dow-etched magnesium plates or other forms of letterpress block. But offset-lithography has made such strides in the past twenty years that it is now used for both the cheapest highest-speed printing (on giant web-offset machines) and for the highest quality reproductive work, in black and white or colour. 300-line screen lithography, pioneered by Dr Harold Hugo at the Meriden Gravure Company in Connecticut, is so successful that it has replaced collotype (previously the best printing method for reproducing tone subjects, since no screen was used, but subject to severe restrictions in the length of run that could be obtained from one set of plates) and is capable of producing far finer definition in line and tone than the finest work obtainable by letterpress.

Printing from movable type, on the other hand, has the advantage that corrections can be made easily and instantly without removing the type from the printing machine, and this may be an important consideration for things such as price lists and timetables. (In lithography and offset lithography, almost any correction – except a very simple small deletion – requires a new plate.) Movable type is used today only for short runs, since it may begin to show signs of wear even after, say, 50,000 impressions (depending on the skill of the printer, paper surface, machine speed and so on). For longer runs, relief plates are made, of stereo metal, polymer, rubber and various other special materials. Many newspapers and journals are printed letterpress on high-speed

ROBERT NATHAN

Winter in April

ALFRED A KNOPF : NEW YORK
1938

rotary machines. But it is probably true that, today, anything letterpress can do, lithography can do better; and letterpress printing has the serious disadvantage that it involves – in large scale printing of, say, books – enormous quantities of heavy metal. This is cumbersome and expensive to move about; and the type, set up for a book, a booklet or even a leaflet, has to be kept 'standing' – i.e. in store – in case of reprint, which may never be needed, and ties up a lot of money and space.

Letterpress printing will no doubt continue in use in small businesses for many years, because of nostalgia and the costs involved in changing, but it has been rendered obsolete by the combination of offset-litho, filmsetting and computerization (of which more in Chapter 5).

Tailpiece drawn by Edward Bawden for the *Twentieth Century* magazine, 1960.

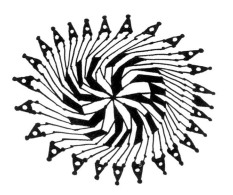

2   Studio and equipment

STUDIO AND EQUIPMENT

N.B. Information which was correct at the time of writing may have become out of date by the time you read it, as models are superseded and new equipment is introduced. The latest information should be obtained from the manufacturers and suppliers. A list of recommended firms is given at the end of the book.

The conditions in which a designer works are highly important, but they are personal; what suits one person does not suit another. I cannot work with either music or even a clock ticking near me; many designers cannot work without background radio and other noises. Every designer requires both daylight and artificial, controlled lighting, and a steady table – more than that will depend on the designer's nature and character, and on the kind of work that is being done.

As a small boy I was taught that the way to learn golf was to play first with only one club, just as young anglers often begin, not unwisely, with a bent pin and a piece of string on a stick. Later, I deliberately taught myself typography using only one typeface, Caslon. The danger in starting with too much equipment is that your work may be influenced to suit your gadgets, and become mechanically, not thoughtfully, produced. But that *may* turn out to be right for the kind of work you do. A simple illustration of the danger of tools can be provided by the ruler. A typographer spends much time drawing lines of type in pencil: it is how a design is first of all worked out, before it is shown to the client for approval. If you always draw parallel guide-lines before drawing type – two lines for the x-height, or three to include the ascenders, or even four to include the descenders as well – you are preventing yourself from learning to draw typefaces free-hand, which you must do, simply for speed. A typographer who has to draw an elaborate system of pencil lines before pencilling in the type will take two or three times as long as a practised typographer who can trust his eye; and to make matters worse, when finished, the job may be quite wrong, just because you have trusted mechanical aids and *not* your eye. This may sound puzzling, but after practice you will appreciate its truth. The technique of drawing layouts is discussed more fully in Chapter 8. The purpose of tools is to make life easier and to produce work more efficiently. Except in very specialized circumstances, they are not (and must not be allowed to become) a substitute for the creative processes.

Nevertheless, typography is for a given purpose, which is different from the artist's motivation. The draughtsman may offer his drawing for sale quickly, or after months, or years: it may even never be sold. A typographer works for a client or employer, and always – if he wishes to stay in business – to a time schedule: so some organization is essential.

Students on graphic design courses in Art and Design Colleges should find available every book and piece of equipment they are likely to need and the opportunity to try them out. What you will need in your own workshop depends on yourself, your circumstances and, in particular, the kinds of work you do. I have been happier, all my life as a typographer, with very little special equipment. I have always worked at a solid desk or table, and do not possess an adjustable drawing board or easel, but if you get used to one as a student, you will probably want one in your own studio, and may be the better workman for it.

Previous page: woodcut by Thomas Bewick, from *A General History of Quadrupeds*, 1790.

Opposite: basic and advanced studio worktables.

34

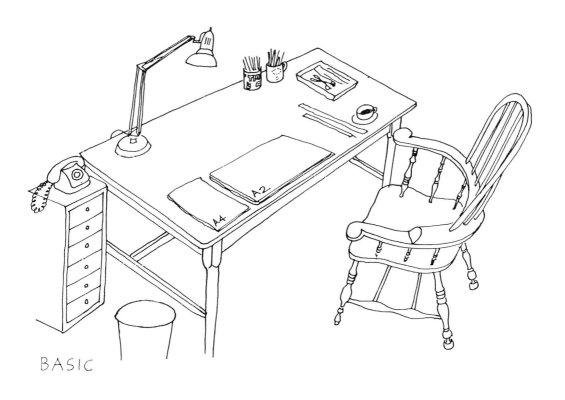

BASIC

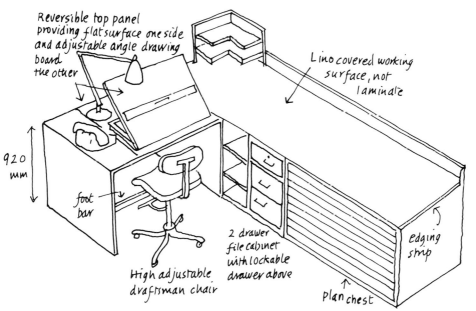

Reversible top panel
providing flat surface one side
and adjustable angle drawing
board
the other

Lino covered working
surface, not
laminate

920
mm

foot
bar

High adjustable
draftsman chair

2 drawer
file cabinet
with lockable
drawer above

plan chest

edging
strip

ADVANCED

In my opinion, it would be utterly wrong to say that a designer must use this or that tool: you may work better without it, and in any case it depends on what sort of work you are doing. But you should know what tools and time-savers exist, and should evaluate them. It is also axiomatic that a designer should surround himself only with articles that are pleasing to his eyes and not – if he can help it – have any object that is ugly. When you decide you need something, buy the best you can afford. It is nearly always cheaper in the end to buy one good thing, and save up for the next, than to buy two inferior things. You are going to use them all your life.

Here is a list – it could never be definitive or complete – of the principal articles of equipment and materials that a typographer may be expected to use or at least know about.

FURNITURE

A designer's work table or desk must be absolutely steady. The smallest convenient working surface is about 60 × 34 in. (152 × 86 cm), but larger is better. A second table of similar size is desirable for laying out proof sheets, galley proofs, illustrations, etc., but it need not be so strong, if it is not used to draw at. Some designers have both a table or fixed desk to write at, and an adjustable desk or easel for drawing. British Thornton make a 'Double Top' series of desks which provide two alternative work surfaces: flat on one side, or an adjustable drawing unit in either A1 or A2 size on the other. Complete 'work units' are available or can be made (see illustration) combining easel, working surface, shelves and drawers. 'Rotobord' rotating drawing boards and 'Rotring' and other drawing boards with sliding or movable fitted rulers are extremely useful alternatives.

The designer's chair is of course important and must match his working surface, both for appearance and height. Swivelling steel seats, ergonomically designed with an adjustable back support and a foot rest, are efficient; they are expensive, so do not buy one until you have thoroughly tested it.

A plan chest or plan file (with large shallow drawers) is the only safe way to store posters, printed sheets, drawing paper, etc., and its top will also provide a working surface. You will need flat surfaces at table height for operations like cutting paper, laying out illustrations and weighing and wrapping up parcels. Bookshelves and cupboards are required *ad lib*, and you will probably need a filing cabinet: you must have an efficient filing system for all business correspondence.

You will also need at least one large wall board, for pinning up work to look at from a distance, and for exhibiting specimens, urgent notices or whatever. Your studio is probably the most convenient place to interview clients and discuss work, so you will require comfortable chairs for this. Larger studios usually have a special room for interviews, so that conversations can take place without disturbing others who are trying to work.

LIGHTING

Artists' studios in the northern hemisphere traditionally have north-facing windows, because direct sunlight is too bright, especially for those working on white paper. If your studio has south-facing windows, you will need some kind of adjustable blind to take away the glare. Light should come from your left, if you are right-handed. You will need an adjustable lamp (e.g. Anglepoise or '1001') to bring strong light to your work when you need it. If it can be fixed to a wall or elsewhere, rather than stand on your desk, it will save a little valuable space.

Fluorescent lighting gives a steady diffused light economically for the whole room, if you want it, but it may affect colour values slightly and you must test this carefully. Transparencies and colour printing should never be checked by ordinary artificial light: they should be checked either by daylight or on a controlled light table.

BASIC EQUIPMENT

It would be absurd to try to list every kind of pencil, pen, brush and drawing instrument that a typographer may need; designers learn best by experience which tools suit them and which don't, and the range is dictated by the nature of their work.

The basic equipment needed by a typographer to design a book could be:

Pencils (only 2B and HB are essential).

Technical pens (e.g. Rotring, Kern, Leroy) in the required range of points. For an evaluation of brands, see *Design*, 371 (November 1979), pp. 62–4.

Chinagraph or wax pencils for use on film.

Felt-tip pens and colour sticks, in as wide a range of colours and tips as possible. The PMS (Pantone Matching System) range of markers, matching with Pantone papers, film and colour selectors for printing inks, marketed by Letraset, is recommended.

Ball-point pens.

Blue pencil for making marks that will not be picked up by a camera, with other colours as needed.

Pencil sharpener.

Sharp knife, scalpel (with spare blades) for trimming layouts and film, scissors. If you are working with sheets of proofs, you need scissors with long (5 in. or 6 in.) blades.

Process white, 'Snopake', 'Tippex', and 'Uno' Triple

White Ink (which can be used in technical pens and is stronger than other whites).
Indian ink and other inks as needed.
Camel-hair brushes in a variety of fine points, for retouching lettering, etc., and such thicker brushes as the designer may need.
Needle in holder for pricking holes.
Soft rubbers, ink erasers, and 'putty-rubbers' for picking up rubber adhesives.
Paste, 'Cow' gum (and spreader) and spray adhesive if large areas have to be stuck down.
Masking tape, double-sided tape for mounting artwork, etc., and 'invisible' mending tape, which does not discolour or show up when photocopied, and can be written on.
Compasses, dividers and drawing instruments. If the typographer has to draw for reproduction, or prepare camera-ready artwork, a complete set of the best instruments available (e.g. Kern, or British Thornton) is a necessary investment.
Steel rulers for measuring, marked in inches, points and metric (probably 12 in., 24 in. and 36 in. rulers will be needed).
Geliot Whitman 'Artsquare', a transparent plastic triangle ruled into a 5 mm grid, for quick squaring-up.
Rulers for ink ruling (bevelled edges) and cutting. Beware of cheap plastic rulers which may be seriously in error.
Slide rule and proportional enlargement/reduction disc.
'Pantone' colour guides and Pantone colour specifier with tear-off strips.
'Letraset' and other dry-transfer sheets, available for rules, borders, shading, tints, symbols, and illustrations of all kinds, as well as lettering.
Drawing pins.
Stapling machine (a reliable type is 'Ofrex Nipper').

STATIONERY (see also Chapter 7)

You will need layout pads in all A sizes from A1 to A4. Make sure that paper is sufficiently thin for easy tracing from type specimens.
Tracing paper in all A sizes. Tracing paper is not stable and cockles when coloured or inked, so you will also need blue tracing 'cloth', supplied in rolls, which is stable, and necessary when making colour separation drawings for reproduction.
Heavy black-and-white board for mounting layouts and artwork.
You will also need coloured papers and card in many varieties and weights (see Appendix for names of suppliers).
Also: scribble paper, tissue paper, wrapping paper, corrugated cardboard and cardboard in sheets for protecting

artwork and photographs, 'Jiffy' or other padded bags, and envelopes in various sizes.

For the design of printed stationery, see Chapter 11.

SPECIAL EQUIPMENT

The amount of special equipment needed by a typographer depends on the nature of the work undertaken and the size of the office. Some of the following items are considered necessary by many designers, and are not used by others. It is hoped that all the items mentioned will be available in training colleges and you should certainly familiarize yourself with them and know their capabilities and disadvantages.

Photocopier A photocopier is an almost essential time-saver and, more important, can be an insurance against loss. A designer working alone, without a secretary or typewriter, can annotate a letter or document received, and send back a photocopy as his reply, although this must be done with discretion, as some recipients might find it discourteous. The 3M Dry-Photo-Copier Model 051 is probably the best small photocopier on the market: it will take up to A4 sheets, but does not give good reproduction of half-tones in my experience. Photocopying which requires good reproduction of photographs (some machines can reproduce three-dimensional objects such as bookbindings), enlargement or reduction, quantity production, etc., is best obtained by going to firms which specialize in such services, who exist in nearly all cities today and are quick, cheap and efficient.

High quality copiers are made by Agfa Gevaert (e.g. 'Rapidoprint') and Kodak. They will make copies which will usually be good enough for reproduction, although not as good as will be obtained from a first-class photograph. To evaluate them, you must see what process is involved, what materials are required, how long it takes to make a copy and how good the result is in terms of the sort of work for which you want to use it.

These machines usually do not enlarge, or reverse: for that you need additional equipment.

Light-box This is for viewing transparencies, film, etc., under controlled conditions, and is useful – indeed, essential – for some kinds of tracing, and for checking register. A simple light box consists of a strip-light or bulb fitted under a sheet of glass, preferably clouded, with holes for dispersal of heat. If tremendously accurate evaluation and correction of transparencies is required, standard light values are needed so that designer, printer and plate-maker are using the same references.

For a detailed drawing of a light-table (and much well-illustrated information on drawing equipment) see the

Thames and Hudson Manual *Rendering with Pen and Ink* by R. W. Gill (London 1990).

Guillotine Used for trimming photographs, cutting sheets of paper, etc.: a time-saver, but dangerous. Make sure it has a guard, and that it is out of reach of children.

Grant Projector (in U.S., opaque projector) This is used for producing an enlarged or reduced image from a flat original on a glass screen, which can then be traced on to paper or, on certain machines, photo-printed. It is useful when, for example, an advertisement layout has to be adapted for different page sizes. For colour transparencies, a 'cold cathode box' attachment is required.

The latest equipment can be seen at Cowling & Wilcox Ltd, 26 Broadwick Street, London W1 or Langford & Hill Ltd, 38–40 Warwick Street, London W1.

Hand-held slide viewer, and slide projector, with screen The projector is the best way to view colour slides, and will also be useful if the designer is required to make a presentation to clients, or to give lectures.

Camera A camera is an 'almost essential' item of equipment for the contemporary typographer, but photography has its own literature and cannot be dealt with here.

Electronic calculator Invaluable, and now relatively cheap.

Telephone, telex and fax The uses of the telephone are too obvious to emphasize here. The advantages of telex and particularly fax are that all communication is printed (or written), that all incoming messages are received automatically and that the cost of transmission is lower than the telephone. This is important if your business requires continuous communication with both clients and printers on prices, production details and correction of proofs, and especially if you are dealing with printers and suppliers all over the country and perhaps abroad as well. The fact that the fax can transmit visual material makes it even more useful for the designer.

REFERENCE MATERIAL

The most obvious reference material needed by a typographer is type specimen sheets. It can be said that a typographer in general practice requires every type specimen sheet issued by every firm manufacturing letter assembly systems in the world, whether hot metal or film, and, worse still, every specimen sheet that has ever been issued. Many typographers spend their lives trying to achieve this aim, and it is not a waste of time; but what they will actually use is another matter.

This is 12 pt Times New Roman, a typical seriffed typeface

This is 12 pt Univers Medium, a popular sans-serif

'Legibility' is a dangerous – and interesting – word. It is dangerous because it is so often used as if it had a definitive or absolute meaning, which it does not have. It is a personal word, neither scientific nor precise. If you say 'that is legible', you mean only that you can read it: you do not know whether I can. 'Illegible' is worse, because it is nearly always emotive and expresses annoyance, rather than a fact.

In typographic design, 'legibility' is the word used to define a desirable quality in typefaces, lettering, pages of books, posters, road signs and words in any form. If we say something is legible, we mean that in our opinion or experience the people we want to read it can read it in the conditions in which we think they will see it. When discussing their own work, and in particular book pages, typographers use the word 'legible' to mean 'easily read'; and that is the sense in which it is used here.

To try to make something legible, the designer must know *what* is to be read, *why* it is to be read, *who* will read it, and *when* and *where* it will be read. 'Where' includes the quality of light, for reading is impossible for sighted people without some form of light. The way light is transmitted to the eyes, to and from the matter to be read, and the angle and distance of the viewer, will all affect the typographer's work.

Legibility is obtained by different means when writing on blackboards or on notepaper, or designing books, magazines, newspapers, motorway or street signs, neon lighting, films and display by cathode-ray tube; although the letters to be read may be the same.

To appraise the legibility of anything, therefore, we must know its purpose. A typeface intended for use in books printed in English can properly be appraised only when so used. A display face intended for magazine advertising has an entirely different purpose: its users may want it to be more 'noticeable' than 'legible'.

The legibility of a typeface intended for continuous reading depends first on its inherent qualities and second on how it is used. A good typeface poorly used may in those conditions be less legible (i.e. less easily read) than a poor typeface well used.

Today in Britain and America the two commonest kinds of typeface used for reading matter are 'roman' (with serifs) and 'sans-serif' (which, as the name implies is without serifs, the little finishing strokes at the ends of letters, derived from the pen and the chisel). For the history of sans-serif types and the reasons why they are so much used today, see Chapter 5; here, we must discuss their 'legibility'. When we look carefully at seriffed and sans-serif types, we find that serifs have three prime functions: (1) they help to keep letters a certain distance apart; (2) at the same time they link letters together to form words, which helps reading (because it has been shown that we read our own language not letter by letter but by recognizing the shapes of words); and (3) they help to differentiate individual letters, particularly the top

Previous page:
Above: nineteenth-century floriated 'A'. *Below:* a contemporary magazine title, which although hardly 'legible' is perfectly 'recognizable'.

halves, which is what we recognize words by, rather than the bottom halves. You can prove this for yourself by taking a straight edge of paper, or a ruler, and laying it over the top half of a sentence and seeing whether you can then read it by its lower half. Whether you can or cannot, you will find it far easier to read if you cover the lower half and can see the top half only.

The letters whose top halves are less easily distinguishable without serifs are generally (for this may vary according to the actual design of the face)

aclmnpqgo

aclmnpqgo

Letters of a language one knows are easier to read when composed in words than when seen singly, because one knows by the context what a given letter ought to be; but if you see the following 'word' out of context, by itself, set in a sans-serif face

you cannot tell whether it says: 'three'
'one hundred and eleven'
'Ill'

or it might be three cricket stumps, or have a mathematical meaning. This reminds us of the definition of legibility once made by the poet Robert Bridges, who was also deeply interested in handwriting and printing: 'True legibility consists of the *certainty of deciphering*; and that depends not on what any one reader may be accustomed to, nor even on the use of customary forms, but rather on the consistent and accurate formation of the letters.'[1] Bridges was referring to handwriting, but his words apply equally to printing.

The 'certainty of deciphering' is an important element in true legibility; and in relation to typography, it bears the message that legibility, or ease of reading, is increased by letters that are clearly distinguishable from each other, and decreased by letters that look too much like each other. The 'certainty of deciphering' therefore brings a positive meaning to the word 'legibility'.

The trademark of the British electronics company Plessey. By themselves, the letters are not letters: together, they make a word.

THREE RULES OF LEGIBILITY

From the foregoing we deduce the first rule of typographical legibility *in text setting for continous reading*:

1 Sans-serif type is intrinsically less legible than seriffed type. It is less legible because it is inherent in sans-serif type that some of the letters are more like each other than letters that have serifs, and so the certainty of decipherment is diminished; and the serifs have other functions that help reading, as mentioned above.

This does not mean that all matter set in sans-serif type is always, or is necessarily, less legible than if set in roman type. It does mean that there is an 'illegibility factor' in sans-serif type that must not be forgotten; and one result of the loss of serifs is that pages of type set in sans-serif have a uniformity and evenness of 'colour' (because the serifs are missing) that makes them look monotonous and therefore unattractive. This can of course be guarded against by various devices: first by interlinear spacing (the appearance and readability of text set in sans-serif type is always improved by this), then by cross-headings, paragraphs, illustrations and so on, to break up the solid area of unbroken text.

Sans-serif, well used, is more legible than seriffed type badly used; and there are occasions when a designer will prefer sans-serif to a seriffed type for special aesthetic reasons. But for all *continuous* reading matter, seriffed type, properly used, is likely to be more easily read than 'sans'.

The second rule of typographical legibility *in text setting for continuous reading is*:

2 Well-designed roman upper- and lower-case type is easier to read than any of its variants, e.g. italic, bold, caps, expanded or condensed versions. This statement is to be taken as a guiding principle only, with many exceptions: a few italics, especially those which are 'sloped romans', not true italics, are as easy to read as romans, and so are some 'condensed' types (see Chapter 5). The basic principle is that roman type has become the 'norm' for most Europeans and Americans. The variants were designed or have come to be used for special purposes, such as emphasis or variety, rarely for increased legibility, and in nearly every case will be less easy to read than normal roman if used for continuous text setting.

For this reason the distinguished typographer Sir Francis Meynell used to advise, perhaps with tongue in cheek, that poetry should be set in italic, because poetry ought to be read slowly, and italic is slower to read than roman.

It must be remembered that in designing a specific book, legibility will always be only one of several factors to be considered; and when using well-designed typefaces, legibility is not an absolute but a comparative term.

The third rule of typographical legibility *in text setting for continuous reading is*:

3 Words should be set close to each other (about as far apart as the width of the letter 'i'); and there should be more space between the lines than between the words. The space between the lines – called in the old technology 'leading', because the space was created by inserting thin strips of lead metal between the lines, but now called 'interlinear spacing' – is a vital factor in legibility, and it can be stated as a rule of thumb that all continuous text matter is made easier to read by interlinear spacing.

These are the basic principles of legible setting in roman upper- and lower-case type. Since the practised eye reads word by word, or in word clusters, recognizing the shapes of the words, not letter by letter, it does not need more than a small gap between words; if the gap becomes too big, it may be bigger than the space between the lines, thus tempting the eye to jump to the next line rather than to the next word; and if the line is longer than about twelve words, the eye has got to go too far back and has difficulty in picking up the correct next line.

There are many other factors which affect 'legibility', which will recur throughout this book, and will be dealt with at their appropriate places. Many are matters of common sense, many are matters of judgment and experience and guessing, many depend on a number of interrelated factors, some of which may be outside the designer's control; and, finally, legibility of printed matter will also depend, most importantly, on the quality, surface and colour of the paper used by the printer, and how he machines the type on to it. The above three 'rules' are all that can be safely set down as 'rules of thumb'; but two other points may be made here.

First, legibility is not always a prime requirement of printed matter; and we are not now thinking only of continuous reading matter. Legibility, in its strict sense, may be less important than both noticeability and recognizability. For example, the prime requirement of an announcement on a notice-board or in a newpaper may be that it should be noticed, for if it is not noticed, it will not be read. To make it noticed, methods may be adopted which make it apparently less legible, e.g. it may be printed upside down, or in white on black ('reversed out'), or with some other form of distortion. Again, with logotypes, such as trademarks or magazine titles, legibility is less important than recognizability and memorability. The famous 'Plessey' trademark (*opposite*) is not legible out of context; but it does not have to be. It has to be recognizable and memorable, which to a high degree it is. Exactly the same applies to the title of a magazine or newspaper that will be repeated in every issue, or lettering on a shop front: instant legibility, the first time it is seen, is far less important than that it should remain, for its intended life, distinctive, attractive and recognizable.

A typeface called 'Indépendant' (*c.* 1930), with some built-in illegibility.

Secondly, to quote from Beatrice Warde again: 'Type . . . can be legible and dull, or legible and fascinating, according to its design and treatment. In other words, what the book-lover calls readability is not a synonym for what the opticians calls "legibility".'[2]

The difference between legibility and readability must be pondered on by every book designer. Mere 'legibility' is now easy, with over five hundred years of printing practice to look back on; 'readability' is where the command of one's craft is truly tested.

In yet another definition of legibility, Francis Meynell once said: 'By legibility I mean a proper observance in all its infinite details of that principle of order and convention which is the basis of written communication. Printing is the vehicle; legibility is the well-greased bearing that allows the wheels of sense to revolve without squealing.' He was not, in fact, defining legibility in the oculist's sense, at all, but readability or the skill of designing books.[3]

SEE STANDEASY AT MODULEX 78

Right: an ingenious face by Letraset, called 'Stop': to be used with caution.

Below: lettering or type from a travel advertisement which is difficult to read even when the words are recognized.

gran canaria

Letters some of which are legible
only when helped by other, more
easily recognizable, letters.

LEGIBILITY RESEARCH

A great deal of research has been carried out during this
century into the legibility of print, and also into the
psychological and physiological processes of reading and
comprehension. I believe that no research so far published
has been seriously helpful to designers concerned with the
design of a straightforward reading matter for literate adults,
except insofar as it has, in general, confirmed their practice.
Research in legibility, even when carried out under the most
'scientific' conditions, has not yet come up with anything
fundamental that typographic designers did not already
know – or believe – with their inherited experience of five
hundred years of printing history and their specialized
observation of the civilization in which they live. For
example, one authority, Tinker, had concluded that 'black
print on a white background is over ten per cent more
efficient than white on black'.[4] I am glad to hear it, but after
even ten years as a typographer it would never have occurred
to me to think otherwise. I believe that research once
'proved' that maximum legibility for posters lay in black type
on yellow paper; it is useful to remember, but no such dictum
will hold good for every poster design problem that arises:
just for a start, what black, what type, what yellow, what
paper and where? Research has shown that red is a 'dense'
colour, as is black, so that black on red, or red on black, are
poor in legibility: that *is* useful to know, as one might not
have guessed it. Experience adds that red ink and red paint
fade in sunlight, often quickly.

The findings of most 'laboratory' tests of legibility prove,
if they prove anything, what suited those people, of that age
and sex, at that time of day (tired? well fed? hungry? in good
or bad temper?), in that month, in those conditions. But
every job a typographer tackles is in a different set of
conditions, and his skill is first to find out what those
conditions are, and then to design particularly for them.

It is in special cases – in which the typographer's work
abounds – that research must be respected. Research into the
legibility of lettering and print *has* been helpful in specialized
areas, such as print for children and for those with poor
vision or for handicapped or elderly people, the design of
bibliographical entries, telephone directories, and motorway
signing – where only research, and nobody's guessing, could

47

logica

A perfectly acceptable logotype; it is surprising how easily it can be read.

Live births

Deaths

Wheat

Shipping

Armed forces

Isotype symbols, invented by Otto and Marie Neurath in Vienna in the 1920s, represent stated quantities of the items shown, and are used to present statistical information in graphic form.

discover how tall, and in what forms and colours, letters should be if they are to be legible at a safe distance by a car driver travelling at speed on a motorway.

Research of one kind or another is indeed required before almost any important typographical problem is tackled. If an airline approaches a designer and asks for a new livery and symbol for its aircraft, vehicles and staff, research is certainly required to ascertain the exact designs, colours and systems of every other airline in the world. If a bus company requires new timetables, research is required into the precise services the company offers, what other transport is available in the area, who uses the transport and why, what forms of communication already exist between the company and its public, how often and how dependably the buses actually run, and much more besides.

It must be remembered that there are different kinds of reading: a novel, a cookery book, a dictionary and a telephone directory are all 'read', but in different ways, which will affect the typographer's choice of type and type size, length of line, use of bold and italic, and so on. Businessmen and cabinet ministers, for example, have to read hundreds of reports, usually typewritten, and the way these documents are presented may make a lot of difference to their readers. Some reports have to be carefully read all through and absorbed: they should follow the normal principles of book readability, i.e. about 10–12 words a line and with some interlinear spacing. Other reports can be more quickly scanned, to see whether they mention certain subjects or not; they could be typed with shorter lines and greater interlinear spacing, possibly with main topics underlined. The designer must always ask 'What, why, who, when and where?'

Whatever the problem appears to be, it has to be researched, and sometimes it is found to be quite different from what someone supposed. Some research can be undertaken by an individual designer, or by his staff; but on major jobs, professional researchers may have to be employed. Let their qualifications and methods be the subject of some close research too!

Research into reading, learning, comprehension and teaching processes can make a significant contribution to much work by typographers, particularly those who work in teaching or educational publishing. If the problem is how to convey different kinds of information – sometimes extremely complex – to different kinds of people – e.g. children in the Third World, who have a totally different cultural background and speak a different language – words may no longer be the best medium. The typographer/communicator must therefore study communication in other forms than words: e.g. illustration of all kinds, diagrams, isotypes (pictorial diagrams designed by the Isotype Institute), algorithms ('a set of rules or directions for getting a specific output from a specific input'[5]) – typography is by no means the only kind of communication.

4 Lettering and calligraphy

Symbols by Jock Kinneir for British Rail Hotels (symbolizing night and day service) and vehicle testing stations.

'Lettering' is the drawing of letters by hand: 'calligraphy' is 'beautiful writing' or, as Stanley Morison defined it, 'freehand in which the freedom is so nicely reconciled with order that the understanding eye is pleased to contemplate it'.[1] In fact, it is difficult to establish any real difference in meaning between the two words, and they are often used synonymously.

The connection between lettering (or calligraphy) and typography is fundamental. Typography is lettering adapted for a special purpose. Lettering, or calligraphy, lies behind everything that a typographer does. And today, when types no longer have to be cut in metal, the influence of drawing on typography is going to become stronger. 'Type' now means anything you can get out of any composition system, and it may not be long before you can draw your own letters and images into it, as well as command the types that are already there. Calligraphy and drawing are today much more a part of typographic design than ever before.

It is worth remembering that the calligrapher Edward Johnston designed the first modern functional sans-serif, which is still used by London Transport (on London bus-stop signs, on the buses themselves and their destination indicators).

How far should a young typographer go in the study of lettering? The answer must lie in himself or herself. It should anyway be a labour of love – but it does mean hard work and practice. The more calligraphy you can learn, the better. Certainly, you must practise with different tools, such as pens of all kinds, perhaps goose quills and/or reeds which you have cut yourself, and brushes. Letters should also be *cut*, both positive and negative, in linoleum (which is easy) and, if possible, in wood, metal and stone.

Just as freehand drawing is an essential part not only of the work, but also of the life, of any designer, so drawn lettering is an integral part of a typographer's function. How much use you make of it in your professional work depends on yourself, and on the opportunities that come your way. Lettering to go on buildings, and for outdoor and indoor signing, are legitimate tasks for typographers. You may actually specialize in type design: this is a highly technical business, but a very important one. There are many opportunities to design special alphabets, for signing, for private use by big companies, on buildings, vehicles or advertising, and for several other purposes, quite apart from the requirements of the dry lettering and typeface companies.

You will certainly find occasions in book, magazine and newspaper design when existing typefaces do not provide an adequate solution to the problem, and it will be necessary to draw the initial, the title, the spine lettering or the logo – if there is time and the client will pay for it.

Lettering on buildings, and signing, are specializations for which the typographer is better trained than anyone else. It is not enough to pick a typeface from a specimen book and

Previous page: first brush-drawn rough for a monogram by S. L. Hartz.

enlarge it to stick on a building, although this has been done regrettably often. Typefaces are designed to be read from close to; they need modification, or total re-thinking, for use out of doors, in varying conditions of light, in a three-dimensional context. Although this is a logical extension of a typographer's work, it is unfortunately not often a re-munerative one, as provision for it to be properly done is often omitted from architects' estimates. Britain's motorway signs, probably the best in the world, were designed by a typographer, Jock Kinneir, who has also designed some of the most successful logotypes in Britain today (e.g. for Ryman shops, British Rail Hotels and the three triangles for vehicle testing stations).

The use of lettering for writing out continuous texts is not the typographer's business, and is in a sense a contradiction of typography. Lettering should be used for text only when it provides a better solution to a problem than type.

LETTER SHAPES

All typography stems from the various shapes of our alphabetical letters and numbers. These must therefore be learned: and the best, the most enjoyable, way to learn is to practise. As you draw, you learn, you explore, you will 'invent' (which means 'find').

One of the most interesting things to study is the *essential* character of each letter. Each letter has its own essential nature. It is very hard to say how or why or where the line is drawn; but some departures from the basic shape of a letter look far and fantastic, yet the letter is clearly identifiable. Other variations seem slight, yet it is no longer that letter: its recognizability is destroyed. This curious question, of when a letter ceases to be itself, is illustrated in Eric Gill's delightful *Essay on Typography* (1936), and is fundamental to typographic design.

One of the best books from which to start learning how to draw lettering is still Edward Johnston's *Writing & Illuminating, & Lettering*, first published in 1906: its illustrations, by Johnston and Noel Rooke (particularly Rooke's marvellous drawings of hands holding pens, etc.) and general presentation have caused it to be called the best manual about a craft ever produced. There are also many other books; but the best way to learn how to letter is as the pupil of a good teacher.

The connection between lettering – or calligraphy – and type design is evident all through the work of the men who have designed typefaces. As far as I know, no drawings exist that can be attributed to the hands of Claude Garamond or any of the other early type designers (including Caslon and Baskerville); but plenty of drawings exist – although not many have yet been published – from the hands of Eric Gill (designer of Perpetua), Fred Goudy (Goudy Old Style),

When is an A not an A? The last three examples are from Eric Gill's *Essay on Typography*, 1936.

*The incised capital letters on
Trajan's column in Rome (AD 114)
were for long regarded as the
'perfect' Roman letter, and the only
kind taught in many British art
schools, although a different, and
some think a better, tradition exists
in England. See Nicolete Gray,
Lettering on Buildings (London 1960),
and James Mosley, 'English
Vernacular', *Motif,* 11 (1963).

W. A. Dwiggins (Electra), Jan van Krimpen (Romanée), Jan Tschichold (Sabon), Sem Hartz (Juliana), Berthold Wolpe (Albertus), Hermann Zapf (Sistina), Max Caflisch (Columna), Will Carter (Klang) and so on. Those were all typefaces of a certain formality: if, behind them all, the Trajan capitals* parade like Puritans, remember that there are also other virtues. Roughness and dash, unevenness and informality also have their place in type design. Think of the note-book page of scribbling (but it is not scribbling) by F. H. Ernst Schneidler reproduced in *Typographica,* 1 (1949), and the same designer's types Legenda and Graphik. Think also of Imre Reiner's Sinfonia and Reiner Script; of Johannes Boehland's Balzac and Ashley Havinden's Ashley Script.

The freedom of these types is something that badly needs exploring at the present time, to enrich book, magazine and even newspaper design. Yet, in the words of the French typefounder, Charles Peignot, 'A clear distinction must be made between lettering and type design. In lettering, fantasy is of the essence. In type design discipline is the first requisite. In both cases education and a proper sense of tradition are all important.'[2]

ITALIC

Whereas 'lettering' is formal (concerned mostly with small groups of letters or words, as on book jackets, posters, signs and so on) calligraphy may be less formal, because it is writing; and writing to be practical has to be fast. But fast writing can still be beautiful, and the script that has solved this problem most successfully is the kind of writing known today as 'italic'. It originated in Rome in the first half of the fifteenth century as a hand for writing official documents, and was known as *Littera Cancellarescha,* 'chancery script'. It was first cut as a typeface by the Venetian humanist and publisher Aldus Manutius in about 1500, who used it as a text face: he set entire books in it, because he considered it the most appropriate kind of letter for that kind of book. Italic did not become the 'partner' of Roman type, as it is today, until several centuries later.

Italic type appeared in the first known printed writing manual, that of Ludovico Vincentino (known as Arrighi) in 1522, and became the normal hand used by people educated under the influence of the Renaissance, all over Europe. It was used in the Court of Henry VIII, and Queen Elizabeth I learned it as a girl: she wrote it most beautifully, and you can buy postcard reproductions of her writing in the British Museum, the Bodleian Library in Oxford and elsewhere.

Italic handwriting is accepted today as the best way for ordinary people to learn to write in a way that combines speed, legibility and beauty. It is easy to learn – if you have some aptitude, which as a designer you almost certainly will have. The best way to learn is very simple: find a model

feceris. Deinde vt teperatę sit
gracilitatis rostrū, quo sensim per
hoc, quatum singulis creandis sufse-
cerit literis, atramentū fluat .
Contractum eni atq̄ ampliū plus
aequo alimeti literis mittit, tenel-
lum Verò & longius minus .
Postea vt extremā cuspidem ea
parte modicè altius refeces, qua te
scribente calamus prominet, quip-
pe vt resectionis huius linea, dum
calamus officiū prebet, tota in pa-
pyri planiciem cadat. Deniq̄
    vt eadem hęc medio sui
        sec tionem prius
    fac tam   admittat .
    Exempli   causa

Mercator's treatise on writing italic,
Louvain 1540. *Left*: a page engraved
by Mercator on wood (reduced).
Below: a woodcut illustrating how to
hold a pen for calligraphy (reduced).

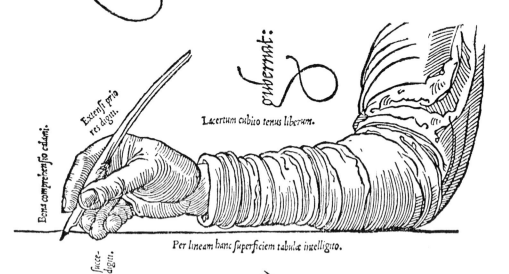

53

Dwiggins' personal device for himself and Dorothy Abbe, used on compliments slips, address labels, envelopes etc.

Letter of Protection issued by King Christian III of Denmark, c. 1556.

which pleases you, and copy it, with any sort of pen or pencil. There are plenty of books which give all sorts of elaborate instruction, to be found in every good library: have a look at them, and see if they help you. But if you are not moved by the beauty of a genuine italic model, it will be hard work and not, as it should be, a pleasure.

Italic handwriting, and its attendant flourishes, for its most natural execution requires an obliquely cut and flexible nib, which can make both thin and thick strokes: but it *can* be done with any pen, even a rapidograph. And let it not be thought that it will mask the character of the writer who practises it: character shows through italic as through any other kind of writing. Look at any collection of calligraphic hands and you will see.

A typographer's business is to enhance communication: let him start with his own handwriting.

LETTERING AS DESIGN

The use of lettering in conjunction with typography is of the greatest importance in every kind of modern design, and the young designer should form a collection of all the examples of it that come to hand. It can enliven book jackets, title-pages, letterheads, advertisements, almost everything. Nearly all Imre Reiner's books are full of examples; Dwiggins was another typographer whose pen was always dancing off into decoration, illustration or calligraphy, often all three being completely integrated.

It is a strange fact that beauty in lettering has nothing to do with the meaning of the words lettered. Lettering and calligraphy are in fact abstract arts: the traits and swirls of Bickham and Reynolds Stone are equally fair, whether the word written is 'Amaranth' or 'Dolcis'. The famous Edward Johnston letter to Fred Phillips which begins with what look like three great P's (but are not) is visually, rather than verbally, exciting. Persian and Chinese calligraphy are entrancing to people who cannot read them. Indeed, there need not even be any words: a page of A's and B's can be lovely. What moves us is something formal and, in the last resort, inexplicable.

*Slesuici Holsatiæ, Stormariæ et Dytmariæ Dux, Comes in Oldenbo
nibus et singulis, pro cuiusq; statu, dignitate, ordine et officio, pace
amus, simulq; significamus quod qui literas has nostras exhib
ditus noster et incola, præsentiisq; nauis, Vacca appellatæ, præfect
ad impiam et scelestam piratarum quorundam comprimendam ei*

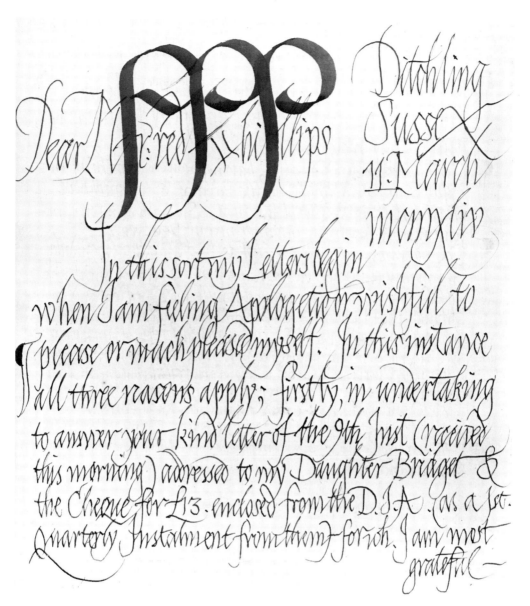

Dear Mr. Fred Phillips

Ditchling Sussex 11. March mcmxliv

In this sort my Letters begin when I am feeling Apologetic or wishful to please or much please myself. In this instance all three reasons apply; firstly, in undertaking to answer your kind letter of the 9th Inst (received this morning) addressed to my Daughter Bridget & the Cheque for £13. enclosed from the D.I.A. (as a 1st Quarterly Instalment from them) for wh. I am most grateful—

Letter from Edward Johnston to
Fred Phillips dated 11 March 1944
(reduced). Courtesy Victoria and
Albert Museum.

La belle écriture demande un esprit gai pour son exécution

'Beautiful writing requires gaiety for its execution.' Apparently written by Alfred Fairbank: see _Calligraphy and Palaeography_, London 1965, p. 176.

To a very limited extent, lettering may help to express a feeling or a mood that is in harmony with the meaning of the words. On a book jacket, or in a magazine or newspaper article title, lettering should help to make the article look like what it is, as well as stating what it is: it may be ecclesiastical, or delicate, or chunky, or traditional, or avant-garde. Can lettering, by its form, express grief, or hope? That surely is the province of words or drawing. When rope is coiled to form the words 'Ship Ahoy', or branches writhe into 'Our Trees', or there is a heavy snowfall on the serifs, that is illustration, not calligraphy. The loop and lift of a flourished letter expresses nothing that has anything to do with the words involved.

5 Letters for printing

Do not take this one.

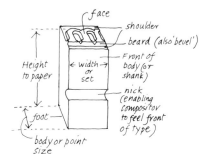

The shoulder at head and foot of the type (also sometimes called the beard) supports the ascenders and descenders of lower-case type.

An italic 'f' in metal type is 'kerned' on both sides, and the kerns are supported by the shoulders of the adjacent types.

Previous page: drawing by van Krimpen for 'Sheldon', a typeface commissioned in 1947 by Oxford University Press for use in Bibles in 7 pt. (The instruction is in van Krimpen's hand.)

DESCRIPTION AND CLASSIFICATION

Letters for printing require to be described and categorized by typographers, just as plants need to be described by botanists, in universally accepted terminology. Even when all types were cast in metal, no common language or code existed for their description; now that the restrictions of metal manufacture have been removed, a new 'language' for type description, classification and measurement (inside a metrical system) is urgently required. Whatever system is adopted must be on an international basis, since publishing today is an international business. Typographical students must keep an eye open for all attempts to find a solution to this problem.

A further problem is that many words used by printers, designers and publishers have different meanings; the word 'page', for example, is used to mean one side of a piece of paper only and also both sides, which in a book is more correctly called a 'leaf'. The word 'roman' can mean a type with serifs, or it can be used to indicate the opposite of 'italic'. 'Roman' figures are set in capital letters (I, II, III, IV), as opposed to 'arabic' figures (1, 2, 3, 4). 'Folio' means a sheet of paper folded once, to give four printed pages; a book made up of sheets so folded; and the number of a page. The words 'fount' and 'font' have the same meaning: 'font' is used in this book, for a complete set of type characters of the same design and size.

CLASSIFICATION OF TYPEFACES

Since many words describing typefaces (e.g. gothic, antique and Antiqua, grotesque, modern) have different and sometimes opposite meanings in different languages, the French designer Maximilien Vox (1894–1974) devised a new system for which he invented artificially composed names which did not carry associations of ideas liable to perpetuate the old confusions. This is the only system of classification that has had enough support to be adopted as a British Standard (BS 2961: 1967) and by A Typ I (Association Typographique Internationale) and is accordingly given here. It must be emphasized that in any one group there will be few 'pure' examples – many typefaces have characteristics that belong to other groups – but the Vox system is a useful aid to communication and description. Not all the Vox titles are easy to turn into English. Where I have preferred a different title to that used in BS 2961 (which is due to be revised in 1980–81) the BS title is given in brackets.

Group I: Humanist
These are the earliest roman types, based on humanistic script, first seen in Venice in the fifteenth century. Examples: Verona, Rogers's Centaur, Goudy's Kennerley.

Aa	**Aa**	**Aa**
Centaur I. HUMANIST	*Caslon* II. GARALD	*Baskerville* III. TRANSITIONAL
Aa	**Aa**	**Aa**
Bodoni IV. DIDONE	*Rockwell*	*Grot 215* VI. LINEAL (a) Grot
Aa	**Aa**	**Aa**
Univers VI. LINEAL (b) Neo-Grot	*New Clarendon Bold* V. MECHANISTIC	*Futura Light* VI. LINEAL (c) Geometric
Aa	**Aa**	**Aa**
Gill Sans VI. LINEAL (d) Humanist	*Albertus* VII. INCISED	*Ashley* VIII. SCRIPT
Aa	**Aa**	**لن**
Mercurius IX. MANUAL	*Old English Text* X. BLACK LETTER	*Farsi* XI. NON-LATIN

The journey will
They specialized in
ABCDEFGHJK

Monotype Garamond 18 pt

the diversity, quali
Become expert in th
ABCDEFGHIJKL

Monotype Bembo 18 pt

When jobs have
When jobs have
ABCDEFGHIJ

Monotype Plantin 18 pt

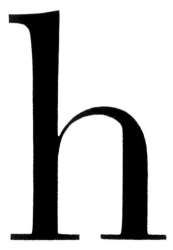

Linotype Caledonia, of which the designer, W. A. Dwiggins, wrote: 'We turned to one of the types that Bulmer used, cut for him by William Martin around 1790 . . . an attempt was made to add weight to the characters and still keep some of the Martin swing . . . about the "liveliness of action" that one sees in the Martin letters . . . that quality is in the curves – the way they get away from the straight stems with a calligraphic flick, and in the nervous angle on the under side of the arches as they descend to the right.' (From *Caledonia, a new printing type . . .* Mergenthaler Linotype Co., New York 1939).

Group II : Garald (name formed from *Gara*mond and *Ald*us)
These are the roman types deriving from those cut by Francesco Griffo for the Venetian printer-publisher Aldus Manutius. They include Garamond, Bembo, Caslon, Ganeau's Vendôme, Mardersteig's Dante, Novarese's Garaldus, Tschichold's Sabon.

The normal English term 'old face' makes no distinction between Groups I and II. It is an unsatisfactory term because intrinsically meaningless.

Group III : Transitional
These types are transitional between 'old face' and 'modern'. The prototype is the French typecutter Grandjean's Romain du Roi (1694), based on a report made by the Académie des Sciences in which an elaborate construction of each letter was made on a mathematical basis, in which each letter was drawn on a square containing 2,304 small squares, an odd anticipation of digitized letter forms. The Romain du Roi, private to the Imprimerie Royale, was echoed sixty years later by the types of John Baskerville; both embodied 'the spirit, simultaneously rationalist and realist, of the Age of the Encyclopedists'.[1]

Examples: the types of Fleischmann and Rosart; modern examples are Monotype Fournier, Baskerville, Bell, Times and Photina, and on Linotype, Dwiggins's Caledonia.

Group IV : Didone (name formed from *Did*ot and Bod*oni*)
These types, invented by Didot and perfected by Bodoni, are classified in England by the meaningless term 'modern'. They are characterized by vertical shading and hairline serifs, introduced in the middle of the eighteenth century when improvements in presses and paper-making made such fine lines possible to print. Didot's types are still the most commonly used book faces in France. Examples: Didot, Bodoni, Falstaff.

Group V : Mechanistic (Slab serif)
The title, perhaps sounding unintentionally pejorative to English ears, denotes that these types originated in the high flowering of the Industrial Revolution; the large area of their faces made them ideal for decoration, sometimes of the most extravagant kind. These types are also known in England as 'Egyptian'. Examples: Memphis, Jost's Beton, Clarendon, Ionic, Rockwell, Zapf's Melior.

Group VI : Lineal
Types without serifs, known today as 'sans' or 'sans-serif'; known also as 'grot' (from 'grotesque') in England, 'grotesk' in Germany and 'gothic' in USA. For notes on the history and use of sans, see below. BS 2961 gives four subdivisions: (a) 'Grotesque', which are sans of nineteenth-century origin (e.g. Monotype 215 and 216, and Headline Bold; and Stephenson Blake's Grot no. 6).

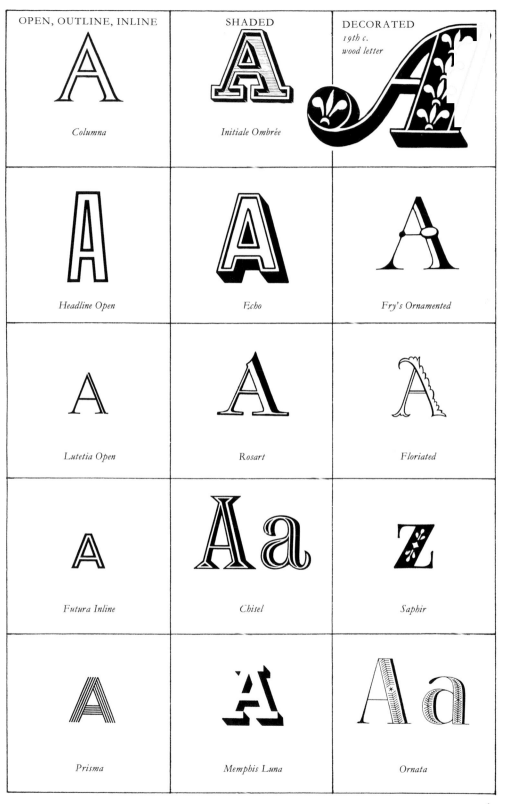

OPEN, OUTLINE, INLINE	SHADED	DECORATED
Columna	*Initiale Ombrée*	19th c. wood letter
Headline Open	*Echo*	*Fry's Ornamented*
Lutetia Open	*Rosart*	*Floriated*
Futura Inline	*Chisel*	*Saphir*
Prisma	*Memphis Luna*	*Ornata*

abcdefghijklmn
MNOPQRSTU

Bauer Futura

QRST

Ludwig & Mayer Erbar

QRST

Monotype Gill Sans

QRST

Monotype Perpetua

QRS

Stempel Optima

Legende abcd

Bauer Legende

Jonathan Swift

Amsterdam Reiner Script

Shak

Stempel Balzac

(b) 'Neo-grotesque', the modern sans such as Frutiger's Univers, and Miedinger's Helvetica. It is to be noted that these are drawn with great subtlety both for artistic reasons and to allow for deformation in printing (see pp. 69–70).

(c) 'Geometric': these are 'theoretical' faces constructed on geometrical shapes, usually monoline, and since the same curves and lines are used deliberately in as many letters as possible, there is the least differentiation between letters. Examples: Renner's Futura, Erbar's Erbar, Eurostyle.

(d) 'Humanist': these are sans based on the proportions of inscriptional Roman capitals and Humanist or Garald lower case. They may have much stroke contrast and may not be monoline. Examples: Gill's Gill Sans, Zapf's Optima, Mendoza's Pascal.

Group VII: Incised (Glyphic)

These are types based on letters cut in stone; the most characteristic 'incised' letters therefore tend to be capitals. Eric Gill's Perpetua can be called an 'Incised-Garald'; Gill was a stonecutter. Examples consisting only of capitals are Max Caflisch's Columna, Van Krimpen's Open Roman, and Goudy's Hadriano. Berthold Wolpe's Albertus, designed by a man trained in metalwork and other crafts, has a strong incised feeling and has been widely successful both as a typeface for display, and for inscriptional use on buildings.

Group VIII: Script

This denotes types that copy hand*writing*, as opposed to the next group, Manual, that denotes types that are *drawn*. The distinction is not always easy to maintain.

Italic is based on a kind of writing, but Vox excluded it from this category, presumably because today the word has come to mean a sloping face that is always associated with an upright version on which the categorization is based.

In English printing, 'copperplate' script is type that imitates the fine engraved writing that used to be used on copperplates, and which was for long the kind of handwriting most taught in English schools.

'Cursive' is used to describe types which resemble handwriting that is flowing rather than formal.

Examples of modern script typefaces are Excoffon's Mistral, Schlesinger and Dooijes's Rondo, Reiner's Reiner Script, Trafton's Trafton Script, Schneidler's Legend, Boehland's Balzac, Bernhard's Bernhard Cursive, Ashley Havinden's Ashley Script, Wolpe's Hyperion.

The difference between a 'Script' and a 'Manual' (the next category) may be difficult to define.

Group IX: Manual (Graphic)

This group includes types obviously based on hand-*drawn* originals, drawn with brush, pen, pencil or any other instrument but not representing *writing*, and therefore probably unsuitable for text setting: they are intended for publicity purposes. Most of the wildest creations of the transfer lettering manufacturers come in this group. Examples: Will Carter's Klang, Excoffon's Banco, Jacno's Jacno, Reiner's Matura, de Roos' Libra, Trafton's Cartoon.

Group X: Black letter

Black letter, the type in which printing in Europe began, is essentially a letter drawn with a wide nib, which originated, and remained, north of the Alps: the term 'gothic' was applied to it contemptuously by the humanist scholars of Italy. It is still widely used in Germany and other European countries.

'Black letter' is not a satisfactory term, because it is vague, but it is the word most commonly used by English-speaking printers for this kind of type, and it seems better to go on using it than to try and invent a new word. The alternative 'Gothic' is, by derivation, positively inaccurate when applied to lettering, and has other meanings. The German name *gebrochene Schriften* ('broken letters') describes the breaking of the curved main strokes of letters, and their terminals, into angles, but it does not sound happy in English.

Black letter has been classified in four main groups:[2]

1 Gotisch (English, 'Textura'). These types are compressed and angular, without curves in the lower case; the lower-case letters terminate, at both head and foot, in oblique rectangles. Examples: Hupp-Gotisch, Trump-Deutsch, Rudolph Koch's Wilhelm Klingspor, Cloister Black, Goudy Text, Minster Black, Monotype Old English Text.

2 Rundgotisch (English, 'Rotunda'). This was the Italianate version of the textura, transitional between it and *Schwabacher*. The letters became rounded, and did not end in rectangles. Examples: Rudolph Koch's Wallau, Weiss-Rundgotisch.

3 Schwabacher. This was a vernacular, popular type: the reason for the name is not known. Alexander Nesbitt says it has 'mandorla' rounds in lower case, and can be used where a religious feeling is to be avoided.[3] It was based on a cursive writing; the French variety was called 'lettre bâtarde'. Caxton's first types were of this character. Examples: Renata, Ehmcke-Schwabacher.

4 Fraktur. This has become the most common kind of black letter used in Germany today. Nesbitt says: 'It is the result of Renaissance influence upon Gothic letters – to be more definite, the influence of the baroque element of the Renaissance . . . one need but examine some of Albrecht Dürer's title-pages to see the introduction of the baroque flourishes and movement.'[4] The lower-case ascending letters characteristically have pronounced forked tops; lower-case 'a' does not have a loop at the top, and lower-case 'g' has an open curved tail. Examples: Unger-Fraktur, Fette Gotisch, Zapf's Gilgengart.

4a Fraktur-variants. Examples: Rudolph Koch's Claudius, Koch-Kurrent, Weiss-Fraktur, Heinrichsen-Kanzlei.

abcdefg
ABC

Monotype Old English Text

ABCDEFG
abcdefghijklmno

Monotype Goudy Text

ABCDE
aabcddee

Wilhelm Klingspor-Schrift

EINTRAGUNG RUDOLF
Das Herz ist

Klingspor Wallau Light & Bold

Frankfurt·

Stempel Alte Schwabacher

Start zum

Stempel Fette Gotisch

Der Starke ist am

Klingspor Kleist-Fraktur

abcdg

Original Unger-Fraktur

Group XI: Non-latin type forms

These, traditionally known by English printers as 'exotics', include all cyrillic, arabic and oriental typefaces.

For other terms used to describe typefaces, see ill. p. 76.

SANS-SERIF TYPE

The serif, as we have seen, is a small stroke added to the ends of roman letters, when written with a pen, or cut in stone, for reasons that are both functional and decorative. It came naturally to both chisel and pen; and was naturally incorporated in the versions of roman lettering cut as typefaces.

Serifs form a link between letters that help to 'bind' them together as words, while at the same time (in metal type) they create a thin white space between the main strokes of letters that helps recognizability and legibility.

A roman letter without serifs, caps only, first appeared as a typeface in 1816. It was then known as 'English Egyptian' (apparently for reasons connected with a vogue for things Egyptian derived from Napoleon's dreams of Asian empire)[5] and was intended as a display face for occasional use in advertising, although it does not seem to have been very widely used during the nineteenth century. The first lower case cut in London without serifs came from the typefounding firm of Thorowgood; it was called 'Seven Lines Grotesque', and appeared in 1835. It seems to have been called 'grotesque' because it looked grotesque to its contemporaries; and 'grotesque' (shortened to 'grot') became its ordinary name to British printers, until gradually superseded in recent years by 'sans-serif', soon shortened to 'sans'.

It is worth noting that sans was used on buildings and by signwriters, before it was cut as a typeface – for the obvious reason that it is easier to draw, paint or carve, than letters with serifs. An example on Brighton Pavilion, incorporating the date 1784, is shown in *Motif*, 6 (1961), p. 91. The sans letter, cut or painted on stone, goes back to the days of ancient Greece.

Sans can be found occasionally on book title-pages, and more often in advertisements, all through the nineteenth century, but I cannot remember ever seeing it used as a text face, at least for more than a paragraph, during the Victorian period.

Sans came into its own at the beginning of the twentieth century, when designers, especially in Germany, called for a typeface *unsere Zeit* – 'of our own time'. Curiously, the first new sans, designed to express 'our own time', was the one made in England in 1916 for the London Underground Railway, and still in use.

It was commissioned by Frank Pick from the calligrapher Edward Johnston, as we have already remarked: a reproduction of one of the preliminary drawings (now in the Victoria and Albert Museum) can be seen in *Motif*, 6 (1961),

p. 76, and sheets containing the full font can still be obtained from the London Passenger Transport Board. Eric Gill was actually present at the meeting between Pick and Johnston, on 29 October 1915, when the new face was discussed. In Beatrice Warde's words: 'What was afoot was the first "standardisation" of lettering forms for systematic use by a large organisation in signs, posters, and printed matter - and the designing, for the needs of a modern transport system, of the first twentieth-century sans serif of aesthetic merit. There is no reason to assume that Eric Gill played a creative part in the design of the famous "London Underground" letter. But there is every reason to note that he was drawn-in upon what must have been memorable conversations.'[6]

Of the Johnston alphabets, P. M. Handover wrote in *Motif*, 6 (1961): 'The alphabet was exceptionally economical of space, it was monoline [the strokes were of uniform thickness; but it was drawn in varying weights], it was legible, and in every detail it has been debated and considered. Johnston not only worked out the relationship between counter (the white space inside the letters) and mass (the general shape), but the spacing between letters, a nicety unknown to the grotesques of industrial jobbing. The use of such a designer's work on such an institution as the London transport system gave unseriffed letters an authority they had not before achieved.'

The letters designed by Johnston deserve close study and comparison with the more famous Gill Sans, designed by Johnston's pupil, assistant and friend, Eric Gill. Gill Sans was first cut by the Monotype Corporation in 1927 and eventually the family consisted of twenty-four related series.* Features of Johnston's alphabets that may seem strange to us (accustomed to Gill and Univers) are the square full points (set obliquely when above 'i' and 'j'), the lower-case 'g' (but a better 'g', like Gill's, appears in the trial drawings reproduced in *Motif*, 6 (1961), p. 7 *l*) and the cap 'S'. Johnston's lower-case 'l', however, cannot be confused with the cap 'I' (as happens in both Gill Sans and Univers) because he gave it a hook: an aid to legibility that has been followed by Jock Kinneir in the British motorway signs.

The 'modern movement' was based on ideas welling up all over the world, not only in Germany; Ruskin's and William Morris's dissatisfaction with the industrial system made an important contribution before the end of the nineteenth century, and started what became known as the Arts and Crafts Movement. But it was in Germany that the need to 'start again', to destroy the old, was felt with the greatest urgency. After the First World War, in 1918, sans-serif types were hailed in Germany as *the* typeface for the new age, the typographical expression of the new movements in art, sculpture and design which inspired, and were explored at, the Bauhaus, in that remarkable educational experiment founded in Weimar in 1919 by the architect Walter Gropius. The movement was concerned fundamentally not with art or

*See *The Versatile Gill Family of Type Faces*, The Monotype Corporation, n.d. The twenty-four series included some very minimal variations, available in one size only, and are not comparable with the scientifically planned twenty-one versions of Univers.

design ('art for art's sake' was specifically repudiated by the Bauhaus), but (following Ruskin and Morris) with how people should live and make use of, rather than become slaves of, the new technologies such as electricity, whose implications were then just becoming evident. As Kurt Rowland writes in *A History of the Modern Movement* (New York 1973): 'The concepts of standardisation and pre-fabrication in architecture and architectural design were explored in the Bauhaus . . . the concept of teamwork was explored and tested . . . under realistic conditions, defining the position of an individual designer within a team and the responsibility of the team to society.'

The Bauhaus under Gropius was concerned primarily with training people rather than designing products; but many concepts which still seem novel today were first worked out there. For example, 'In 1922 Moholy-Nagy had made the symbolic gesture of ordering the execution of a painting by telephone. With the colour chart used by an enamel factory and a squared up design in front of him he transmitted his "work of art" square by square. Art had become industrialized, or to put it another way, art and industry had moved closer together.'[7] Paul Klee, also on the staff of the Bauhaus, wrote at this time: 'Art does not render the visible, it renders visible.' The title of a book by Moholy-Nagy, *Malerei Photographie Film* (Munich 1925) (later translated as *Painting Photography Film* (London and Cambridge, Mass. 1969)) is significant.[8] To Moholy-Nagy, the camera (as Rowland points out) was not an instrument for recording life, but for exploring it. While he was experimenting with light and film, Kurt Schwitters and John Heartfield (a German who changed his name from Herzfelde in the middle of the First World War, in protest against the war, in which he had fought in the German army) were using photography in another way to make a new artform, known as 'collage' (paste-ups). The furniture workshop in the Bauhaus was directed by Marcel Breuer from 1925 to 1928, and from him came the classic tubular steel and plywood chairs that still do not look dated, chairs for mass production that are still being produced, and the concept of 'knock-down' furniture.

All this may sound a little far from typography; but typographers are designers. Some knowledge of the contributions made both to modern thinking and to our own surroundings by men such as (to name only a few) El Lissitzky, Theo van Doesburg, Kurt Schwitters, Piet Zwart, Laszló Moholy-Nagy, Man Ray, Walter Gropius, Herbert Bayer, Paul Klee, Josef Itten and Wassily Kandinsky is basic to the education of all typographers.

To return to sans-serif types. In the 1920s, the 'modern' typographers felt that sans represented letter design in its fundamental form: Jan Tschichold, in *Die neue Typographie* (Berlin 1928), wrote that its proper name should not be 'grotesque' but *skelettschrift* or 'skeleton lettering': it was the bare bones of the alphabet. Herbert Bayer (the principal typographer at the Bauhaus, but a lot of other things besides) designed a single-alphabet type, a simplification that appealed in theory but ignored the useful function of capital letters, and never caught on. Fifty years after the opening of the Bauhaus, Bayer designed the Bauhaus Exhibition Catalogue of 1968 entirely without capitals: the great size of this catalogue (364 pages) makes it easy to see that this is not an improvement that should be widely adopted, but is an interference with communication because it leads to ambiguities.

Tschichold, in 1929, also designed a single-alphabet sans-serif type, with a phonetic version,* but neither his nor Bayer's were accepted for use. Another German typographer, Paul Renner, after making experiments to find the 'pure' essence of the roman alphabet in sans-serif, designed a more conventional sans called 'Futura', which appeared in 1927 and is still often seen. In the same year, 1927, Rudolf Koch produced 'Kabel', another sans intended to express the spirit of the age, and Eric Gill's sans first appeared in Britain. Harold Curwen, a pupil of both Johnston and Gill, also designed 'Curwen Sans', first cut as a typeface, caps only, in 1927; the lower case was cut in 1931.

*Reproduced in Spencer's *Pioneers of Modern Typography* (London 1969) and my *Jan Tschichold, Typographer* (London 1975).

It was the essence of all these typefaces not only to have no serifs, but to have an even (or almost even) weight of line (i.e. no contrasts of thick and thin) and to have as many interchangeable components (e.g. the bowls of 'a', 'b', 'p', 'd', 'g', 'q') as possible, on the analogy of a factory production line. This seductive theory had to be paid for in loss of legibility, since the effect was, of course, to reduce the differences, and increase the similarities, between the individual letters – especially in the top halves, by which most of the recognition in continuous reading takes place.

The final *reductio ad absurdum* of their theory (that the capital 'I', lower case 'l' and figure '1' end up as identical – see Chapter 3) does not matter so much in continuous reading matter, where sense (provided you know the language) will tell you what the words are, but it might matter very much indeed in, for example, codes, alphabets for children, architecture or signs. Eric Gill's sans was different from Erbar's and Renner's in that it was drawn by an artist and designer who was already deeply involved with the classical roman alphabet as a letterer and carver of inscriptions, and whose classical roman typeface, 'Perpetua', was to appear in 1929. Gill is even reported to have said, of his sans, that it was a good face, but would have been better if it had had serifs. T. M. Cleland, the American graphic designer, remarked: 'Cutting the serifs off roman letters in the name of "simplicity" may well be compared to simplifying a man by cutting off his hands and feet!'[9] The letters of Gill Sans contained subtleties and refinements which the German designers, preferring the logic (or dictatorship) of ruler and compasses, could not admit.

It is also interesting to note the completely different climate of typographical taste in England during the period up to 1939, compared with that in Germany. In Germany, for many reasons which did not apply in Britain – including a much uglier general standard of both book and advertising typography – there was a greater need for revolutions, both in typography and architecture. Consequently, modern architecture, modern art and modern typography all thrived in Germany, while in England they were little understood and rarely seen. When the Nazis came to power in Germany in the 1930s they hated what was truly modern in art, because it was free and questioning: they labelled it as 'decadent' and proscribed it. In typography, they chose a bogus historicism and adopted black letter, which was nationalistic as opposed to international.

The revival of typography in Britain between 1918 and 1939 was, in contrast with the modern movement in Germany before the Nazis squashed it (when it continued in Switzerland), rooted in tradition and shared with America. The first freelance 'typographer', in the present-day meaning of that word, as mentioned in Chapter 1, was the American Bruce Rogers; Beatrice Warde, one of the most important and lively influences in the typography of the first half of the twentieth century, was an American who spent all her working life in Britain. Stanley Morison, the great English typographer, spent much time in Chicago and New York. American influence on British typography came from Updike, the prolific type designer Frederic Goudy, Bruce Rogers (who among other activities was typographic adviser to England's Cambridge University Press for some years), Frederic Warde, T. M. Cleland, W. A. Dwiggins, and the publications of the Limited Editions Club of New York, directed by George Macy. Influences on America from England came from, for example, Bernard Newdigate at the Shakespeare Head Press, Harold Curwen and Oliver Simon at the Curwen Press, Francis Meynell and his Nonesuch Press, Eric Gill, and the fine work of many British printers, notably the Oxford and Cambridge University Presses and the firms of R. & R. Clark of Edinburgh under William Maxwell and of Robert MacLehose of Glasgow. During the entire inter-war period, sans-serif type hardly ever appeared in Britain or America in any matter intended for continuous reading: one can remember it in railway and bus timetables, industrial catalogues and price lists, and that is about all.

One of the very few men in England before 1939 connected with printing who also understood and appreciated the modern movement in art and design was Eric Gregory, the London director of the Yorkshire printing firm of Lund Humphries in Bradford, who for many years printed and published *The Penrose Annual*. Gregory invited Jan Tschichold over to London in 1935, mounted a small exhibition of his work in Lund Humphries' London office, and commissioned him to redesign the firm's letterheading and the 1938 volume of *The Penrose Annual*. At the time, this had no effect at all on British typography, since a very good traditional or 'national style' already existed, but a few eyes were opened.

After the war, Lund Humphries appointed a young typographer, Herbert Spencer, as their design consultant, with the stated intention of using 'modern typography' for all their work. Spencer's influence, both as a designer, writer and editor of the periodical *Typographica* (1949–67) (and also the appearance of a few books meticulously designed by Anthony Froshaug), were factors in introducing to British designers an understanding and appreciation of the 'modernism' which typographers on the Continent had been practising since the 1920s.

The belief, originally preached by Tschichold and others in the early 1930s, that sans-serif was the only typeface suitable for use in the present century, and that it expressed the essential 'spirit of the age', has long since been abandoned; nevertheless, sans-serif did become the most used kind of type for almost every kind of printing (other than conventional book printing), and still holds that position today across Europe and the United States. To meet the demand, a new sans-serif typeface was specially commissioned by Charles Peignot from the Swiss designer Adrian Frutiger, and was by inspiration christened 'Univers'. It was first issued in 1957 by Deberny and Peignot and later by the Monotype Corporation. It was designed to be suitable for every kind of composition (hot metal, foundry type, filmsetting) and to be available in the greatest number of planned weights, and variations of width, that had ever been made for a single design. There are 21 fonts, in 5 weights and

How different weights and widths of Univers are balanced. Reproduced from *Graphismes by Frutiger*, Monotype House, London 1964, by kind permission of Adrian Frutiger.

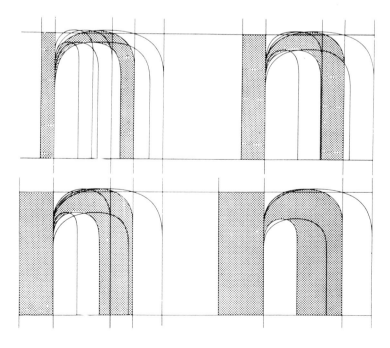

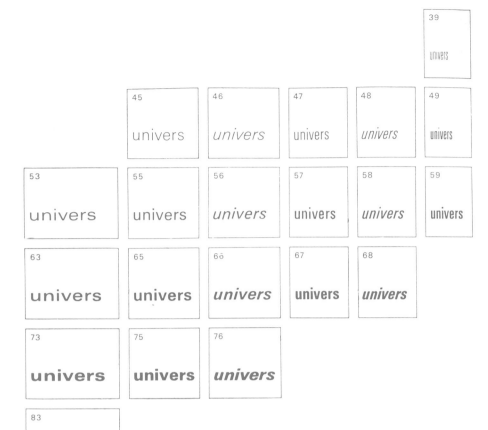

The original grid classification of Univers when first issued by Deberny and Peignot: weight is indicated by the tens figure, and width by the units figure; odd numbers are roman, and even numbers italic. Reproduced from *Graphismes by Frutiger*, 1964, courtesy Adrian Frutiger.

Optical, not mathematical, rules govern the weight and height of Univers letters. Reproduced from *Graphismes by Frutiger*, 1964, courtesy Adrian Frutiger.

4 widths, and all 21 were planned in detail before the first matrix was struck. No manufacturer has yet made all 21 for filmsetting; Monophoto makes 20. Many versions seen today are not true representations of Frutiger's designs.

Optical, not mathematical, rules governed the design of every letter in the series, as can be seen in the accompanying illustrations.

The very fact that Univers is used so much at present means that designers and advertisers will soon be looking for change, so that their work does not look like everybody else's; and as good filmsetting systems gradually, one hopes, oust the less good, the choice of excellent typefaces will widen.

But Univers will stay with us for a long time to come, and it is a very good face. It must, however, be remembered that all sans-serif faces used for text need leading (space between the lines) more than other faces; that the adjustment in filmsetting that sets letters closer to each other than normal (known as minus-setting) will diminish legibility quicker in sans than in seriffed faces; and that even when set and printed in the best possible way, pages of continuous reading matter set in sans tend to look more 'uniform', or featureless, than pages set in seriffed type, and require a little more effort to read.

Monotype

How can consistently high standards of typography be achieved and maintained ? Naturally much depends on the ability of the designer and on the technical accuracy of the layouts sent to the printer. Nevertheless, perfection in design and the technical accuracy in the marking of the layout for printer are only beginnings.

abcdefghijklmnopqrstuvwxyz   1234567890
ABCDEFGHIJKLMNOPQRSTUVWXYZ

Compugraphic

How can consistently high standards of typography be achieved and maintained? Naturally much depends on the ability of the designer and on the technical accuracy of the layouts sent to the printer. Nevertheless, perfection in design and the technical accuracy in the marking of the layout for printer are only beginnings.

Photon

How can consistently high standards of typography be achieved and maintained? Naturally much depends on the ability of the designer and on the technical accuracy of the layouts sent to the printer. Nevertheless, perfection in design and the technical accuracy in the marking of the layout for printer are only beginnings.

Monophoto

How can consistently high standards of typography be achieved and maintained ? Naturally much depends on the ability of the designer and on the technical accuracy of the layouts sent to the printer. Nevertheless, perfection in design and the technical accuracy in the marking of the layout for printer are only beginnings.

Linotron

How can consistently high standards of typography be achieved and maintained? Naturally much depends on the ability of the designer and on the technical accuracy of the layouts sent to the printer. Nevertheless, perfection in design and the technical accuracy in the marking of the layout for printer are only beginnings.

IBM Composer

How can consistently high standards of typography be achieved and maintained? Naturally much depends on the ability of the designer and on the technical accuracy of the layouts sent to the printer. Nevertheless, perfection in design and the technical accuracy in the marking of the layout for printer are only beginnings.

Six different versions of Univers Medium, 10 on 11 pt (the Monotype example is 9D on 11 pt), which demonstrate the variations from Frutiger's original designs (shown opposite) introduced with different filmsetting systems. Courtesy H.M.S.O.

A FONT OF TYPE

A font of type (the word is derived from 'found', as in typefoundry, and has no relevance in these days of filmsetting) was 'a set of letters and other symbols in which each sort was supplied in approximate proportion to its frequency of use, all being of one body-size and design. A fount of roman type consisted of CAPITAL LETTERS, SMALL CAPITALS, small ('lower case') letters, accented letters, ligatures (tied letters such as ffl, made from a single punch and matrix), punctuation marks, figures, and a few special symbols such as &, *, R, etc. (also %, $, £); this usually added up to about 150 sorts, and there were in addition spaces to go between words (short pieces of type of various thicknesses without letters cast on them) and quads (very wide spaces) for filling out blank lines, which were specific to the body but not to the design. Italic founts, which lacked small capitals, generally had about the same total number of sorts as roman because of the addition of extra ligatures and decorated (or 'swash') capitals.'[10]

In the days of hot-metal setting, a Monotype font (i.e. what was available on a single die-case, and could therefore be set without changing the die-case) sometimes included seven alphabets, viz. roman caps and lower case, roman small caps, italic caps and lower case, and bold caps and lower case.

The concept of 'font' does not have the same meaning in filmsetting, when the possibilities of enlargement, reduction and distortion are added to the supply of letters and symbols: but the designer still needs to know the full range of what is available on one disc, or whatever, in the system to be used, and this varies considerably.

Various extras are available in various faces: any face that is likely to be used for school or university textbooks should be provided with all necessary foreign accents, mathematical fractions and scientific signs. Catalogues or sheets should be, but are often not, provided for all the figures and symbols which manufacturers offer.

Where bold types have been designed, it is normal for a bold italic also to be provided; possible additions include semi-bold, extra bold, light, condensed and expanded.

Note should be taken of the difference between 'old face' and 'modern' or 'lining' figures (see illustration below). It is historically incorrect to use modern figures with an old-face type, but it is pedantic to insist on this. However, the designer should be entitled to choose, and it is disturbing to find that in many filmsetting systems, no choice is possible: all figures, even for old-face types such as Imprint and Bembo, are lining.

Monotype ampersands: reading downwards, Albertus, Caslon Italic, Goudy Extra Bold, Bodoni Bold, Falstaff Italic, Goudy Old Style, Bodoni Bold Italic, Garamond, Old English Text.

modern figures: 1 2 3 4 5 6 7 8 9 0 (Century Schoolbook)

old face figures: 1 2 3 4 5 6 7 8 9 0 (Bembo)

In my opinion, non-lining figures are always preferable, either for ordinary use in text setting, or settings which are entirely in figures, e.g. Reports and Accounts, or statistical tables. Non-lining figures are more different from each other and therefore easier to distinguish. Pages of lining figures, all the same height, look uniform and monotonous, and therefore less attractive, than pages set in non-lining figures.

The Monotype system of hot-metal composition provides alternative sets of figures for many of its faces: e.g. Times, which was originally designed with only lining figures, now has excellent non-lining figures. Bembo, and certain other faces for which non-lining are historically correct, have been provided with lining figures as an alternative. Because of this, a typographer who cares what figures are used in his setting must now specify which kind of figures he requires, because if he does not, he will (by Murphy's Law, 'Anything that can possibly go wrong will do so',) get the kind he does not want; and to change all the figures in a job after it has been set may cost a large sum in corrections.

THE POINT SYSTEM AND MEASUREMENT OF LETTERS

Types cast in metal in regular sizes used to have names, such as nonpareil, brevier, pica, etc. In 1737 the Parisian typefounder Pierre Fournier le jeune invented the point system of measurement: his unit was 0.349 mm. About forty years later, another Parisian typefounder, François-Ambroise Didot, introduced his point system with a unit of 0.3759 mm. Eventually a standard point of 0.013837 in. (0.3515 mm) was adopted by the American Type Founders' Association in 1886[11] and by the British in 1898; this is still the standard system in America and Britain, but on the Continent the Didot system is still used. The Anglo-Saxon system roughly equates 72 points with 1 inch (2.54 cm), so that six lines of 12 point type are 1 inch deep.

The description of a type as 6 pt, or 12 pt, or 24 pt, indicates only the size of the metal *body*: it does *not* indicate the 'appearing' size of the letters of a typeface on the paper (see ill. p. 75). The 'face' of a type, which is its appearing size, can be small on the body, with long ascenders and descenders, or large on the body, with short ascenders and descenders: in both cases, it would be the same point size. The actual appearing size of a face can be conveniently described by defining the x-height, the size from head to foot of the lower-case 'x'. The letter 'x' is chosen because all its terminals touch a line of measurement.

Monotype ampersands: reading downwards, Braggadocio, Garamond Italic, Temple Script, Caslon, Gill Sans, Univers Extra Bold, Perpetua Italic, Imprint Italic, Plantin Bold Italic.

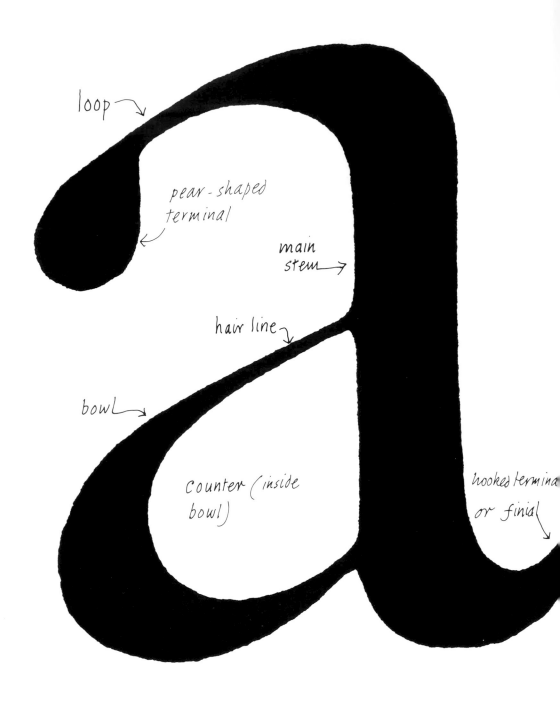

loop

pear-shaped
terminal

main
stem

hair line

bowl

counter (inside
bowl)

hooked termina
or finial

THE PARTS OF A LETTER

No definitive nomenclature for describing all the parts of a letter has yet achieved universal acceptance. The most familiar terms in common use are shown *above* and on p. 76. Other terms must be self-explanatory and will depend on common sense.

SET

The word 'set' is used as a noun to define the width of a type, and for a series of books which when complete are a 'set'. It is also used as a verb for composing type, and for the drying of ink. A Monotype leaflet explains the first meaning: 'The width of a piece of type or a phototypeset character is expressed in 'set points', one set point being the same as the point which defines the body size of the type. For example, an em quad of a font of 9 pt, 9 set, will measure 9 points wide.

'Every character of each size of every "Monotype" and "Monophoto" face has a unit value which is a fraction, in eighteenths, of the set size. For example, in Times New Roman (327) 10 pt. $9\frac{3}{4}$ set, the lower-case 'e' is 8 units wide: so in physical terms, the 'e' measures eight-eighteenths of $9\frac{3}{4}$ points wide.

'Unit values range from 5 to 18. The lower case 'i' and the comma are likely to be 5 units wide and the capital 'M' and 'W' 18 units wide; and numerals are normally 9 units wide for ease of tabular composition in ens.

'... Is it important for you to know about set? For the vast majority of typographical layouts, knowledge of set is of little practical value. However, there is the occasional job where it can make all the difference between whether or not a keyboard operator can make a typographer's layout work.

'A timetable is an obvious example ...

'If a tabular job is set in columns, the keyboard operator will work to ems of set and not to pica ems. If, for example, the font is 'Monotype' Gill Sans (262) 6 pt, it is no good making out the column width in multiples of 6 points. The set size is $6\frac{1}{2}$, and so you must work in multiples of $6\frac{1}{2}$ points.'[12]

Set width does in fact often influence a designer's choice of typeface for a book to be set in hot metal, since a font with a narrow set (such as Ehrhardt or Fournier) will accommodate more words per page than one with a wide set (such as Baskerville).

A 'pica' is 12 points. The pica is traditionally used to indicate the width to which a line of type is set (the 'measure'): the text type on this page is set to a measure of 20 picas.

The other traditional units of typographical measurement are the 'em' and the 'en', i.e. the letter 'm', which is roughly square, and the letter 'n', which is half the width of 'm'. Compositors in the nineteenth century were paid by the number of ens they set in an hour.[13] An average speed was 1000 ens an hour, but Philip Gaskell, in his *New Introduction to Bibliography* (Oxford 1972), mentions 'skilled American compositors being able to keep up 3,000 ens per hour in favourable circumstances'.

BEMBO

← 10 ¼ pts →

GARAMOND

← 11 ¼ pts →

PLANTIN

← 11 ¾ pts →

TIMES

← 12 pts →

These letters were all cast on the same size body but have a different width or 'set'. The set width shown is based on a 12 pt body size.

Opposite and overleaf: the main characteristics of letters and the terminology used to describe them.

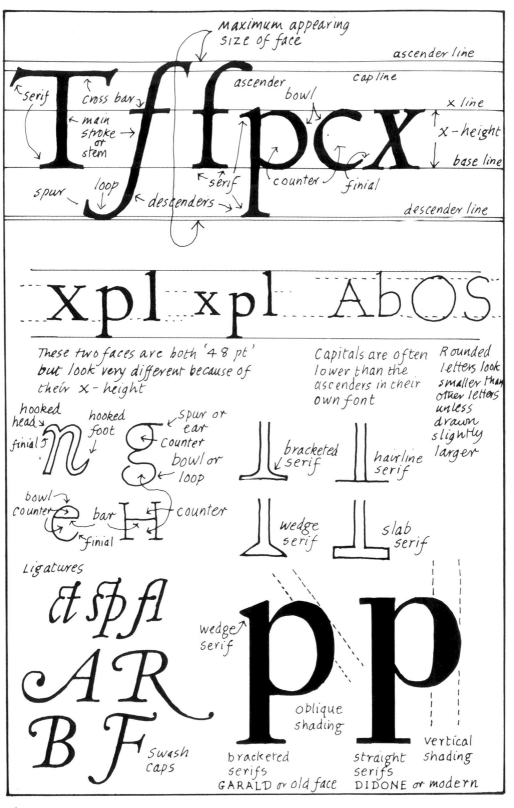

Maximum appearing size of face

ascender line

serif — cross bar — ascender — cap line — bowl

main stroke or stem — x line — x-height — base line

spur — loop — serif — counter — finial — descenders — descender line

These two faces are both '48 pt' but look very different because of their x-height

Capitals are often lower than the ascenders in their own font

Rounded letters look smaller than other letters unless drawn slightly larger

hooked head — hooked foot — spur or ear — counter — bowl or loop — finial

bracketed serif — hairline serif

bowl counter — bar — counter — finial — wedge serif — slab serif

Ligatures

ct sp fl

AR BF — swash caps

wedge serif — oblique shading — bracketed serifs GARALD or old face — straight serifs DIDONE or modern — vertical shading

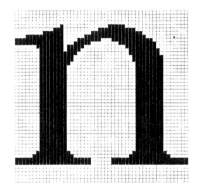

It must be remembered that any measurement given in ems is not a fixed size, but is meaningful only in relation to the size of type in use; 'one em indent' in 8 pt type is 8 points, but in 10 pt type is 10 points. The instruction '24 ems wide' is technically meaningless if no type size is given; but '24 pica ems wide' is definitive.

Metrication and the obsolescence of metal types has meant that a new system for measuring types is required; but international agreement has not yet been reached by the bodies concerned. When and if agreement is finally reached, it will be published in Britain by the British Standards Institution. For the time being, any measurement of a letter in millimetres must be accompanied by a drawing showing the precise limits of the measurement. The best measurement for giving a general indication of the size of a type is the x-height; but it is a fairly vague method of defining size.

A critical requirement for designers is to know how many lines of a given typeface can be fitted into a given depth of page. With hot metal, this is defined by point size: we know that 30 lines of 12 pt type, set without leading, will be 30 pica ems or about 5 in. deep. Since no accepted standard for measuring filmsetting yet exists, most filmsetters and printers still use the point system, although filmsetters are not calibrated in points. The typographer must therefore be extremely careful to understand what measurement terms are being used and what they mean, in any given job. He may have to specify in points, millimetres and inches on the same layout sheet; illustrations may have to be sized in inches or millimetres, to the width of columns of hot-metal type set in picas.

A lower-case letter digitized for generation in a cathode-ray tube typesetter. At actual output size, the 'steps' on the curved parts become, or should become, invisible.

Below: Apollo roman and bold, designed by Adrian Frutiger for Monotype filmsetting in 1962. It was required that the drawings should, from a single set of originals, provide satisfactory characters in all sizes from 6 to 24 pt. Secondly, the weight of the roman had to be sufficiently heavy to produce a good impression when printed by photolithography on smooth paper, while at the same time be light enough to contrast with the bold, which is not so heavy as to exclude its use as an independent reading face. Reproduced from *Graphismes by Frutiger*, Monotype House, London 1964, by kind permission of Adrian Frutiger.

Hmg

24 p

Hmg

10 p

Hamburg

10p

Hamburg

24p

Hamburg

How a metal face, in which every point size was cut, or drawn (and therefore designed), separately, is adapted for film composition. *Above*: Monotype Plantin in 24 and 10 pt, enlarged for comparison. The text size (10 pt) is bolder and wider, the 24 pt much narrower and lighter. *Below*: a text word set in the old 10 pt and 24 pt, beneath which is the new type design: a compromise, with weight, angles, serifs and proportions designed as the best for reduction and enlargement.

6 Methods of composition

From the invention of movable type in the fifteenth century down to the middle of the twentieth century, all printers' types for continuous reading (i.e. in sizes suitable for book pages) were cast in metal. As explained in Chapter 1, until the invention in the late nineteenth century of typecasting machines, all types were cast by hand, letter by letter, in hand-held moulds. The shape of the letter was obtained by *cutting* its shape, in relief (and in reverse), on the end of a bar of steel, called a punch, which was then struck into a softer bar of copper, thus creating the matrix into which the molten type metal would be poured. Although the shapes of our letters were originally evolved and determined by the instruments (latterly quill pens) with which they were written, the fact that to turn them into types meant cutting the shapes on steel punches brought another influence into their shaping: an influence that very subtly affected the curves and the way that the curves joined the straight lines. Another factor in the design of metal types is that type metal, in the process of printing, gets worn, and thickens: the old typecutters therefore anticipated this and allowed for it in designing their types.

When all type was metal, all typographic design was conditioned by the constraints of a metal technology; and although these constraints and limitations no longer apply to filmsetting, it is necessary for the typographic designer of today to understand what the constraints were, and still are, as long as metal types remain in use; and to understand also the terms and concepts of the old technology, because they still apply to, and affect, the new.

HOT-METAL MACHINE COMPOSITION

As long as the production of a new typeface involved cutting every letter and every numeral and every punctuation mark by hand on a steel punch, making a matrix for every item in copper and then casting every single item in a hand-held mould, the amount of human labour required (and highly skilled labour, at that) meant that not many new typefaces *could* be produced: there were never more than two or three men in the world with the necessary skills. But the invention of the punchcutting machine by the American Linn Boyd Benton in 1884, using the pantograph, removed the laborious element from the process; and by 1900, two successful machines for casting and composing types had been invented, both in the USA. These were the 'Linotype' and the 'Monotype' systems, which remained the standard systems for book, magazine and newspaper composition until the introduction of filmsetting.

The Linotype was invented by Ottmar Mergenthaler and was first demonstrated, in New York, in 1886; by 1890 the machine was in regular production. The Linotype has one operator, who types the 'copy' on a keyboard; as he types, the

Previous page: peacock drawn by Lovat Fraser.

matrices are assembled in the machine, and when a whole line is complete, it is cast in type metal as a 'slug'; the complete line, cast as a single piece of metal, emerges at the bottom of the machine, within seconds of its having been keyboarded. The prime advantage of the 'slug' system is speed and ease of handling, but if only so much as a comma has to be corrected, the whole line has to be reset. Typographically the system is not perfect: for example it will not produce 'kerned' italics (as the Monotype can). The most certain way of telling Linotype setting from other kinds is to look at the italic 'f's', which in Linotype have to be slightly distorted in order to condense them to fit on their own bodies.

The Monotype system was invented by Tolbert Lanston, of Ohio, and was in production by 1894. It cast and composed movable individual types which were virtually identical with the old types cast by hand. It required two separate machines, each with its own operator. The keyboard operator, with a keyboard like a typewriter, produces a paper ribbon perforated with a code of holes. Towards the end of each line, the operator decides how much he can get into the line and whether he will break a long word or not, and finally presses a key which divides the remaining space in the line by the number of spaces between words, determining the actual space that will appear between each word (a crucial factor in ease of reading or 'legibility').

The paper tape is then fed *backwards* into the casting machine (one operator can operate two or more casting machines) so that the signal determining the word spaces is given before the line is set. The caster provides column after column of type, in brand new metal, which can be corrected very easily, since every letter and punctuation mark is separate; but it has to be handled with the traditional care required ever since printing was invented, since if a single line is dropped (or 'pied', in printer's language) it has to be re-assembled letter by letter.

The implications of this are serious. If a page set by Linotype is dropped on the floor, the worst that can happen is that a line can be replaced in the wrong order, which a proof-reader could hardly fail to notice. But if a page set by Monotype is dropped, it would have to be entirely reset, and re-read; and every correction by hand of even a single letter in Monotype composition brings with it the possibility of further errors.

Monotype composition is typographically preferable to Linotype, but it requires two separate machines and therefore operators, and is slower. This usually makes it more expensive, though not for complicated setting (e.g. mathematics, or foreign languages) which is likely to need a lot of correction.

COLD-METAL (STRIKE-ON) SETTING

This term covers all instruments which, on the depression of keys, produce an immediate image on paper: e.g. typewriters, including IBM 'golf-ball' machines. Conventional typewriters cannot justify, but certain IBM and other machines can now do so. Conventional typewriters also have the important characteristic that for every depression of a key, the carriage moves forward the same amount, which is not so in electric typewriters. This is significant for two reasons: (a) all the letters occupy the same space-width, a design 'fault' that introduces distortion ('W' must occupy the same space as 'i') and therefore prevents typewriter faces being quite as legible as typefaces; (b) since all letters occupy the same space-width, every line of the same length has exactly the same number of letters. This means that it is necessary only to count the number of lines in a typescript to obtain the number of letters when making an accurate 'cast-off' (see Chapter 8).

IBM 'Selectric' composers are in effect electric typewriters that can set camera-ready copy up to 72 picas wide, in type sizes from 6 to 12 pt, or magnetic tape for higher-speed composition, in excellent versions of the classic typefaces. Each font is held on an easily changeable sphere, the size of a golf-ball. The 'golf-ball' carries 88 characters in one size of one typeface. The quality of the composition is not quite so even as in the best hot-metal or filmsetting systems, and quality of printing will depend on the plate-making and printing machines available; but the advantages to both designers and publishers of setting one's own copy in one's own office are obvious.

The latest information on IBM machines and typefaces should be obtained from IBM United Kingdom Ltd, 389 Chiswick High Road, London W4, or branch offices. IBM literature is extremely well designed, and available freely on request.

FILMSETTING

The introduction of filmsetting is a revolution which is still in progress. Its implications are not yet fully understood, nor has the new technology reached a final state of development. But the limitations imposed by types being objects made of metal no longer exist. The material on which types are now assembled, prior to making a printing plate, is usually film; and the images (i.e. the shapes of the letters) start either as black-and-white prints or drawings, or as instructions, probably on tape, for 'digitization' by CRT (cathode-ray tube) or laser: i.e. they are scanned and built up in dots or other progressions. If they start as actual images inside a filmsetter, they may still be transferred on to film by digitization, as in the Monotype 'Lasercomp' phototypesetter.

The introduction of filmsetting is a revolution which is still in progress. Its implications are not yet fully understood, nor has the technology reached a final state of development. But the limitations imposed by types being objects made of metal no longer exist. The material on which types are now assembled, prior to making a printing plate, is usually film; and the images (i.e. the shapes of the letters) start either as

The introduction of filmsetting is a revolution which is still in progress. Its implications are not yet fully understood, nor has the technology reached a final state of development. But the limitations imposed by types being objects made of metal no longer exist. The material on which types are now assembled, prior to making a printing plate, is usually film; and the images (i.e. the shapes of the letters)

The introduction of filmsetting is a revolution which is still in progress. Its implications are not yet fully understood, nor has the technology reached a final state of development. But the limitations imposed by types being objects made of metal no longer exist. The material on which types are now assembled, prior to making a printing plate, is usually film; and the images (i.e. the shapes of the

The introduction of filmsetting is a revolution which is still in progress. Its implications are not yet fully understood, nor has the technology reached a final state of development. But the limitations imposed by types being objects made of metal no longer exist. The material on which types are now assembled, prior to making a printing plate, is usually film; and the images (i.e. the shapes of the

The introduction of filmsetting is a revolution which is still in progress. Its implications are not yet fully understood, nor has the technology reached a final state of development. But the limitations imposed by types being objects made of metal no longer exist. The material on which types are now assembled, prior to making a printing plate, is usually film; and the images

The introduction of filmsetting is a revolution which is still in progress. Its implications are not yet fully understood, nor has the technology reached a final state of development. But the limitations imposed by types being objects made of metal no longer exist. The material on which types are now assembled, prior to making a printing plate, is usually film; and the images

This book is set in 10 on 11 pt Monophoto Garamond. Illustrated here are six alternative versions of 10 on 11 pt Garamond (set using 'track 1', or 'normal' letterspacing), all available from a London typesetter (Filmcomposition Ltd). Reading downwards: Amsterdam Garamont, ITC Garamond Regular, ITC Garamond Light, ITC Garamond Book, ITC Garamond Light Condensed and ITC Garamond Book Condensed.

The result of digital scanning is that every letter will have a ragged outline, since it is built up in steps. In the reading sizes of type, this will be discernible only with a magnifying glass. Digitized letterforms may however be more consistent (i.e. less susceptible to variation in weight) than film-generated letters, but again, it depends on various steps in the process.

Film-generated letters should always be sharper in outline than hot-metal types, although not many filmsetting systems achieve this yet. They may also be subject to some distortions, inherent in light-exposure on to film. It is the amount of control available for these variables that differentiates the systems, and makes some preferable, in terms of typographic design and printing, to others.

So the shapes of letters for printing no longer have to be cut in steel: the original is anything that can be photo-graphed, or scanned. Letters can be set touching each other, or even superimposed, or set at controlled distances apart; they can be enlarged, reduced or distorted, to taste; any size is obtainable. Not every one of these facilities is available on every filmsetting system, but they are all available on some. Computerization has also brought new facilities: for example, work can be stored on tape, and subsequently programmed for setting in any number of different ways (different measures, different typefaces) without having to be re-keyboarded. This has obvious advantages for long, frequently reprinted works like the Bible, the British Pharmacopoeia or telephone directories.

In theory, filmsetting offers more possibilities to designers than they had before. In a few years from now it may be normal for a designer to have his own keyboard at home and be in complete control of everything that he designs up to and even including plate-making. But at present the use of filmsetting is still in its early stages and in many cases designers are faced with serious problems which often result in less choice and worse quality than before.

The first thing a typographer needs to know about a filmsetter is what typefaces and fonts are available and what is the quality of image definition. Under the heading of typefaces, the designer must know what typefaces are available with the actual operator, and what other faces can be obtained from the suppliers, how quickly, and at what cost. It is not enough to be told 'Times' or 'Univers' (which are the only faces available in many plants): it is necessary to see specimens of the general output, and also the exact constituents of the fonts. Are ligatures provided for fi, fl,* etc.? Are small caps available (they are usually not)? What is the italic like, and the bold, and is there a bold italic? Are the figures lining or non-lining? What are the fractions and other special sorts available? How many fonts are simultaneously available and what are the constraints in mixing them? What printed specimen sheets can be provided, showing the range of sizes, for the typographer to work from? (The answer, too

*It will be noticed that the composition system used for this book (Monophoto) has ligatures for fi, fl, but not ffl or ffi.

often, is 'none'.) How are type sizes obtained and specified, and how is inter-letter spacing controlled? What sort of proofs will be provided? Bromide proofs (i.e. on photographic paper) are not easy to write corrections on, and if more than one proof is needed, they may have to be xerox copies at an extra charge. In some computerized filmsetting systems, every line of type in the proof is preceded by a number (to identify every letter, for corrections): the proof does not, therefore, show what a finished page will look like. Is the final product (required for plate-making) positive-film, or bromide print?

Other facilities which differ from filmsetter to filmsetter are maximum and minimum point sizes, maximum line length, and output speed, all of which may be important to the designer. All these variations (usually largely a function of cost) are considerably greater than the variations between one hot-metal machine and another. With the increase of computerized typesetting, 'software' differences can also be important, e.g. hyphenation and justification (known as 'h & j'), ability to set accents and exotic scripts and other programmable typographic refinements.

All this information is required by the typographer, and it may be difficult to obtain, because the operators often, and the manufacturers (or sales officers, who are the manufacturers' 'communicators') sometimes, do not know themselves.

One drastic result of these variables is that no specification of type in the old terms (e.g. 'Times 10 pt') has a fixed meaning any longer. This is because a range of sizes of a typeface is usually made photographically by filmsetters, but in hot-metal manufacture, every size has to be cut separately. The necessity of recutting gave the opportunity for slight redrawing (as explained in Chapter 5). Generally, smaller sizes are wider and more loosely fitted; larger sizes are narrower, tighter and with proportionally finer hair-lines.

Most filmsetters alter the point size by straightforward photographic enlargement and reduction of the master image. It is possible, then, that a comparison of the *same manufacturer's* hot-metal and filmset versions of the *same typeface* may show them to be exactly the same in design at one point size and one only – the size chosen for the filmsetting master. Equally, a film face may be completely redrawn to allow optimum typographic 'feel' right through the range – and is not the same as any metal size. Some manufacturers offer different masters for different size ranges, typically three, one for composition (up to 10 or 12 pt, say), one for the middle range and one for display (above about 18 pt). The drawings for the different masters will be modified to compensate for scale, and here a closer match between hot metal and film is possible. Another example of the differences between metal and film versions of the same face is italics designed originally for slug-machine composition where they were often treated as the poor relations of roman, obliged to fit on uncongenial widths and deprived of an even slant by the lack of kerns. The opportunity to redraw these italics when adapting them for filmsetting is irresistible, and the resulting faces much improved, but the typographer who casts off one version from a specimen of the other is due for a surprise.

Nearly all filmsetting systems offer, among their basic typefaces, versions of Times and Univers; yet any six systems, setting the same copy to exactly the same specification, may produce six different results – worse, it is probable that even the differences will not be consistent, and each system may produce different versions at different times, from different operators, on different days.

The first source of variation is in the preparation of the master font, which may be positive or negative, on glass or film, or digitized on floppy disc, tape or whatever. Although Times and Univers start off in definitive versions, variations, deliberate or accidental, may occur in the process of being adapted to the technical requirements of a particular system.

The second source of variation occurs within the filmsetter during the process of reproducing or regenerating the image. This may involve rapid mechanical movement of the font on a disc or drum, and of mirror or prism in the optical path, and be subject to mechanical problems that interfere with critical timing. CRT output tubes are capable of all the distortions familiar on a maladjusted television set. The fact is that some filmsetters are better engineered than others, and some have more reliable electronics. In the good ones a character comes out on film precisely as it went in on its font: sharp, correctly positioned and undistorted. Inferior systems produce inferior output, but it must be said that they often cost less to buy and run.

A third source of variation occurs when chemicals are required to develop the image on photographic paper, and qualities of paper, temperature, humidity, etc. may all introduce further variables.

A fourth kind of variation which is predictable, but not always predicted, is the deliberate variation, in weight, slope, width or compression, and space between letters, that can be controlled by the operator. Perhaps the most important, because the least obvious, is the amount of space between the letters. Letters can be set closer to each other by minute progression until they actually overlap: this is called 'tracking', or 'minus-setting', because the increments are subtracted from the number of units allotted to each letter. Minus-setting can be done for separate characters – for instance, to improve the fit of an awkward combination such as 'AV', 'LT', 'OW', 'Ty' or 'gy' (this is known as 'kerning') – or throughout the font to tighten its fit consistently. If text set in a sans-serif face such as Univers is given minus-setting, it becomes progressively less legible: the space between the even vertical strokes, which is not much to begin with, is soon lost, and the letters merge into each other. But faces with serifs may actually gain in legibility from minus-setting (see examples, ill. p. 91). Such an adjustment, not possible in hot metal, is available with some but not all filmsetting systems. It can have a decisive effect on legibility and *must* be specified by the typographer, not by the operator.

So filmsetting is, or may be, full of surprises. We have a completely new tool, we do not yet fully understand how to use it and we do not know how to communicate what we know to other interested parties. The designer is responsible for the appearance of the finished product, and must safeguard himself, or herself. A typographer who specifies for a job that is to be filmset must place the responsibility for accurate cast-off (i.e. the number of pages the job will make) firmly on the typesetter; to be satisfied with the look of the result, as well as its extent, it is essential to insist on seeing and approving (and if necessary adjusting and revising) a specimen setting of not less than a page, making sure that it contains all the features of the text to be set, e.g. italics, numerals, caps and small caps, footnotes or margin notes if applicable. The approved specimen page must be established as the definitive style to be followed, and it should be stipulated that any significant variation from it in the finished product may be regarded as a reason for rejection. All this takes time; and when a job has been printed, there often isn't time to reprint it, even if it is wrong. Clients who do not or cannot allow for such contingencies risk an inferior final result.

It is now common for printers to install a filmsetter and be unable to supply any specimen sheets from which an accurate layout and specification can be made. It is like being asked to design a house without knowing the size, shape or colour of the bricks. In such unsatisfactory circumstances, the typographer has to ask for a previous job produced by the same system and specify from it.

It should be mentioned here that Mergenthaler Linotype, manufacturers of the Linotron and VIP filmsetting systems, provide excellent literature for their products, including a general catalogue of typefaces and individual booklets for most of their recently released faces, which show a complete font, all sizes and weights, lettercounts and specimen settings. Setting is possible in three variations of letter-fitting, or 'tracks'. Track 1 is normal; Track 2 is 'tight'; and Track 3 is 'very tight, as tight as possible without overlapping O's'. All the settings shown are in Track 2.

Linotype, who are associated with Mergenthaler, Stempel and Haas in their typeface programmes, will send any literature requested by any practising typographer, as will also the Monotype Corporation, which provides reference sheets for Monophoto faces similar to those available for hot-metal faces.

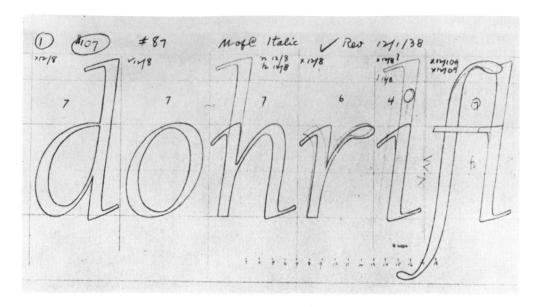

Drawings by F. W. Goudy of italic
letters for his typeface 'University of
California Old Style' – the only
drawing that survived the burning
down of his workshop in 1939. See
F. W. Goudy, *Typologia*, University
of California Press, Berkeley 1940,
ch. VI.

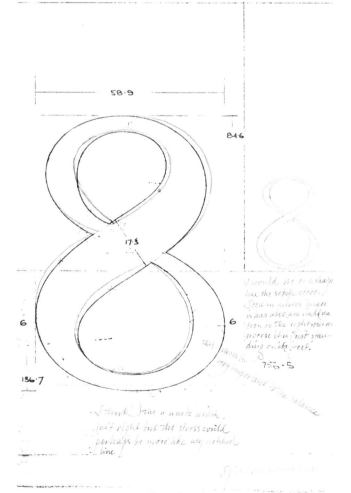

Drawings of a figure '8' for
Spectrum Semibold, designed by
S. L. Hartz, with his pencilled
comments.

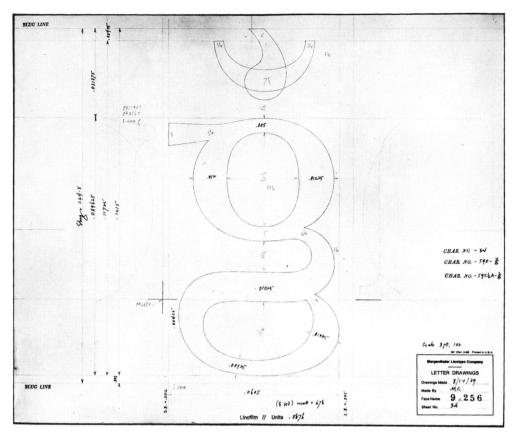

Drawing by Matthew Carter of a lower-case 'g' with diacritical marks, from a 9 pt 8 set teletypesetter newspaper text face for the Mergenthaler Linotype Co. of New York, 1969. Photographic reductions of such drawings are used to make masters for photocomposition machines. The drawing is made to a scale about 100 times actual size. The dimensions are entered on it by the designer in order that measurements may be checked during manufacture. The character is unit drawn, i.e. its width is a multiple of eighteenths of the set size, in this case 11 units, of 8 pt. To increase the apparent size of the face without reducing the number of characters per line, the body – the vertical dimension – is one point greater than the set.

Up to this point the affair has been pretty much under your control. You have made your individual letter= shapes good according to your lights, and have got them through to metal type. . . . Will they behave decently when they are combined into words? You can't tell yet. All you can do about this question, in your drawing stage, is to lean hard on the hunches you have picked up as to what letters do to each other when they are fitted together.

FITTING *is the process of working out the ex= actly right amount of space to go between letters.*

Left: a passage about letter-fitting written by W. A. Dwiggins, from *WAD to RR*, Harvard 1940.

subjects at different levels. It is emphasised, however, that the outline of organisation in paragraph 10 is not meant to be uncritically copied: schools are urged to try to make better arrangements and many will undoubtedly succeed in doing so. The purpose of the study was not to provide a model but rather to see whether with present standards of staffing a school with as few as 300 pupils could be viable in the age range 11 + to 16 + . The conclusion was that it could be viable, but that time-tabling and organisation would be easier and options more closely related to pupil rather than to teacher election if the normal standards of staffing could be improved. Such an improvement would, of course, entail improvements in standards of accommodation.

Above: an example of 'plus-setting', i.e. extra space has been set round each letter so that the whole book has been apparently letterspaced – making it harder to read. This was not specified by the typographer, but it can happen in filmsetting. It is not acceptable.

This should be good news to the land management profession. The new awareness is in large part due to a disillusionment with planning in its widest sense. After World War II, we embarked upon the planning era. Planning departments of Government were set up in numerous countries. They were empowered to draw up land use plans and to plan for the entire economy of nations; a national plan was usually a five-years prognostication. The UNEP, for example,

Sir,
I refer to Iain Cuthbertson's article in the October issue, and having just been in the area planned to lunch at Tayvallich but on arrival the place was shut.

psychologists, educationalists and civil servants let him get away with it for so long? – for any reasonably careful inspection shows Burt's work to be careless, riddled with implausibilities, and inadequately documented. As late as 1977, after the *Sunday Times* had exposed Burt's famous work on identical twins as valueless or worse, Professor Cohen wrote in furious defence:

all I enjoyed the superb flashes of football from the Maori out-half Dunn, the strength of Osborne and Jaffray in the centre and the creative running of Wilson on the wing
Cardiff, although they generated a strong forward

Right: examples of unacceptable poor typesetting in narrow measures, which is why unjustified 'ragged right' setting is usually preferable for narrow columns. The letterspacing of single words is absolutely unacceptable – unless it is used for emphasis, which is a common usage in Germany, but not elsewhere. In the top example, the actual image of the typeface is a parody of what Univers ought to look like.

Humber Bridge Board, which is responsible for the project; British Bridge Builders; Freeman Fox and Partners, the consulting engineers, and the unions which have been in touch with the Minister. He will have to reconcile violently opposed viewpoints.

How can the quality of a typeface be judged? Why do the master:
raphy use a few specific type designs? What do they see in them?
ays practical design. What they see in a good type design is the q
itness to perform a task. It has a balance in all of its parts just ri

How can the quality of a typeface be judged? Why do the masters i
phy use a few specific type designs? What do they see in them? Gc
practical design. What they see in a good type design is the qualit
to perform a task. It has a balance in all of its parts just right for

How can the quality of a typeface be judged? Why do the masters in t
use a few specific type designs? What do they see in them? Good desig
design. What they see in a good type design is the quality of practical
ask. It has a balance in all of its parts just right for its size, as any goo

Three examples of ITC Garamond
Light Condensed, set in 12 pt with
normal, tight and very tight
letterspacing.

How can the quality of a typeface be judged? Why
in the art of typography use a few specific type desi
hey see in them? Good design is always practical de
y see in a good type design is the quality of practica

Galliard 12 pt, track 3 (very tightly
letterspaced).

How can the quality of a typeface be judged? Why do the
rt of typography use a few specific type designs? What do
Good design is always practical design. What they see in
n is the quality of practical fitness to perform a task. It ha

Galliard Italic 12 pt, track 3.

How can the quality of a typeface be judged? Why dc
he art of typography use a few specific type designs? \
e in them? Good design is always practical design. Wl
good type design is the quality of practical fitness to p

Frutiger Light 12 pt, track 3.

COMPUTERS

A computer is an electronic machine designed to accept
information ('data'), to process it according to a prede-
termined scheme (a 'program') and to store or deliver the
results back to the user. A computer can perform in a few
seconds laborious tasks (e.g. counting the number of 'e's in
the Old Testament) which would take a human being so long
that they might even be beyond the capabilities of a single
person.
    In typesetting, a text of any length (e.g. the works of

Shakespeare, *Who's Who*, the Pharmacopoeia or a telephone directory) can be keyboarded into the computer, which stores it as data: for example, by recording it on magnetic tape. The computer can then be programmed with instructions for setting the text in whatever style is required: the revised tape is then fed into a photosetter. Corrections or additions to the stored text can be made at any time without difficulty.

When the text is keyboarded into the computer no length of line is specified, and therefore no breaking of words is necessary. The rules for the breaking of words at the ends of lines, which of course vary from language to language, are included with all other rules of style (e.g. the setting of the names of books and ships in italics) in a set of rules which form an exact specification of the required style. This set of rules is accepted by the program as input data along with the text to be processed. Styles can be altered, or new styles introduced, merely by altering the relevant specifications.

WORD-PROCESSING SYSTEMS

Word-processing systems are a revolution in business organization. They are of various kinds and varying capabilities, but are intended not only to replace 'typing pools' and the system of one man, one secretary + typewriter + dictaphone, but also to provide storage and retrieval facilities for all kinds of information.

Text can be keyboarded or recorded and then stored on tape or floppy discs. The stored text can then be used later in any way that may be needed. It can be fed, for example, into a VDU (visual display unit) or VDT (visual display terminal) and read on a screen, it can be obtained as a bromide print-out in a single copy (which can then be copied by xerox, etc.) or it can be fed into a photocomposition system (which may be 'in-house', i.e. in the company's own office, or may be in another city or continent) and emerge as a printed document for publication. The design of such a document may be undertaken by a typographer in the normal way, working from some kind of print-out produced in the office; but it is also envisaged that companies will be offered 'Design Menus', that is, examples of perhaps twelve different solutions to a standard problem – e.g. a Report and Accounts – from which they can choose the solution that suits them best, and fit that solution, by a pre-written program, to their already keyboarded text.[1]

The production of printed text is only one of the by-products of a word-processing system. The instant (and simultaneous, in different offices) retrieval of previously stored information is an important facility – e.g. the existing stock of any item can be called up on the VDU, or the names and addresses of staff or customers. But their potentialities in many different kinds of printing are very great.

7   Paper

WHAT IS PAPER?

Typographers need paper, and a wide knowledge of it, as sailors need rope. But whereas there are now many kinds of excellent rope made from man-made fibres, all paper for printing is made from vegetable fibres. The kinds of fibres determine the qualities of the paper. Paper is made most commonly from linen, cotton, straw, esparto grass and wood, but can be made from a host of other raw materials, including bamboo, mulberry bark and nettles. Dard Hunter, an American who has spent a lifetime studying, making and writing about paper, in his *Papermaking* (2nd edition, London 1957), first quotes Webster's Dictionary definition of paper as 'a substance made in the form of thin sheets or leaves from rags, straw, bark, wood, or other fibrous material, for various uses' and then says: 'To be classed as true paper the thin sheets must be made from fibre that has been macerated until each individual filament is a separate unit; the fibres intermixed with water, and by the use of a sieve-like screen, the fibres lifted from the water in the form of a thin stratum, the water draining through the small openings of the screen, leaving a sheet of matted fibre upon the screen's surface. This thin layer of interwined fibre is paper.'

The fibres, the basic constituent of paper, are *cellulose*. Cellulose is a chemical compound of the elements carbon, hydrogen and oxygen and is 'found in nature as the *cell* walls of plants'[1] in the form of minute threads which have certain remarkable properties. The fibres vary greatly in size, strength and exact nature from plant to plant, and in ease of extraction. The main qualities they have in common, which make paper what it is, are:

(a) cellulose as a chemical substance is rather inert: that is, it is not easily attacked by chemical reagents. It is for this reason that papers can be made that have a high degree of resistance to the deleterious effects of light and air and that will remain unaffected by the solutions used in photography or by the inks used by the printer;

(b) the fibres are tubular in form, and swell when immersed in water. In the swollen state, a suspension of the fibres in water can be deposited as a layer of pulp, and, when the excess of water is squeezed out, a coherent mass remains on drying. In other words, the fibres act as their own cement if they are soaked in water and allowed to dry in close contact with one another. Because the fibres absorb water easily, paper is naturally porous, and absorbs the liquids used in writing and printing inks (it can be made less porous by adding other substances);

(c) the fibres are colourless and translucent: they naturally make a substance (paper) that is white and opaque;

(d) the fibres are strong, light and flexible. Paper can be made so strong that is is virtually untearable. Individual fibres have remarkably high tensile strength and, when a sheet of paper is torn, the fibres themselves are seldom fractured to any

Previous page: unpublished design by Edward Bawden.

great extent; it is rather the bond between fibre and fibre that breaks down. This bond between fibres in dry paper, however, is very drastically loosened by water, so that a wet sheet of paper has greatly reduced strength compared with a dry sheet. When beaten in water, the surface of animal fibres such as wool and silk are not gelatinized or fibrillated, nor do they swell in water or bond together physically or chemically; in consequence, a coherent sheet of paper cannot be made from them.

QUALITIES OF PAPER

Paper can be manufactured to have a range of qualities and characteristics hard to find in any other material. It can be very thin (e.g. 'India' paper for Bibles, airmail paper, tissue paper) or very thick (e.g. cardboard). It can be very weak (e.g. newspaper) or very strong (e.g. for legal documents, for watercolour painting, packaging, certain building and engineering uses). It can be very porous (e.g. filter and blotting papers) or very resistant to water (e.g. for building and wrapping purposes).

Paper can be transparent (e.g. 'glassine', for wrapping, window envelopes and tracing paper), or opaque; it can be white or coloured; it can be made greaseproof; it can be made to stand much erasure (e.g. for artists) or none (for security). It is used for cigarettes; for insulation in the electrical industry (from thin capacitor papers to coverings for power transmission cables); for surgical dressings; transfers, stencils, handkerchiefs, towels, underclothes, bed linen, wall coverings, and even in the plastics industry.

Papers used by publishers and printers, which are the kinds of most interest to typographers, represent a small percentage of the total output in the paper industry: we are far from being the paper industry's biggest customers.

A BRIEF HISTORY OF PAPERMAKING

The word 'paper' is derived from the Greek word 'papyrus', the name of a plant which grows on the banks of the lower Nile and was used as a writing material three thousand years before Christ. The exact way that papyrus was prepared has been disputed, but basically, strips were cut or peeled from the stem, laid transversely and hammered together to form sheets. It was therefore not 'paper', by our definition, described above.

Paper as we know it was invented in China, but the exact details are not established.* The invention of paper was officially announced to the Emperor by a Court official, Ts'ai Lun, in AD 105. This was true paper, since it was made entirely from vegetable fibres, including tree bark, hemp,

*See Tsuen-Hsuin Tsien, *Written on Bamboo and Silk*, Chicago 1962, which reproduces photographs of the earliest known paper and quasi-paper.

Detail (reduced) from a woodcut of Nuremberg, in Schedel's *Liber Chronicarum*, 1493, showing Ulman Stromer's paper mill, the first in Germany.

rags and fishing nets. Specimens of this kind of paper, bearing writing, and dating from Ts'ai Lun's period, were found in China by a Chinese expedition in 1942. But almost certainly paper of a kind, made from pulped silk (i.e. non-vegetable fibres) and called today 'quasi-paper', was being made in China at least a hundred years before the birth of Christ: from this kind of paper to paper made from vegetable fibres was a natural step.

The art of paper-making soon spread through China and via Korea to Japan. Paper has always played a much larger part in the life and civilization of the Orient than in the West. It took a thousand years to reach Europe: the route was via Persia, Arabia, Egypt and North Africa. The probable dates for the first paper mills in Europe are: Spain, at Xativa, *c.* 1150; France, at Hérault, *c.* 1189; Italy, at Fabriano (a name still famous in paper-making), *c.* 1260; Germany, at Nuremberg, *c.* 1389; England, in Hertfordshire, *c.* 1490. Paper could be made only where there was suitable water and plenty of it: hand-made paper may require as much as 120,000 gallons of water to make one ton of paper.[2]

All paper was made by hand until the nineteenth century, so that the size of the largest sheet for practical manufacture was determined by the largest size of tray that could be conveniently held by a man. The tray (known as the mould) was dipped into the vat of pulp and given a 'joggle' by the man holding it, in order to 'mix' the fibres evenly. The knack of giving this joggle was said to take thirty years to learn.

The largest sheet of paper made by hand in Europe is Whatman's *Antiquarian*, 31×53 in. (78.7×134.6 cm) (first made by James Whatman at Maidstone, *c.* 1770), but Dard Hunter mentions *Emperor*, 48×72 in. (121.9×182.9 cm), and a Chinese paper 48×84 in. (121.9×213.4 cm), both of which must have required two men to hold the mould.

The first paper-making machine was invented by a Frenchman, Nicholas-Louis Robert, and was made in France, about 1798. Robert's patents were, however, eventually taken over and developed in England by Henry and Sealy Fourdrinier, and their paper-making machines were operational before 1810. From then on, paper could be made 'on the web', i.e. in a continuous roll, which is then reeled up, to be cut later into sheets if required. Most printing paper today is still made on Fourdrinier machines, which are not only colossal (among the biggest single production machines in the world) but dramatic: you see a white liquid, which looks like cream (but is actually 99 per cent water) flowing along, and quite suddenly it has become solid – it is paper.

THE RAW MATERIALS

The kind of paper made is defined, first of all, by the kind of raw material that provides the fibres. Since all fibres have different characteristics, they are frequently mixed, in varying proportions. Other factors that affect the end product are the way that the raw materials are pulped, cleaned, bleached and otherwise treated, the way the fibres are separated, the other ingredients that are added to the pulp (e.g. for sizing and colouring) and the 'beating' process, which makes the final mixture, known as the 'furnish', that goes into the paper-making machine. The machine itself, and ancillary rollers, etc., determine not so much the basic character of the paper as its thickness, or weight, and its surface and finish.

The most important raw material used for printing papers in Europe and America today are cotton rags, hemp, jute, manila and sisal rope, esparto grass, straw, bagasse (the residue of sugar cane after extraction of the sugar), and wood, both coniferous and broadleaf. Of these, by far the greatest in quantity is wood.

Wood-pulps are either 'mechanical' or 'chemical'. Mechanical pulp is made by grinding de-barked wood logs on a grindstone under a stream of water, which fragments the fibres. It cannot produce a pure white, strong or durable paper, but it is cheap and opaque; it is used extensively for newsprint, popular weekly magazines, and the cheaper grades of wrapping and printing papers. Chemical pulp depends on the use of solutions to dissolve away the encrusting substances that cement the fibres together in their natural state. In this way, the fibres are separated with minimum physical damage and are mostly whole. Chemical pulp is therefore of a higher quality and whiter than mechanical pulp.

When beaten for maximum strength, sulphite (coniferous) wood-pulp loses opacity, and some pulps can be beaten to such an extent that they give a highly translucent sheet, used for greaseproofs, glassines and tracing papers. Hardwood pulp is in general more opaque and bulky than coniferous pulp and can be a substitute for esparto. By choosing suitable woods and varying the cooking conditions in the chemical processing, a range of pulps can be produced that used singly or in blends provide as wide a range of papers as may be obtained from cotton. Papers made from chemical pulp are known, illogically, as 'woodfree' or 'pure', which means 'without mechanical wood'. They are extensively used for books of all kinds and many good quality printing papers.

Esparto grass comes from North Africa and Spain. As the fibre is small and flexible, it confers on paper a closeness of texture and smoothness of surface that are unique. Furthermore, esparto papers expand rather less when wetted than do papers made from almost any other fibre. The combination of these factors renders esparto particularly suitable for the manufacture of printing papers, especially when multi-coloured printing makes good colour register essential. Esparto is also used for the 'body paper' for coated papers and for good-quality writing papers, as it watermarks very clearly. Because of the shortness of the fibres, however, high

Jost Amman's woodcut of a paper-maker (reduced), *c.* 1568, showing a boy carrying sheets, behind him the machine for beating rags (driven by water) and, right, the papermaker himself dipping the mould in the vat of pulp.

resistance to tearing cannot be expected and for this reason it is usual to add a proportion of longer and stronger fibres (such as wood-pulp or rag) to the furnish. Esparto as a paper-making fibre is almost unknown in the United States.

In Britain, the best esparto papers are made in Scotland, because of the almost unlimited supplies of rain and soft riverwater. The use of esparto has, however, decreased in the U.K. in recent years: other pulps, such as that from the Eucalyptus tree, have been found to be satisfactory substitutes.

Straw, being home-grown, was used in Britain during the Second World War as a substitute for esparto: it makes a less strong paper (i.e. easier to tear) and tends to be spotty if held to the light. Straw may be used alone, but it is more frequently mixed with longer fibres such as wood-pulp or rag. This blend finds wide application in the production of thin, hard writing (*bank* and *bond*) and other papers, although its use during the war was extended to printing and to many other papers for which it is less suitable than is wood-pulp. The hardness of straw-based paper also makes it specially suitable for book jackets. Straw is not widely used in the U.S. for papermaking except for a few kinds of rough board, in cigarette papers (flat straw), and never in printing paper.

The strongest and most durable paper for books and other purposes is known as *rag paper*, and is usually made from rags* of cotton, linen, and hemp. Until the end of the eighteenth century, cotton and linen were almost the only material used; and the paper in surviving fifteenth century printed books can be seen to be as white and strong today as it was when it was made. The close relationship between the kind of raw material available and the finished product was borne in on me when I visited a paper mill on the river Medway shortly after the end of the Second World War: the mould-made paper (destined for legal documents) being made that day was blue in colour, because it was being made from a delivery of ex-RAF shirts.

Paper made from rags may cost perhaps six times as much as paper made from wood and is therefore too expensive for normal book production; but its qualities of strength, durability and opacity are pre-eminent, and it is used when 'the best' is demanded, e.g. for a few special books, legal documents, banknotes, charts and so on. It is often mixed with other fibres to give additional strength.

Only two mills in England, Hayle and Wookey Hole, still produce hand-made paper, and none do so in the USA. A characteristic of hand-made paper is 'deckle edge', which as Dard Hunter points out is an imperfection. The hand-mould method of making paper leaves a rough, uneven edge which no printer wants, because he cannot 'lay' to it easily; if each sheet has a different edge, the printing will tend to fall in a slightly different position each time, so that sheets will not back up correctly, and colour printing in register will be almost impossible. For this reason, both in the Orient and in

*True rags are less and less used in paper-making because of the common occurrence of man-made fibres, useless in conventional papermaking, in modern textiles. Most 'rag' paper today is made from Cotton Linters, a by-product of the preparation of cotton yarn.

Europe, the deckle edge was always cut off and the sheet trimmed to be perfectly square, with a straight edge. Dard Hunter says: 'It was not until the inception of the machine age that deckle edges began to be considered artistic and desirable; at the present time more hand-made paper is sold on account of the deckle edges than for any other characteristic. As a matter of fact, if the four rough edges were cut away, scarcely a dozen printers and bibliophiles in America would be able to tell whether the paper had been made on a hand-mold or upon a paper-machine.'[3]

Hand-made paper has other defects when compared with machine-made paper: the sheets may vary in thickness, not only between sheet and sheet, but from one part of a sheet to another, and they may not even be square, all of which causes great difficulty to the printer. Hand-made paper is also usually heavily sized,* to make it hard and give it a surface more suitable for writing than for printing: if this is so, it has to be dampened before printing. Dard Hunter also points out that if the same stock, or 'furnish', is put into a hand-mould and a paper machine, 'There is no reason in the world why the machine-made product should not last as long as that formed in the hand-mold. Provided the same stock is used, the only possible advantage the hand-made sheet would have over the machine-made paper in lasting quality would be the fact that the fibres are shaken four ways, while on the traveling wire of a paper machine their course is limited to the cross-shake, which has a tendency to lay the fibres in one direction. For this reason paper formed on a machine tears more easily one way than the other, while hand-made sheets will tear almost equally in either direction with the same resistance.'[4]

Hunter comments finally that a printer using hand-made paper should logically print on a hand-press, using hand-cast types; it is an anachronism to print a book on hand-made paper when the text has been composed on a machine.

The use of hand-made paper is in any case limited by the relatively small size of sheet that can be made; it is entirely uneconomical for use on large modern printing machines.

Mould-made paper is made (usually, at least in the UK) from rag, but by machine, and is a cheaper substitute for hand-made paper.

Hemp is the bast tissue of an annual shrub grown extensively in India, Russia and America. It usually reaches the paper-maker in the form of spinning waste, or used twine, cordage and ropes. It has shorter fibres than either linen or cotton, but bonds well, and makes paper which combines extreme thinness with strength and opacity, e.g. 'India' or Bible paper, and airmail paper.

Manila fibre comes from the leaves of a plant that grows chiefly in the Philippines, and is used for ropes: it gives an extremely tough, almost untearable sheet. It is used chiefly in the manufacture of stencil, insulating, envelope and wrapping papers, for which great strength is required and a high

*Size here means an additive, formerly gelatine, now usually a wood resin and aluminium sulphate complex, that reduces the rate at which paper treated with it absorbs water.

white colour is not necessary. It is not much used in the U.S. for papermaking (the same is true of Jute) because of the abundance of strong kraft pulp made from wood.

Jute, used for sacking, and *sisal*, used for making rope and twine, when they come to the paper-makers go chiefly into wrapping papers.

THE FINISHES OF PAPER

Paper is made on Fourdrinier machines by flowing the pulp on a wire mesh and draining off the water: the surface of the paper is therefore conditioned by the wire mesh. The wire mesh is usually closely woven, and the resulting paper is known as 'wove': no discernible pattern can be seen on the paper, but usually one side is less smooth than the other. A refinement of this is the twin-wire Fourdrinier, in which two separate wire meshes make two separate sheets of paper, which are pressed together while still liquid, with the wire-mark of each paper inwards. The resulting paper is perfectly even-sided. Another kind of wire mesh is known as 'laid'; it imitates the appearance of old hand-made papers by means of the thick lines (in the watermark) which run across the sheet and the thicker lines, nearly an inch apart, which run the length of the sheet (i.e. in the direction of the grain, or the way the fibres lie) and served originally to strengthen the hand-held mould.

WATERMARKS

The 'watermark' in paper is caused by a shape, made deliberately in wire (or bamboo, in an oriental mould), fastened to the mould (or the 'dandy roll' in a paper-making machine) which causes the pulp, and therefore the paper, to be thinner at that place. The earliest paper makers in Europe used watermarks perhaps as their own personal trade marks, perhaps also to convey secret religious or political signs. However, some of the marks they used have remained in the language to denote paper sizes (e.g. foolscap, crown, elephant). If paper is being specially made for a particular job, as it often is, the cost of introducing one's own watermark may be negligible in relation to the total cost of the paper. 'A well-designed water-mark should always fall in the same position on the sheet. The best position is perhaps near the edge of the sheet, so that the water-mark will appear in the margins of the page, where it will be clearly visible and will not interfere with the printing. A conspicuous water-mark may weaken a solid printed over it.'[5]

Watermarks need not be merely simple shapes in line. The most extraordinary detailed pictures, based on photographs or reproductions of paintings, have been turned into watermarks, and have been effectively used both as anti-forgery devices and for publicity.

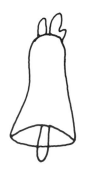

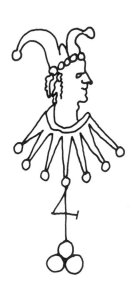

Watermarks. *Above*: ox-head used by Ulman Stromer; *middle*: a bell; *below*: the foolscap which gave its name to a size of paper. These all occurred in many variations.

PAPER KINDS AND TERMS

The surface of a sheet of paper is conditioned by (1) the material (the 'furnish') that goes into it, (2) the treatment given to it during or after the making (e.g. rolling or hot pressing) and (3) coating it with an artificial surface, as in 'art paper', or by lamination.

The main descriptions of paper that a designer will come across are given below, with brief definitions; but it must be remembered that trade terms vary, and new processes and terms are frequently introduced while others fall out of use. The designer must compile, and keep up-to-date, his own 'dictionary of paper'.

Tub-sized: the paper is dipped in a tub of gelatine or starch, to make it suitable for writing and erasure. The process is mainly used for writing and document papers.

Super-calendered: a cheap method of producing a shiny surface is by super-calendering, which entails damping the paper and passing it between alternate metal and composition rollers separate from those on the Fourdrinier. The method has now been largely superseded by the cheaper grades of machine-coated art paper.

Coated or art paper: the paper is coated on one side or both, either by hand or by machine, with a mineral surface, usually (in Britain) china clay from Cornwall, to provide a smooth surface for printing fine screen half-tone blocks or litho plates. Coated paper has the disadvantages of being liable to crack when creased, of sticking together if it becomes wet (but modern coated papers have waterproofing substances added to counteract this), and of being shiny (reflecting light), glaring to the eye and unsympathetic to the touch. It is available in several different grades and finishes. The best qualities may be several times more expensive than uncoated papers. Coated paper can be obtained in different colours and even with different colours on each side of the sheet.

Machine-coated paper: the base paper is coated on the actual paper machine by rollers carrying a mixture of adhesive and mineral matter; these are usually inserted near the end of the drying cylinder system. The best of these machine-coated papers have a surface that is not markedly inferior to that of a second-grade art paper, and they are appreciably cheaper as they can be made at high speeds and from body papers containing mechanical wood-pulp. They are therefore replacing imitation art papers.

Imitation art paper (called 'English Finish' in the U.S. and now obsolete) is not a coated paper, but paper in which a large quantity of mineral loading is added to the pulp in the beater. It is water-finished or damped and super-calendered, the result being a paper decidedly inferior to a good-quality coated paper from the point of view of appearance and finish, but sufficiently smooth to give reasonably good results with fine-screen half-tone blocks.

Matt art ('dull-coated' in U.S.) is art paper without a glaze, and may look better than shiny white art paper, and be more suitable for matching with cartridge. It may be more difficult to print on and may require coarser-screen blocks: the printer must, as always, be consulted. A machine-made matt art with less coating is known in the U.S. as 'matte coated'. Both are made for offset printing.

Antique is an unsmooth, bulky paper used for books, usually creamy in shade; but the demand is now for a smoother surface, to suit fast-running litho machines. It is also used to describe a kind of rough-surfaced drawing paper used for watercolour painting.

Drawing paper. A good quality drawing paper must be strong, permanent, white and opaque, take Indian and writing inks well, accept colour wash without mottle and withstand the action of india rubber or an erasing knife. The best drawing papers are still hand-made rag papers, but these are costly; machine-made papers from rag, or rag and chemical wood-pulp mixtures, are cheaper and often satisfactory substitutes.

Featherweight antique ('high bulk antique' in the U.S.) is thick and fluffy and used to make books (e.g. children's annuals) thicker than they would otherwise appear; it is now used only by a very few publishers.

Cartridge paper (so called because it was originally used for making cartridges) is strong and not necessarily white: coloured cartridges are used for end-papers, booklet covers, jackets, etc. White cartridge is used for drawing paper. 'Offset cartridge' is a well-sized paper, often made on twin-wire machines and perfectly even-sided, used for better-quality offset printing.

Newsprint is the cheapest kind of printing paper, and is available in various qualities. It is not suitable for books if any permanency is required, since it soon discolours and becomes brittle, due to high mechanical wood-pulp content. Most newsprints have a 'good' (i.e. the top) and a 'bad' (i.e. the lower, or wire) side, and half-tones printed on the 'bad' side are often completely illegible, as can be seen in almost any Sunday newspaper.

Bond papers are strong, thin, hard-surfaced papers used for printing and duplicating stationery, and are available in various colours.

Wrapping papers are made to be strong and provide protection to wrapped goods, especially in the rain. Wrapping papers are often glazed on one side (in the U.S. known as MG, machine glazed), making them suitable for printing, and rough on the other, which provides a key for adhesives. Some wrapping papers are bitumen-laminated or impregnated to make them impervious to water.

Tissue papers are very light, thin papers made from chemical woodpulp and are often highly coloured.

Boards (in U.S., 'cover' papers) are used chiefly in binding booklets and books. Thin cardboards suitable for printing on and using as booklet covers can be single-sided (i.e. with one smooth side, suitable for printing, and the other not) or double-sided, and can be plain or laminated, in various weights and thicknesses.

The three main kinds of board used for books, to be covered with a binding material, are chipboard (the cheapest), strawboard (the most usual), and millboard (the heaviest and most expensive). Strength and resistance to warping when dry are the qualities that matter most to the designer: books being exported to America nearly always require millboard if it is hoped to avoid warping. U.S. binders use 'chip' or 'binders board'.

PAPER SIZES

(See British Standards 4000, *Sizes of Paper and Boards*, and 1413, *Page Sizes for Books*.)

Paper that is supplied in sheets (as opposed to reels) comes, in Britain, in two ranges of sizes: the traditional British sizes whose exact dimensions are impossible to remember (foolscap, crown, post, demy, etc.) and the international paper sizes, known as ISO (International Standards Organisation) sizes, formerly known as DIN (Deutsche Industrie Norm, 'German Industrial Standard') (see ISO 216, 1975 [E]).

Metrication has not yet been adopted in the American paper industry. The basic North American unit of size for business papers is $8\frac{1}{2} \times 11$ inches. If metrication is adopted, it seems likely that it will remain based upon $8\frac{1}{2} \times 11$ or some close approximation thereof. Canada's paper industry has changed to the metric system but not to ISO sizes.

It must be remembered that the size of a sheet of printing paper is given as *untrimmed*, before it is printed; but when it is printed and folded, it is nearly always *trimmed* (otherwise the pages cannot be opened at the 'bolts' (see illustration), nor will the edges be flush); therefore the size of a printed page is normally given as *trimmed*, which is the size it actually is, when in use. To avoid mistakes, which could be costly, the phrase 'trimmed size' should always be used when that is what is meant. In Britain, when describing book (or picture) sizes, the depth (vertical dimension) is always given first.

Page, leaf, sheet: the word 'page' can mean: (1) one side of a leaf in a book, which normally has a number (if a book contains 32 leaves, it has 64 pages); (2) the leaf of a book, comprising two pages. 'Sheet' means any whole piece of paper, which is folded to make pages.

A sheet of paper printed as one page is called a *broadside*:

when folded once, it becomes a *folio** (4 pages);

folded twice, it becomes *quarto* (8 pages);

folded thrice, it becomes *octavo* (16 pages);

folded four times, it becomes *16mo* (32 pages);

folded five times, it becomes *32mo* (64 pages);

folded six times, it becomes *64mo* (128 pages).

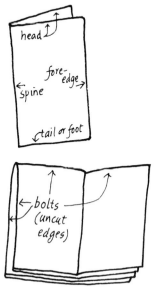

Terminology used in describing paper folded into pages.

*It should be remembered that 'folio' is still used, loosely but commonly, to mean a large book. It is normally larger than a 'quarto', just as a 'quarto' is normally larger than an 'octavo'. 'Folio' is also the regular publisher's term for the page number, written or printed, on a page.

It is a curious fact that no sheet of paper, however thin, can be folded more than seven times.

The phrases 'folio'*, 'quarto', 'octavo' etc., when applied to a book, do not indicate the *size* of the book unless the original sheet size is also given; they only indicate the number of times each printed sheet has been folded. 'Broadside' is the basic sheet size. 'Double' is when the short side of the sheet is doubled, and 'Quad' is when both dimensions are doubled. Crown Broadside is 20 × 15 in.; Double Crown is 20 × 30 in.; Quad Crown is 40 × 30 in.

The main traditional British sheet sizes and folded sizes are as follows (N.B. *untrimmed*), in inches and millimetres:

	FOOLSCAP	CROWN	DEMY	MEDIUM	ROYAL
Broadside	17 × 13½ in.	20 × 15 in.	22½ × 17½ in.	23 × 18 in.	25 × 20 in.
	432 × 343 mm	508 × 381 mm	572 × 445 mm	548 × 457 mm	635 × 508 mm
Folio*	13½ × 8½ in.	15 × 10 in.	17½ × 11¼ in.	18 × 11½ in.	20 × 12½ in.
	343 × 216 mm	381 × 254 mm	445 × 286 mm	457 × 292 mm	508 × 318 mm
4to	8½ × 6¾ in.	10 × 7½ in.	11¼ × 8¾ in.	11½ × 9 in.	12½ × 10 in.
	216 × 171 mm	254 × 191 mm	286 × 222 mm	292 × 229 mm	318 × 254 mm
8vo	6¾ × 4¼ in.	7½ × 5 in.	8¾ × 5⅝ in.	9 × 5¾ in.	10 × 6¼ in.
	171 × 108 mm	191 × 127 mm	222 × 143 mm	229 × 146 mm	254 × 159 mm
16mo	4¼ × 3⅜ in.	5 × 3¾ in.	5⅝ × 4⅜ in.	5¾ × 4½ in.	6¼ × 5 in.
	108 × 86 mm	127 × 92 mm	143 × 111 mm	146 × 114 mm	159 × 127 mm

Metric book papers

In 1967 the British government adopted the metrically based International Standards Organisation range of paper sizes for all government printing, where feasible, and the British printing industry has, in principle, followed suit. Since 1976 the British paper trade has agreed that only the following should be considered as stock sizes for book printing:

Metric Quad Crown 1010 × 770 mm (which gives an *untrimmed* 8vo size of 192 × 126 mm).

Metric Large Quad Crown 1060 × 820 mm (*untrimmed* 8vo size: 205 × 132 mm).

Metric Quad Demy 1130 × 890 mm (*untrimmed* 8vo size: 222 × 141 mm).

Metric Small Quad Royal 1270 × 960 mm (*untrimmed* 8vo size: 240 × 158 mm).

In addition, the following secondary sizes are recommended for use but not for holding in stock:

Metric Quad Cap 860 × 690 mm (8vo: 172 × 107 mm).
Metric Large Quad Crown 1060 × 820 mm (8vo: 227 × 146 mm).
Metric Quad Royal 1270 × 1020 mm (8vo: 255 × 158 mm).
RAo* 1220 × 860 mm (8vo: 215 × 152 mm).
(N.B. These sizes may vary slightly in practice, e.g. Quad Demy can be 888 × 1128 mm, or 890 × 1130 mm, or 890 × 1140 mm.)

*The 'RAo to 2' and 'SRA' series are papers intended to be trimmed to ISO-A sizes. They are listed in BS 4000:1968 (*Sizes of Papers and Boards*), p. 11.

The ISO paper sizes are in three ranges, 'A' (for general printing), 'B' (for posters, wall-charts, etc.) and 'C' (for envelopes). Full details are available from the British Federation of Master Printers. In the ISO 'A' range, the basic sheet, Ao, is 841 × 1189 mm, one square metre. Smaller sizes are derived from Ao by progressive halving but the significant feature of the ISO range is that the proportions remain uniform i.e. 1:2 or 1:1.414.

The ISO 'A' trimmed sizes are:

	Size in mm	Size in inches
2A	1189 × 1682	46.81 × 66.22
Ao	841 × 1189	33.11 × 46.81
A1	594 × 841	23.39 × 33.11
A2	420 × 594	16.54 × 23.39
A3	297 × 420	11.69 × 16.54
A4	210 × 297	8.27 × 11.69
A5	148 × 210	5.83 × 8.27
A6	105 × 148	4.13 × 5.83
A7	74 × 105	2.91 × 4.13

THE WEIGHT OF PAPER

The weight of paper is expressed in grams per square metre, and is shown as gm^2 (or gsm).

Ranges of printing paper are made in various weights and not in other weights: the weights available in any range must therefore be ascertained by the designer before discussing with his client the sort of paper that will be most suitable for the job. If a book or booklet is being posted in large quantities, the difference in postage costs between one weight of paper and another may be a very large sum of money.

PAPER AND DESIGNERS

Paper is a vital component in the design and appearance, the manufacture and the cost of any printed job. The designer must therefore obtain, and keep on file ready for looking out at any time, as many samples of as many different kinds of paper as possible; and he must know how to find, at short notice, if not on his own shelves, whatever other samples and information he may need.

In a book page the 'Grain' of the paper should run up & down

Run one edge of the sheet between two finger nails. If it crinkles like this ~~~~~ that is the edge across the grain

Paper is supplied by both manufacters and merchants. Whereas a manufacturer can supply only what is made in his own mills, a paper merchant buys from any mill anywhere in the world, so he can supply, at least in theory, any kind of paper that is made. An intelligent and co-operative paper merchant is therefore an important friend of any designer. Designers must also remember that they are important to suppliers, since it is, or should be, chiefly on their advice and specification that papers are bought.

In general, paper manufacturers and merchants are most helpful, and will supply samples and prices quickly to designers who are specifying for a job. Many manufacturers will send sheets for trial pages or dummies without charge (in the hope of an order) and many of them offer 'designers' packs' containing sheets of every colour and weight of paper available in a given range, in large enough sizes to use for drawing, designing, or printing covers, jackets, etc.

Apart from its aesthetic qualities, paper represents a considerable proportion of the cost of any printed job. For many books and other jobs, the paper will have to be specially made, since large stocks are kept only of a few of the most frequently used kinds. It is therefore evident that the selection of the right paper, from every point of view, is a heavy responsibility and if the designer undertakes it, he must be certain that he has *in writing* the approval and agreement of whoever is going to pay for it, or anyone else who could say, after the job is printed, 'this paper is not what I agreed to'. Paper should never be decided on without consulting the printer and getting his agreement to it; and since, if it has to be specially ordered, the exact extent of the book (i.e. the number of pages) and the number of copies required must be known, the designer must remember that once these figures are ascertained, any change may have serious repercussions, and also that there will always be a certain delay, not only in making the paper, but then in transporting it from the mill to the printer. The calculation of the amount of paper needed for a particular job should always be the printer's responsibility: certain operations, e.g. colour printing, require a higher proportion of spoiled paper than others. In high speed web-offset printing, the alarming figure of 25 per cent is sometimes incurred for wastage, which represents a lot of money.

Machine-made paper has a *direction* or grain, i.e. the fibres tend to lie in the direction that the paper moved in the machine. In book production, the direction of the paper matters: the grain must run up and down the page. If it runs across, the pages tend to 'bow' and an open book will not lie flat. Every printer knows this and it is not normally necessary for the typographer to specify the grain, any more than it is necessary to say that anyone in the printing works who handles paper must have clean hands: it is taken for granted. But it is something to remember if the designer is involved in the ordering of paper for a large and costly job.

Paper is a lifetime's study and lifetime's job for many people, and no designer can expect ever to know enough about paper. It cannot be stressed too much that it is *always* necessary to consult the printer, who will have to print on it; *never* order paper without the printer's agreement. In an article in *Typographic*, 11 (1977), the designer Derek Birdsall is quoted as saying: 'Another thing I have learnt is never to specify paper. I say, all these sorts of paper are OK by me but you pick the one that is right for the job. I say I'd like a shiny paper. I never say I'd like a blade coated cartridge. I use common sense terms.'

Those are words of wisdom. But there is something to add. Paper, in every printing job, is a component of absolute importance: it must perform its complex functions (for a start, satisfy typographer, printer, binder and reader) perfectly, and without necessarily calling attention to itself. But, like silk, feathers and gossamer, paper can also give deep aesthetic satisfaction, both visual and tactile. It is essential for a designer to know what qualities paper can have, in order to try to obtain them when needed, or even to create occasions when they can be used. In book-making for literature, i.e. words that matter, the most needed qualities are thinness, strength, opacity, and 'feel' – which may be soft, hard, or in between. It is more than ever necessary for the designer to appreciate that paper can be a relatively inexpensive luxury, when luxuries – so often 'illegal, immoral, or fattening' – are also harder and harder to obtain, because they are 'un-economic'.

Designers should, therefore, collect experiences of paper, as well as samples. It is not enough to look at beautiful books under glass. If you can feel the paper used, for example, in a Jenson, or other great books of the fifteenth and sixteenth centuries, you will not forget it. You must collect examples of Chinese and Japanese and Italian and any other rare, exotic papers that appeal to you, and some day you will have, or create, the opportunity to use them.

Horn watermark, England, 1683. From Gaskell, *A New Introduction to Bibliography*, Oxford 1972.

COMPOSITION INSTRUCTIONS for *MANUAL OF TYPOGRAPHY*

Author *Ruari McLean*

Series *Thames and Hudson Manuals*

Date _____ sent to *B·A·S*

The editor should ensure that all items are either filled in or deleted. Use space on page 2 for additional notes if further clarification is required.

Trimmed page *24.1×15.9* cms. *9½ × 6¼* ins. (upright) _____

Layouts herewith _____

Copy herewith *Main Text, footnotes*

Copy to follow *Prelims, captions, endmatter*

Typeface *Monophoto Garamond 156* Text area _____

Margins:
Head (after trim) *3½ Pica EMS* Backs (each page) *4 EMS*

Fore edge *13½ EMS* Foot *5 EMS*

Type sizes and measures:

Main text *Garamond 156 10/11 pt. (and Bold 201)*

Prelims *156 + Special Setting (to follow)*

Quoted matter *Set as main text in Quotes* full out/indented _____

Footnotes *156 8/8 unjustified (10 Pica EMS Max)* at end of chapter/end of text/ *in margin* foot of page _____

Footnotes references _____ superior/bracketed/old style/modern/ figures/signs

Marginal references *None* other _____

Reference list _____ Bibliography _____

Notes to illustrations _____ Index *8/8 pt*

Running heads: left *10 pt SC* right _____

left page copy ⎫
right page copy ⎬ *chapter titles*

Folios (position as layouts) *156 10 pt (old style)*

Figures in text lining/non-lining _____

Foreign accents and special sorts: none/list attached.   Use z spellings

Paragraph indent *1 Pica EM*

Part titles *None*

Chapter headings: number *Special setting* roman/arabic _____
title *(Galliard Bold)* _____ for spacing see layouts __

Chapters start on fresh pages *Yes*

Headings in text: *156 10 pt CAPS + 10 pt. Italic as marked*

A *10 pt CAPS* space above *2 lines* below *1 line*

B *10 pt Italic u/lc* space above *10 pts.* below *2 pts.*

C _____ space above _____ below _____

Other _____

Captions:
Type size *156 8/8* Measure *10 EMS Max.* Justified/Unjustified

Additional instructions:

Prelims and illustration pages to be numbered in.
Signature marks where necessary to appear in trim area at foot.
Only stepped collating marks to appear on spine, maximum width 2 pts.
Foreign accents and special sorts must appear in galley proofs.
Printer's errors to be indicated in red on marked set.
Use single quotes throughout, double quotes only within quotes.
Use en dash with word space of line each side.
No full point after Dr, Mr, St, etc.
BC and AD in small caps, 2 unit spaced, no full points.
Use roman parenthesis and roman punctuation after italic titles where punctuation not part of title.

Part of the Thames and Hudson composition instructions to the printer for this Manual.

8   Cast-off and layout

To find out exactly how many lines a given manuscript will make in a certain size of type, it is necessary to count the letters or 'characters' ('casting off'), counting 1 for every punctuation mark and 1 for every word-space. Then divide this total number by the number of characters in the length of line, of the intended type size, which for Monotype, Linotype and IBM types can be looked up in copy-fitting tables. In other words, let us suppose there are 70 characters (including spaces and punctuation marks) in a line of type. You multiply this figure by the number of lines of type to be set on each page, to find out how much copy will fit on a page. If it is intended to have 40 lines of type to a page, the number of characters that would appear on that page would be 70 × 40 = 2,800. So in 96 full pages you could fit 268,800 characters. A chapter opening or any page with fewer lines of type set on it will have fewer characters.

As most typewriters use non-proportional letter spacing (every letter occupies the same space), every line of the same length has the same number of letters. If the copy has been typed on such a typewriter, rule a pencil line down the right-hand edge of the typing so that the number of characters to the right of the line equals approximately the number of spaces in short lines to the left of the line – in other words, establish the average number of characters (including 1 for every space, even if the typist has typed more than one space between words or after punctuation) in every line. If the whole manuscript has been typed consistently on the same machine to the same line-length, your average will hold good for the whole work; if the typing is inconsistent and/or on different machines, you will have to adjust your calculations accordingly.

For general purposes, it is an accepted rule that words in English texts average 5 letters + 1 space, so that the total number of characters divided by 6 equals the number of words. (In a scientific text, the average length of word might be more.) So,

$$\frac{\text{No. of Characters}}{6} = \text{No. of words}$$

$$\text{No. of words} \times 6 = \text{No. of characters}$$

Having established the average number of characters in a line, you must then count the lines. If the manuscript has been typed with the same number of lines on every page, you have only to count the number of pages, but this is rare (unless the publisher has taken the trouble to insist on it). If you have to count all the lines in a long typescript, count every chapter separately, and make a mark at every hundredth line, so that your counting can be checked by someone else – and so that the contents of any section can be known from your first count.

Then count the number of words in the page you have designed, and you will find out how many pages the manuscript will make in type.

Previous page: drawing by Fritz Kredel.

Average no. of characters per typed line = 66 = 11 words

(If the average no. of characters is an odd number, always average it out *upwards*: e.g. if average no. of characters is 67, count it as 11½ or even 12 words, and you will be on the safe side.)

No. of lines in MS = 1042

Total no. of words 1042 × 11 = 11,462

Type to be set in Bembo 11 pt × 24 picas, 40 lines per full page. Copy-fitting tables show that Bembo 11 pt averages 66 characters (11 words) in a 24 pica line, so

$$\frac{1042 \times 11}{11 \times 40} = 26 \text{ pp.} + 2 \text{ lines}$$
$$= 27 \text{ pp.}$$

A less accurate, but sometimes quicker and useful way to cast-off copy, is to count the number of words, rounded *downwards* to the nearest easily workable number, in your page of type, and divide that number into the total number of words in the manuscript, which will give you the approximate number of pages it will make in type.

Another quick way to count the approximate number of words in a MS, which also works if the MS is hand-written in a fairly regular hand (though it should always be typed when finally submitted to the printer), is to count up 100 words several times until you have established the average number of lines that make 100 words. If on average 8 lines contain 100 words, then mark off every 8 lines, and the number of '8 line groups' × 100 = total number of words.

If you are designing a magazine or report, where every page may be different, a quick way to cast-off is to find out how many lines of your copy equal how many lines when set: you may find, for example, that every five lines of copy make seven lines when set, which is easy to pencil in. Casting-off quickly but safely (i.e. never finding that the copy makes *more* pages that you had calculated) soon becomes instinctive.

One of the tools you will need is a gauge for measuring the size of printed type matter (see Appendix for suppliers). A simple kind printed on plastic is shown in the accompanying illustration.

It must be remembered that books are normally printed and bound in sheets of 16, 32, 64 (or multiples upwards) pages, and this exact figure for any job must be known by the designer at the point of designing: it will be the designer's job to see that the book makes the required number of pages *exactly*. If a book is being printed and bound in sheets of 32 pages (16 on each side of the sheet), it is generally *possible* to add one leaf of 2 pages by 'tipping in', or 4, 8, or any other multiple of 4 pages extra by an additional binding operation, but the former will mean hand-work, and even the latter will involve disproportionately higher cost.

Points:

	6/12	7/14	4/8	9	5/10	5½/11
	1					
2	2	1	1	1	1	1
4	3	2	2	2	2	2
	4	3	3	3	3	3
6	5	4	4	3	3	3
	6	5	5	4	4	4
8	7	6	5	5	5	4
	8	7	6	6	5	5
10	9	8	7	6	6	6
12	10	9	8	7	7	6
	11	10	8	8	7	7
14	12	10	9	8	8	8
	13	11	10	9	9	8
16	14	12	11	10	9	9
18	15	13	12	10	10	9
	16	14	12	11	11	10
20	17	15	13	12	11	11
	18	16	14	13	12	11
22	19	17	15	13	13	12
	20	17	15	14	13	13
24	21	18	16	15	14	13
26	22	19	17	15	14	14
	23	20	18	16	15	15
28	24	21	19	17	16	15
	25	22	19	17	16	16
30	26	23	20	18	17	16
32	27	24	21	19	18	17
	28	24	22	19	18	18
34	29	25	22	20	19	18
	30	26	23	21	20	19
36	31	27	24	22	20	20
	32	28	25	22	21	20
38	33	29	25	23	22	21
40	34	30	26	24	22	22
	35	31	27	24	23	22
42	36	31	28	25	24	23
	37	32	29	26	24	23
44	38	33	29	26	25	24
46	39	34	30	27	26	25
	40	35	31	28	26	25
48	41	36	32	29	27	26
	42	37	32	29	28	27
50	43	38	33	30	28	27
	44	38	34	31	29	28
52	45	39	35	31	30	28
54	46	40	36	32	30	29
	47	41	36	33	31	30
56	48	42	37	33	32	30
	49	43	38	34	32	31
58	50	44	39	35	33	32
	51	45	39	36	34	32
60	52	45	40	36	34	33
62	53	46	41	37	35	34
	54	47	42	38	36	34
64	55	48	42	38	36	35
	56	49	43	39	37	35
66	57	50	44	40	38	36
68	58	51	45	40	38	37
	59	52	46	41	39	37
70	60	52	46	42	39	38
	61	53	47	42	40	39
72	62	54	48	43	41	39
	63	55	49	44	41	40
74	64	56	49	45	42	41
76	65	57	50	45	43	41
	66	58	51	46	43	42
78	67	59	52	47	44	42
80	68	60	53	47	45	43
	69	61	53	48	45	44
82	70	62	54	49	46	44
	71	62	55	49	47	45
84	72	63	56	50	47	46
86	73	64	56	51	48	46
	74	65	57	52	49	47
88	75	66	58	52	49	47
90	76	66	59	53	50	48
	77	67	59	54	51	49
	78	68	60	54	51	49
92	79	69	61	55	52	50

Part of a type gauge, printed on clear plastic, for measuring print.

THE LAYOUT

A 'layout' is a representation, preferably in pencil, of a typographical design. It should give a very accurate idea of what the job will look like when printed. It is the designer's most satisfactory way of showing (without going to the expense of time and money involved in having it set up in type) what is intended: if it satisfies both the designer and the client, it should then be photocopied and the photocopy, appropriately marked up for typefaces, will be an exact guide for the printer. Make sure, if you do this, that the photocopy is exactly the same size as the layout; on some machines the copying paper is not stable.

If the layout is right, the job will be right. It is therefore worth taking all the trouble required to make it accurate; a slipshod, careless layout will lead to expensive corrections and probably a poor result, satisfying no-one.

In Chapter 2 it was emphasized that it is an essential part of a typographer's skill to be able to draw typefaces in text and smaller display sizes in pencil, quickly and accurately, and it is surprising how soon this skill can be developed by practice.

To begin with, the designer needs a ruler, thin layout paper, a soft rubber, HB and 2B pencils (other grades as required), a pencil sharpener and type specimen sheets from which to trace. It will also help to have a grid sheet, printed in em or 5 mm squares, to lay under one's sheet to establish squared type areas. Such sheets are included in some layout pads, or could be printed cheaply to the designer's order. Mathematical and graph paper printed in blue or grey is less useful because it is harder to see the ruling through a sheet of layout paper.

Since an accurately squared layout is a vital part of nearly all typographic design, the designer must ensure that he has the equipment to achieve this. Apart from the full-scale draughtsman's and designer's work units described in Chapter 2, there are small drawing boards available with rulers sliding in grooves; and a useful new item is Geliot Whitman's 'Artsquare', a transparent plastic triangle, 350 mm long on its short sides, engraved with a 5 mm grid. It is ideal for laying over both drawings and printed matter to check if they are true.

It is necessary to rule, faintly, base-lines only: the designer *must* learn to draw the right size of type by eye, which can never be done with parallel lines drawn for the x-height, which will usually be inaccurate anyway. The size of type must be judged by eye, even if it is traced, because since HB pencil is usually fainter than type printed in black, 10 pt letters drawn in pencil in *exactly* 10 pt size may in fact look like 8 or 9 pt: the eye may require the pencil to draw the letters slightly larger, so that they *look* right.

An HB lead, kept sharpened, will be found the best for all types to be drawn with a single stroke; 2B will be used for bold type contrasting with roman, and for larger letters requiring a thicker stroke. Thicker letters should be built up with parallel strokes, *not* drawn in outline and filled in: that is not what type looks like.

The tracing of the letters from a type sheet can be done fast, but it must be accurate not only for the visual impression of the type size, but, most important, for the number of characters in the line, and the spacing between both letters and also words. It is not expected that the difference between, say, Garamond and Bembo could be shown in a 10 pt size on a layout, but the character of the type (i.e. old face, or modern) should be clear; and if, say, Univers is being used, any difference of weight must be absolutely clear. All this may sound difficult, but it becomes easy with practice.

A small layout, such as a visiting card, a letter-head or an advertisement, should be drawn with complete accuracy down to the last letter. For the chapter-opening in a book, the heading and perhaps the first three lines of text are usually enough: the rest of the text page can usually be expressed with pencil lines approximating the weight of the type. Some designers keep old galley proofs and find them useful for pasting up pages in a dummy that has to be shown to a client. In any *displayed* layout (i.e. in large sizes), it is essential to use the *correct* words on the layout: invented or wrong words are useless. The design exists only when the right words are shown in the intended way; anything else is meaningless and a waste of time.

Transfer lettering, such as Letraset, should not be used in conjunction with pencil in making a layout, but only for preparing finished artwork or camera-ready copy. It may be used as a time-saver, but it is not a substitute for the designer's pencil and imagination in the designing process. In laying lettering down on a photograph, or preparing a 'finished rough' for a cover design or a poster, it is of course ideal, together with such other aids as coloured film. One of the troubles with mass-produced lettering sheets is that they are available to everybody and, suddenly, one sees this or that face appearing everywhere, *ad nauseam*.

It is normally inadvisable to use a pen for making layouts, since ink cannot easily be rubbed out or corrected; and most type faces are much more difficult – and therefore slower – to draw with a pen than a pencil. When a design has been fully worked out in pencil, and a finished rough is required to show a client, an experienced and skilful designer may use a pen to simulate the blackness of type more accurately than pencil can, particularly if the type is Univers or another sans.

The degree of finish put into a rough to show a client will depend on how much finish you think your ideas, and your client, require. Most designers discover early that some clients are more impressed by neat finish than by good design. For important jobs it is often worth while to have your suggestions set up in type, especially if a number of people in different places all want to see them simultaneously.

A layout to show a client should not have instructions to

the printer written on it, unless it is an understood practice between designer and client, and the client, after approving the design, sends the layout on to the printer. If the layout does carry instructions to the printer, they should be placed neatly in a margin or on an overlay. All critical dimensions, e.g. of margins or illustrations, should be marked in picas, inches or millimetres on the layout or overlay: if a photocopy were made without the designer's knowledge, as often happens, on unstable paper, and sent to a printer or blockmaker, any dimension measured from the photocopy could be a quarter of an inch in error, with possibly disastrous results. All instructions to printers, blockmakers, etc. should be written clearly in ink, not pencil.

For books or other jobs requiring layouts for a large number of pages, printed layout sheets may be a great time-saver. (For a description of these, see under 'Grids' in Chapter 9.) A prudent designer will also have a rubber stamp or adhesive labels made, saying 'This layout must be returned with proofs to . . .'. Printers repeatedly forget to return layouts with proofs, and the layout is essential for comparison. Theoretically the designer should keep a photocopy of every layout he makes, and, theoretically, the printer should make a photocopy of every layout he receives, but this does not always happen. The designer must, however, keep an up-to-date written record of the whereabouts of all layouts and other material provided for a book, with receipts and records of posting where possible, to avoid the annoyance of being wrongly blamed for the loss of something through inability to prove otherwise. Since transparencies are small and easily mislaid, and sometimes extremely expensive or impossible to replace, it is particularly important to keep a careful record of all transactions in which they are involved. Both transparencies and photographs, and indeed all kinds of original, should be *listed* individually, as well as counted, before being sent anywhere.

COPY MARK-UP AND PREPARATION

Before 'copy' (the printer's term for the matter given to him to set up in type) goes to the printer, it must be correct, 'clean' (i.e. decipherable, or better still, easily legible by the operator), and provided with clear setting instructions. It must be correct, because alterations made after type has been set are always expensive and usually money wasted. It must be 'clean' because illegible copy will lead to delay, irritation, mistakes and expense. It must be provided with the instructions that the printer requires to do his job.

As explained at the beginning of the next chapter, the words must be right before the typographic design can be right. Although the words will not actually have been written by the typographer, and in theory are not his responsibility, he will often be the last person to see them before they go to the printer. The text may have been edited (i.e. prepared for the printer) well, poorly, or not at all: in any case, the typographer must be satisfied that the material is ready for the printer, and there are various decisions that are more 'design' than 'editorial'. Most editorial typographers have their own printed instruction sheets, to send to the printer, to save the time of writing out similar instructions for every job. Jan Tschichold's 'Penguin Composition Rules' are well known.[1] A typographer working for a publisher must, of course, find out if that publisher has a house style (often in printed form) to be followed.

The items that most often need to be checked are consistency in punctuation (e.g. full points or their omission in Mr, Mrs, Dr, St), use of capitals, italicizing of book, journal and ships' names, style for dates, and the spelling and/or printing of figures. Recommendations for these and similar matters are given in many style manuals, some of which are listed, as standard requirements on a typographer's shelves, at the end of this book.

If the decision is to print all dates in the style '12 May 1970', or all personal names without full points after either initials or degrees and decorations (e.g. R J Thompson VC MA), but the copy has not been written or typed in this way, it is permissible to give the printer this instruction without correcting the copy (but the printer will probably employ someone to so mark it before passing it to his operators). And if the names of books, journals, ships and railway engines have all been consistently typed in caps, but must be set in italic upper and lower case, that instruction can also be given, since it is clear. However, if such names have *not* been typed or written in a consistent style, then the typographer/editor *must* mark them correctly, since a compositor cannot be expected to know which are the correct titles for italicization.

Among the items that need typographic decision are when to print numbers as figures or spell them out as words. Common sense and consistency must be applied in all such cases, and as an example of this we may quote the house style of the Queen's printers, Eyre & Spottiswoode: 'In text we set numbers as words when they are used simply, occurring only occasionally; and when starting a sentence, or when the numbers are under ten. We print them in figures when the idea of measure or number is important, as in tables, dates, references or statistical use.'

Times should be printed in a consistent style (unless there is a good reason for not doing so, e.g. in a novel, when different characters are entitled to different styles) and this will normally be either the 24-hour-clock system (which in any factual, scientific or business document is preferable) – e.g. 1529 (without full point)* – or the older system with am and pm, e.g. 2.45 pm (there *must* be a point between the hour and the minutes, but am and pm (like many other common abbreviations) are not more easily understood with points and therefore are better without them).

*There must always be 4 digits, e.g. 0115; 'hrs' can be added if it is not clear that the figures mean a time.

Set in 'Monophoto' Baskerville 169, 11/14 pt × 30 picas justified.
Keep word spacing close & even. Spacing parameters 32-16-0

r. left

centre point
thin word #
each side
(16 units)

16pt CAPS
8 unit letterfit 16 16

18pt l.c thin
word #

64 pts

Chapter Six /·/ Some steel engravers
↳ use 16pt CAP

25 pts

] 3pt n
] 3pt
] med n.

] med
] 3pt
] 3pt

31 pts

To give a comprehensive account of individual achievement for nearly

four hundred engravers is quite beyond the scope of the present study,

but it is possible to build up a representative picture by examining about

a dozen of the more prolific exponents. Half of those selcted had close

relatives who were also engravers. While it is recognized that there

were differences between the work of individuals within a family, these

groups (for example, the Brandard, Cousin, Finden, Radclyffe, Wallis and

Willmore families) have been treated together. The remainder are names

eminent in their own right, not associated with relatives or a distinguish-

able group. They include J. B. Allen, J. C. Armytage, J. C. Bentley, E. Goodall,

W. Miller and L. Stocks.

1 pica em
indent
(104 units)

The engraver's occupation is a solitary one, and in order to gain an

informed view of his life, the reader cannot do better than refer to the

account, published in 1877, attributed to Charles William Radclyffe.[1]

Charles was the youngest son of William Radclyffe, the eminent engraver,

and the brother of Edward, also an engraver, so although he himself was

a painter, chiefly in watercolours, he had a first-hand knowledge of the

conditions under which his father and brother worked.

½ line # →

21 pts

quoted matter
set 10/14 pt
× 30 picas
justified.
Spacing parameters
as above

Few men have more lacked the sympathy and appreciation of the

public than engravers; few men have been less known, few have

lived more solitary or more laborious lives. Bending double all

through a bright, sunny day, in an attic or close work-room, over

a large steel plate, with a powerful magnifying glass in constant

A typescript marked up for
filmsetting (*above*) and the printed
result (*opposite*). For technical details,
see note on p. 118.

CHAPTER SIX · Some steel engravers

To give a comprehensive account of individual achievement for nearly four hundred engravers is a task quite beyond the scope of the present study, but it is possible to build up a representative picture by examining about a dozen of the more prolific exponents. Half of those selected had close relatives who were also engravers. While it is recognized that there were differences between the work of individuals within a family, these groups for example, the Brandard, Cousen, Finden, Radclyffe, Wallis and Willmore families) have been treated together. The remainder are names eminent in their own right, not associated with relatives or a distinguishable group. They include J. B. Allen, J. C. Armytage, J. C. Bentley, E. Goodall, W. Miller and L. Stocks.

The engraver's occupation is a solitary one, and in order to gain an informed view of his life, the reader cannot do better than refer to the account, published in 1877, attributed to Charles William Radclyffe.[1] Charles was the youngest son of William Radclyffe, the eminent engraver, and the brother of Edward, also an engraver, so although he himself was a painter, chiefly in watercolours, he had a first-hand knowledge of the conditions under which his father and brother worked.

Few men have more lacked the sympathy and appreciation of the public than engravers: few men have been less known, few have lived more solitary or more laborious lives. Bending double all through a bright, sunny day, in an attic or close work-room, over a large steel plate, with a powerful magnifying-glass in constant use: carefully picking and cutting out bits of metal from the plate . . . working for twelve or fourteen hours daily, taking exercise rarely, in early morning or late at night: 'proving' a plate, only to find that days of labour have been mistaken, and have to be effaced, and done over again; criticised and corrected by painters, who often or always look upon engravers – to whom they owe so much – as inferior to themselves; badly paid by publishers, who reap the lion's share of the value of their work; and treated with indifference by the public – such is too commonly the life of an engraver . . .

John Burnet recalls that he worked from seven in the morning until eight in the evening during his apprenticeship.[2]

Despite this gloomy picture, many men seem to have been dedicated to it, and to have lived into ripe old age; a number of them were still working in their seventies

Note to previous two pages:
Monophoto: specify the phototypesetting system to be used. The Monophoto em is the square of the typesize – in this case 11 × 11 pts – and is divided into 96 units. The mark-up shown here is only good for Monophoto setting. Photon is based on 18 units of a square em but in ½ unit increments; VIP is 18 units, but 54 units on the ATP (Advanced Typography Programme). *Spacing parameters*: lines will be spaced by the computer with word spaces between a minimum of 16 units and a maximum of 32 units (i.e. one third of the 'em' of the typesize used). The zero is a specific instruction not to letterspace lower-case letters should the use of maximum word spaces fail to fill the line. *Mixing of typesizes* is not a problem in phototypesetting. Accurate base alignment is automatic. *Letterspacing* of capitals (or small capitals) is specified in units. *Word spacing* in unjustified setting is specified in units. *Indent*: specify in points or in unit equivalent. *Interlinear spacing* is specified as line feed measured in points from baseline to baseline. (Layout and instructions kindly supplied by Ron Costley and the Scolar Press.)

When preparing copy for the printer, the typographer may save himself trouble by giving general instructions, but if he does so, without marking the copy so that it is *exactly* correct from beginning to end, he is asking someone else, the compositor, to do his work for him, and he need not be surprised if mistakes are made. It is clearly preferable to prepare copy so that it is completely correct, in which case any mistakes are printer's errors and cannot be charged for.

Typographical instructions, such as italicizing, use of capitals or small capitals, letterspacing, indenting, setting in bold or underlining, extra leading or space between paragraphs, and so on, *must* be marked on the copy. They should be marked as neatly as possible, in ink which cannot be smudged or rubbed out (as pencil can), in the margin where possible, using standard printers' marks as shown in British Standard 5261 *Copy Preparation and Proof Correction*, parts 1 and 2, and in many other documents. If a manuscript or typescript has already been marked in one colour of ink, it is important that instructions to the printer should be consistently marked in a different colour, to avoid confusion, for example if some instructions are conflicting. When a manuscript or typescript has been heavily corrected, it is always preferable to re-type it, but there is often insufficient time or money to do so, and it must be remembered that every re-typing introduces the possibility, if not the certainty, of new errors.

Some typographical instructions to the printer cannot easily or clearly be expressed in words. The style for chapter titles and crossheadings, for example, will usually be standard throughout the book, and will require one layout (but if chapter titles vary greatly in length, special layouts may be required for the shortest and the longest). Tables and other contingencies which cannot be standardized will need special layouts as they occur. Tables in the text cannot normally be divided, or turned over from right-hand to the following left-hand page, and if this is likely to happen, the typographer must prepare instructions to cover it: usually the table, if it cannot be compressed or reduced by any means to fit on its proper page, will be set on the next opening, and an appropriate reference given in the text.

9 Book design

IT BEGINS WITH WORDS

A book is written: ideas are set down on paper in the form of words – although pictures may be important too. To turn a written book into a printed book is to take a series of decisions which, when the final words 'passed for press' are written on the proofs, cannot be rescinded. The book goes out into the world looking like *that*.

The decisions to be taken, between manuscript and printed book, include those on spelling, punctuation and general consistency of style; decisions on illustrations, if any (how many, what kind, to be printed by what process); and decisions on the physical style and appearance of the printed page (what size, what typeface, what kind of paper and so on).

These decisions may be taken by different people, but they are all part of a single process, that of making a printed book. To make the written words ready for printing is called 'editing' or 'sub-editing',* and to decide on the typeface, the length of line and the page size, is called 'designing'; *but the one activity is an extension of the other*. In many books, the organization of the chapter titles, the section headings and the picture captions (including the words in which they are written) – not to mention other details like footnotes (which may be in several different categories) and indexes – are as much designing as sub-editing: they affect the look of the book and how it works.

The words have to come first before they can be marked up for type. If they are not right, the typography cannot be right, and sometimes, cannot even be attempted. To take an elementary example (it is surprising how often it happens): (a) and (b) must be followed by (c), not C, or (iii) or even (iv); the titles of chapters and sub-headings and section headings must be consistent in style and arrangement. All this is not in order to make life easier for the typographer; it is to make life easier for the reader. If a foreign name is spelled in one way for three chapters and differently in the fourth, the reader is held up, trying to decide if it is a different place, or character, from the one previously mentioned. The main purpose of typographic design, as of care in spelling, punctuation and style, is to make the communication of the author's words and ideas as easily understandable, direct and pleasant as possible for the reader.

TYPOGRAPHIC STYLE

Books are functional objects: they have a purpose, which is to be read, or consulted, or looked at, page by page. There are many different kinds of book, with varying – often widely varying – functions. Normally, the designer's first task is to design the book so that it performs its intended function in the most appropriate way. The book must also be designed to

*In a publishing house, the term 'editor' refers to an individual, who may be a director of the firm or just a member of its editorial staff, whose responsibility it is to act as contact person and general adviser, on all aspects of publishing a book, to a specific number of firm's authors. The advice will cover everything from rewriting to ideas for promotion; or any other subject that an author wants to talk over with his publisher. Creative editors do a great deal of rewriting themselves, especially in the USA. 'Commissioning editors' think up ideas for books and go out to find the best person to write them.

Previous page: detail from cover drawing for the Autumn Book Number of *The Listener*, 6 October 1960, by Edward Bawden. Reproduced by kind permission of the Editor of *The Listener*.

look attractive, because before books can be read they have to be bought, usually in a bookshop, in competition with other – often many other – similar books.

So when a designer is given the manuscript of a book to design, decisions must be taken on its exact purpose, and information must be obtained from the publisher about everything that will affect the way it should appear: who will buy it, how it will be used, how it will be sold, its intended length of life, and so on. There will also be constraints of manufacture – the costs, the printer, the typefaces available, the process, etc. – but the designer should always begin by thinking of the *ideal* solution, and what would be *best*.

Finally, however, the designer has discovered what the book is about and how it should work, and knows what the manufacturing restraints are: the printer, the process, the costs that have to be observed. These are the tools to be used: how to use them?

I think it is still true that the beginning of typographical wisdom lies in Stanley Morison's essay, *First Principles of Typography*, first published in 1930 as an article in volume 7 of *The Fleuron*, and reprinted in many editions since. It is very short, so it will not take long to read. But, like everything else written on either art or design, it must not be taken as dogma but as something to start you thinking for yourself. For example, when Morison wrote 'the typographer's only purpose is to express, not himself, but his author', it is an important statement, but it is not the last and final word on the design of books. The transmission of the author's words and thoughts to the reader are the sacred responsibility of the designer, indeed: but that can be achieved in a variety of ways. One thinks immediately of the work of the American typographer William Addison Dwiggins (1880–1956), who designed more typefaces and many more books than Morison, and often illustrated or decorated them in an exuberant way that seems to contradict Morison's precepts, but never comes offensively between author and reader. Dwiggins's decorations of books enhance the discriminating reader's pleasure, just as a consummate actor's portrayal of a character helps, not hinders, the enjoyment of a play. There is room for a designer's *style* in book design, and indeed Morison's style is very evident in his own books. One can go further, and say that a book *should* have typographical style: to say that a book has no style is to say that it has been poorly designed.

But there is also 'over-design', just as there is 'over-acting'; and although it is not difficult to identify when it is seen, it is not easy to put into words. The best thing you can do is to study as many books, by as many designers, as you can find, and gradually something, that perhaps you did not know was there, will begin to happen when you sit down with a blank piece of layout paper in front of you.

Being a typographer or designer of books involves both words and images, so it comes as no surprise to learn that the greatest typographers were masters of both. Dwiggins is a good example and it is relevant here to quote some discerning words from the first chapter, written by Paul Hollister, in *Postscripts on Dwiggins*, two little volumes published by the Typophiles of New York in 1960.

'Dwiggins once disclosed to me the formula by which he endows words on paper with more force and color than most people (including the people who wrote the words) ever saw in them. Of course, Dwiggins claimed no such objective; he simply described, as to a humble pupil, a method. He said:

"You take the cork out of the top of your head, and you drop in a word like La Paz, or Congo, or Sindbad. One word at a time. If it's the name of a place, it need not be a place you know. If it's not the name of a place, but just a word, you need not know it so fine as to split hairs. Just put the word in. Then put in a couple of cocktails and some black coffee, and put the cork back in tight, jump up and down for two or three days and then the word will come out of your fingers onto paper. Then you give the result – picture or pattern, or whatever, it is – a high-sounding caption like *'Graphic Response to Verbal Stimulus*: La Paz'. That's all there is to it. It doesn't mean a thing, but it's a lot of fun."

'He has never seen La Paz, nor to his conscious recollection any picture of it. I happen to have seen La Paz and am here to state that his *pochoir* "graphic response" to the name of that town on top of the Andes is far more La Paz than today's news-picture. Sindbad, the Congo, I have not seen, but I'll take his "responses". I will take, in fact, his graphic response to any word, any chapter, any book, as signifying everything on paper the author ever hoped they might imply, usually more than they dared hope, and a great deal more than the reader ever expected. If Balzac could see what this American has done to his words[1] he would feel very much as Deems Taylor says Bach might feel suddenly to come upon the Philadelphia Orchestra playing Tschaikowsky's orchestral transcription of the Bach C-minor Passacaglia, drawing out of it things Bach never knew he heard in the days of the hand-pumped tracker organ.'

There is much truth and wisdom about the process of designing in those words, both Dwiggins's and Hollister's.

The best way to learn what typographical style is, and to develop your own, is to study the work of the masters – which if you have any feeling for typography you will find you can soon identify. For a start, look for examples of the work of three Americans: Dwiggins, D. B. Updike and Bruce Rogers; four Englishmen: Bernard Newdigate, Stanley Morison, Francis Meynell and Oliver Simon; and the Swiss typographer Jan Tschichold. Try to have copies of books designed by them, if they appeal to you, on your own shelves; try to analyse the style that is characteristic of each and why the books are different from other books; and then try to find books with different styles, and identify their designers. Look, for example, for books published by

William Pickering of London, and T. N. Foulis of Edinburgh. Once you have recognized their styles, you will find that you can spot them, just from their spines, with one eye shut, at a distance of 20 yards in a bookshop lit with one 40 watt bulb.

CENTRED OR ASYMMETRIC TYPOGRAPHY?

Hamlet was written by Shakespeare more than 350 years ago, but it does not have to be played in Elizabethan costume: I have seen it in so-called 'modern dress' and I have seen it played in the ordinary clothes the actors had travelled in, because their costume hampers had got lost; in both cases it was marvellous, because the magic of the play made one forget the costumes. In the same way, *Hamlet* could be presented typographically in any number of different styles, and it would not matter which, if it were well done; and 'well done' would mean that the style did not come between the reader and the words.

   Hamlet could, for example, be designed in either a centred or an asymmetric style. It is sometimes said that all typography must be either centred or asymmetric; but this is not so. However, 'asymmetry' in typography signifies a particular philosophy of design which is also known as the 'New Typography'. It was 'new' in the 1930s in Germany, where it was formulated: it is only now becoming fully understood in Britain and America. Asymmetric typography is not simply a matter of ranging everything left, or setting lines vertically or obliquely, or of being otherwise unconventional: it is subtler than that. All typographic design depends on planned relationships between sizes of types, shapes of letters, lengths of lines, areas of type and unprinted space, and so on. The New Typography of the Bauhaus period was first and foremost revolutionary, a protest against the 'old way' of doing things, against the wrongs of the nineteenth century, against the politics and philosophies that had led Europe into a world war; it was also a vindication of the machine, and machine production: it claimed that typography, like architecture, must be functional; and it introduced the idea of 'tension' into typography. Jan Tschichold claimed (in his book, *Asymmetric Typography*, London 1967, first published in Germany in 1933) that the 'old' typography was 'static', 'inflexible', 'purely ornamental' and 'entirely unfunctional': the new was in harmony with modern machine production and with the ideas being explored (in the 1920s and 1930s) in abstract art and sculpture, by El Lissitzky, Laszló Moholy-Nagy, Kurt Schwitters, Hans Arp, Josef Albers and their friends (see Chapter 5).

   The books and other work designed by Tschichold at this period all show extreme sensitivity and subtlety, not only in the typography itself but also in the choice of paper and materials for printing and binding. Tschichold, more than any other book designer of his movement, was aware that all printed matter is three-dimensional and to be *touched* as well as *seen*. Later, he abandoned his previous dogma that asymmetric typography was the only possible solution for all typographical problems in this century. For many kinds of literature, he found that it just did not work. Nevertheless, asymmetric typography, not the centred or 'symmetrical' or 'ornamental' style, remains as the essential, basic approach for all industrial and information typography today, e.g. timetables, reports, accounts and every kind of form; and it will increasingly help the designers of newspapers, periodicals and technical literature.

Asymmetry and symmetry (also known as 'non-axial' and 'axial' design) are not even in total opposition to each other and in fact are often combined in the same book; the fact that we begin reading a line on the left and end on the right makes this inevitable. It is not 'wrong' to design a book with off-centre chapter titles and a centred title page, or vice-versa: it depends on how it looks.

Paul Graupe Berlin W 9 Bellevuestrasse 7

Am 17. und 18. Oktober 1932 : **Auktion 105**

Bücher des 15. bis 20. Jahrhunderts	Die grafische Sammlung Rudolf Tewes	Sammlung Paul Ephraim, Berlin
Inkunabeln	Französische Meister	Gemälde
Holzschnittbücher	des 19. und 20. Jahrhunderts:	Handzeichnungen
Erstausgaben	Daumier, Degas, Manet,	neuerer deutscher Meister
Luxus- und Pressendrucke	Picasso, Renoir	
Kunstliteratur	Eine umfassende	
	Toulouse-Lautrec-Sammlung	

Illustrierter Katalog auf Wunsch

An asymmetric advertisement for an art auction, designed by Jan Tschichold, 1932.

ORIGINALITY

It must be emphasized that book typography (perhaps more than any other creative art) is built out of the materials *and ideas* of the past, so that total originality is not possible, let alone desirable. Imre Reiner, the Swiss typographer and artist, wrote 'A typographer should never limit himself to being modern if modern signifies merely the fashion of his day; he should rather endeavour to produce works of lasting effect which will remain modern in time to come.'[2]

The typographer uses tools – the letters of the alphabet, typefaces which are now three or four hundred years old, ink, and paper – which are older still, but out of all the experience of the past, something new can be distilled. What is new, when he sits down before his drawing-board and his layout paper, is the problem, and perhaps also the book itself. Even if he is designing an old book, it is for a new audience.

In picking up a book to *read*, we want originality in the author's words and ideas, not in their presentation (unless the words *need* to be presented in a new way, which is exceptional). The more profound the author's words are, the easier the actual reading of them must be: we do not want 'originality' in the shapes of the letters, or the way they are arranged and printed: we do not want even to notice the typography.

But not all typographic design is concerned with straightforward text. Not all typography is concerned first and foremost even with 'legibility'; if its object is 'notice-ability', it is concerned with claiming attention to itself in competition with all the other stridencies and attractions in our environment. And much typography just exists and will be 'consumed' whether it is attractive or not. In all those cases, originality, freshness, distinction, even 'beauty', whatever that means, are possible – and badly needed.

HOUSE STYLES

Many firms have 'house styles'. A house style may cover anything from the text (standard style for printing dates, addresses, chapter titles, etc.) to every aspect of typographic design: typeface, justified or unjustified setting, centred or asymmetrical, and so on. The reasons for a house style may be that a publisher wants his books to have a recognizable style, or to save time and argument in a large design and production office, or that he just likes things done in that way. To avoid wasting his own time, the designer must always, when working for a new client, find out what house rules, if any, are applicable.

When books are produced in series, the style may be rigid (e.g. 'Everyman', or 'World's Classics') or flexible (e.g. 'King Penguins'), but it is nearly always a requirement that all the books in the series have a family likeness, because if the series is successful they help to sell each other. Bookshop recognizability starts with the jacket: it takes much skill to design a jacket which instantly proclaims the series but is not boring or confusing *en masse*.

MARGINS

The margin is the white space on a page round the outside of the printed matter or type area. Margins serve various purposes: they form a frame round the text, or illustrations, to separate them from the background against which the book may be held; they provide an aesthetic contrast of quiet to the 'busyness' of the printed matter; they provide somewhere for the reader to write notes or mark passages (in his own books, not other people's); they provide somewhere to put the fingers holding the book (particularly if it is a paperback with floppy sides) without obscuring the text; if a book is damaged they provide a defence before the damage encroaches on the text, and if a book has to be re-bound they provide room for trimming the edges flush without cutting into the text. And in certain kinds of book, like the present 'manual', they provide space for illustrations.

Obviously the smaller the margins, the less the above purposes can be served, but they can sometimes be ignored for the sake of novelty or eccentricity. It is impracticable to design a book with margins less than, say $\frac{1}{8}$ in. or 4 mm, since high-speed machine guillotining cannot guarantee to be so accurate and the printed area may be cut into.

Books that have to go into libraries often have to be re-bound, perhaps several times, and the trim each time may be $\frac{1}{8}$ in., so a margin round the outside edges of $\frac{3}{8}$ in., which will allow two re-bindings, should be regarded as a minimum – and don't forget that the folios must be inside that minimum margin. The amount of margin necessary in the back or 'gutter' depends on the binder and the method of binding; $\frac{1}{4}$ in. may be regarded as an absolute minimum, but 3 picas or $\frac{1}{2}$ in. is more normal.

Books in which economy is paramount, or in which as much type matter must be got on to the page as possible (within reason) to reduce the number of pages, such as most paperback series, will have margins such as: back $\frac{1}{4}$ in.; head (to running head, if any) $\frac{3}{8}$ in.; foredge $\frac{1}{2}$ in.; foot (from folio) $\frac{1}{2}$ in. Look at the paperbacks on your own shelves and measure them.

Books in which economy is not so stringent will have, or may have, wider margins. Much has been written about the proportions of margins to text, and much of it is untrue. Hugh Williamson's *Methods of Book Design* gives a common-sense view and should be studied. He quotes the proportions $1\frac{1}{2}:2:3:4$ for the ratio of back:head:foredge:foot as being 'one popular formula', but every serious designer must collect his own examples and make up his own mind. Nearly all books raise different problems and require different solutions anyway. What is certain is that margins – i.e. white space – are an integral ingredient in page design and must always be a prime consideration. They must look deliberate and not accidental. They need not be in the conventional proportions quoted above; and they need not be symmetrical, i.e. both left- and right-hand pages corresponding. But if they are not symmetrical, then the lines of type or blocks of illustration on each side of the sheet will not back up exactly, and this may result in problems of 'see-through'.

If a book is designed with every page on the same system or grid, with no difference between left- and right-hand pages, including the folios, then the order of the pages can be changed freely and quickly, and this can be an advantage. Remember, however, that folios in the back of a book (i.e. the right hand-side of a left-hand page and vice-versa) are virtually useless; but this may not matter if there is always a folio on the outside of the facing page.

PAGE SIZE AND SHAPE

The size and shape of a book page is sometimes determined by considerations outside the designer's control: it may have to conform to a series, or plates and blocks already in existence must be used, and so on.

When the choice of size and shape is unrestricted, the designer must consider very carefully what the purpose of the book is, how it will be used, who will read it and where, and what the requirements of the illustrations will be, if any.

Books have been, and can be, made in odd shapes, like leaves, and golliwogs, and golf balls, and bottles, and many other shapes; and if the cost can be justified by the result, it is all good clean fun. But the basic shapes are upright, square, or landscape. (A 'landscape' book or booklet is one in which the page width is greater than the depth (oblong). A 'portrait' shape is the opposite.) The 'normal' shape is upright, and it is normal because it is the most efficient shape for holding in the hand, open, for the purpose of reading. There must, therefore, be a good reason for departing from this shape.

The *square* format (including all formats which are nearly square) may be justified when a book is illustrated, when the pictures are important, and when the pictures are in all shapes, vertical, square, circular and horizontal. A square page accommodates all these shapes. A large book in which oblong pictures are printed vertically, so that the book has to be turned to look at them, is an annoyance, an example of inefficient design. In *Typographic* 11 (1977), the designer Derek Birdsall is quoted as saying 'Almost all of my books are in fact *square*: where I've got a choice and where the books are illustrated, which almost all of my books are, I've found it almost impossible to beat the square format.' The flexibility of the square format layout is shown by several illustrations and Birdsall's article deserves careful study by students. However, remember that an open book is not a single page

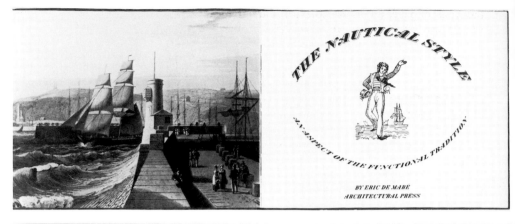

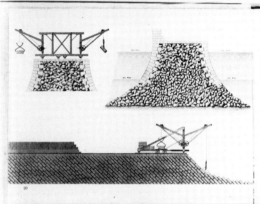

Three openings from Eric de Maré's *The Nautical Style*, Architectural Press, London 1973 (reduced from 202 mm deep) (see p. 135). *Above*: the title-page opening. *Middle*: a chapter opening showing the main text in double column, with the caption to the illustrations on the left-hand page set in italic to the same measure (24 picas) as the text.

Below: an opening of illustrations, with the caption set to a different measure; three different measures are used on three consecutive openings, and for six consecutive pages there are no folios, owing to bleeds and lack of a grid. Marvellous pictures: but would the book's impact – and message – have been stronger if the layout had been disciplined by a grid?

but a pair of pages (a 'double spread'), and if a single page is vertical, an opening of two pages will probably make a horizontal shape, and could be used for a horizontally oblong illustration. Remember also that human beings are vertical, so that an illustrated book dealing with people will almost certainly benefit by having an upright format.

Every illustrated book, catalogue or publication has a different set of requirements and parameters, and successful solutions have been produced in every shape and size: examples can be found to justify almost any shape, and some are illustrated here. A particularly interesting example is Emil Schulthess's *Afrika* (Zürich 1958): the format is upright (315×240 mm or $12\frac{1}{2} \times 9\frac{1}{2}$ in.) and the book consists entirely of superb photographs, superbly printed by Conzett & Huber's photogravure in black-and-white and colour. Most of the pictures are upright, but landscape photographs are printed either as double spreads or as folded pull-outs – an expensive feature, but amply justified when the result is a work of art, as this book is. The folded pull-outs are of different sizes, so that the photographs did not have to be trimmed to uniform proportions.

A landscape format may be justified when all the illustrations are landscape in shape, and particularly if two landscape illustrations need to be shown side by side (and cannot be shown one above the other). But a landscape shape is not a practical shape for a book: the weight of the pages, held in by a shorter spine, tends to break the binding, it is unwieldy to hold, and if the page width is greater than 200 mm or 8 in., it is greater than normal bookshelf depth and will therefore be a nuisance for booksellers and book buyers. The thicker and heavier a landscape book, the worse it is to handle and the shorter its life will be before the pages pull out of the binding.

A justifiable example of the landscape format is the paperback book of Giles' cartoons published by the *Daily Express* every Christmas. I cannot think of a better way of producing them. Another small landscape book that makes sense is *Printers' Trains*, produced and designed by the Allenholme Press, Wylam, for the Wynkyn de Worde Society and the Newcastle Imprint Club. Trains are by their nature much longer than they are tall; the same might apply to books on crocodiles, processions and so on. Another attractive landscape book is Eric de Maré's *The Nautical Style* (London 1973). Its internal design raises questions which I discuss below under 'Grids'.

Then, I find on my shelves a book of 300 pages, 20 mm or nearly an inch thick, on the *Graphic Worlds of Peter Bruegel the Elder* (New York 1963) in which the few upright pictures are printed *sideways*, and that is truly the worst of both worlds!

If a book consists of text only, either prose or verse, or both, and it has no other important purpose in life except to be read comfortably in a normal way, then it must be neither too big, nor too heavy: but of course there are factors like the

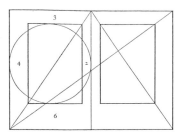

The page proportions discovered by Jan Tschichold to underlie many late medieval manuscripts and incunabula. Page proportion 2:3; text and page area are of the same proportions. Depth of text area is equal to page width. Margins are 2:3:4:6.

number of words in the text, and costs, which cannot be avoided. *War and Peace* makes a staggering 1,744 pages in the Oxford 'World's Classics' pocket format of $5\frac{7}{8} \times 3\frac{1}{2}$ in., and has to be divided into three volumes; and the Bible has been produced in legible single-column format, by skilful typography, at Cambridge University Press.

Royal Octavo ($9\frac{3}{4} \times 6$ in. trimmed page size, see Chapter 7), approximately the size of Hugh Williamson's *Methods of Book Design*, is almost too big for convenience if the book is to be read in bed. Demy Octavo ($8\frac{1}{2} \times 5\frac{1}{2}$ in. trimmed) is, by general agreement and practice, at least in the UK, one of the most 'normal' sizes for books intended to be read. Penguins, although they are now not all uniform, are traditionally $7 \times 4\frac{1}{2}$ in. or $4\frac{3}{8}$ in.; the Birkhäuser Classics, designed by Jan Tschichold, and Hamish Hamilton's Novel Library, designed by Oliver Simon, were 170–173 × 100–104 mm (measurements taken from actual copies of books, which vary) – an extremely elegant and convenient size for books which can be carried about in one's pocket.

The word 'elegant' applied to the proportions of a book page requires attention. Some proportions are definitely more elegant, or pleasing, than others, irrespective of the design of the printed matter. The proportions which seem to have the greatest elegance are those that are known as the 'golden section', or 'golden rectangle', defined as 34:21 or 8.1:5. If you draw a rectangle to these proportions on a sheet of A4, and draw the diagonal, you will find that it makes a page about 26 mm narrower than the A4 sheet; you will also find that it gives the exact proportions of the traditional Penguin page. You will also notice that A5 (210 × 148 mm) is proportionally further away from the golden section than A4: it is about $\frac{3}{4}$ in., or 19 mm, wider. A5 is in fact too wide a page for ordinary reading and is only justified if the page size is dictated by illustrations or the need for diagrams, illustrations, etc. in the side margins.

For further reading on the golden section, study Jan Tschichold's essay in *Calligraphy and Palaeography, Essays presented to Alfred Fairbank on his 70th birthday* (London 1965), the only statement in English about this subject that I have been able to find (and it is translated from German). Jan Tschichold believed strongly in the golden section and discovered methods which medieval scribes used to determine their margins as well as their page proportions. It is an interesting by-way of history, but for contemporary designers the simpler rule of 'what looks right is right' is easier to apply. Make your own collections of examples to train your eye in what does look right.

Large books. The biggest modern book I have in the house is a book of posters, measuring 24 × 17$\frac{1}{4}$ in. (610 × 438 mm), which is slightly larger than the page size of the *Sunday Times*. This is really no longer a book but a bound collection of prints. I much enjoy looking at it, but the only place I can keep it is on the floor beneath the sofa.

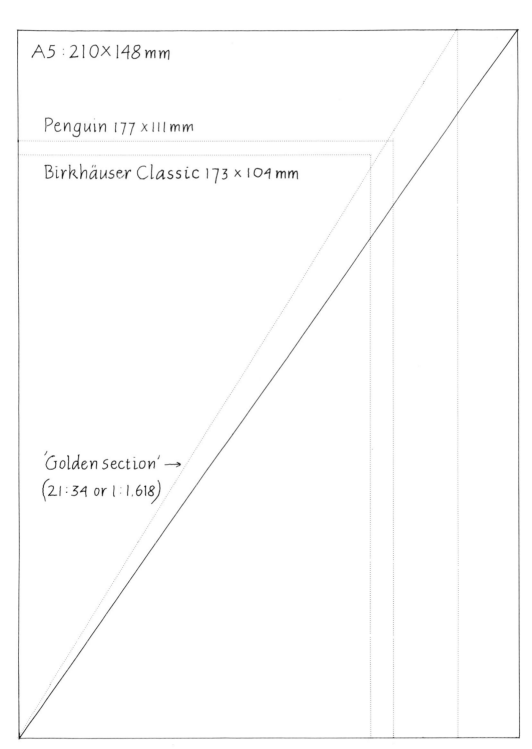

A5 : 210 × 148 mm

Penguin 177 × 111 mm

Birkhäuser Classic 173 × 104 mm

'Golden section' →
(21 : 34 or 1 : 1.618)

The elegant proportions of the
'golden section' superimposed on an
A5 sheet, with the traditional Penguin
and Birkhäuser Classic page sizes for
comparison. (Slightly reduced.)

GRIDS

The grid is the invisible framework within which all books, magazines and newspapers are designed. It is a boon to the designer and the printer; it also helps the appearance of the page.

The simplest grid is the type area of an ordinary book. It must show: (1) the measure, i.e. the length of line to which the text is set (the maximum length if the text is set unjustified) and the number of lines on a full page, which fixes the depth of the type area; (2) the position of the folios which must be identical on every opening, merely because they have got to be somewhere, and it is an unnecessary nuisance, first to the printer and secondly to the reader, if the position varies; (3) the position of the running heads, if there are any; (4) the margins, which must be the same on every opening, unless there are special reasons for varying them.

The grid for an ordinary book of text, like a novel, is therefore very simple. But the more complicated the components of a page, the more necessary and helpful the grid becomes. Any book in which illustrations are an important feature will have (as well as folios and running heads) main text, pictures (which may be of all sorts,

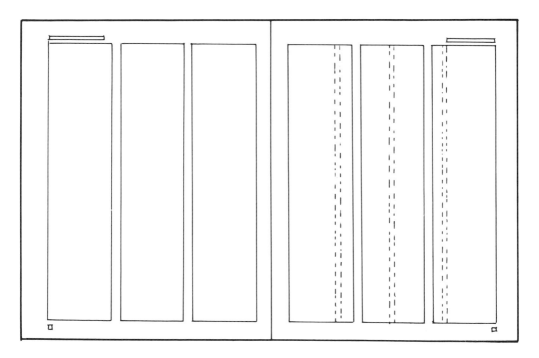

A conventional grid of three equal columns. On the right-hand page a four-column grid has been added: both systems could be used in the same book. One might apply to text, the other to illustrations: there are many possible variations.

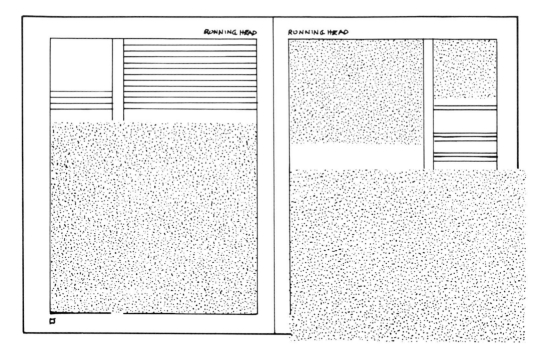

RUNNING HEAD   RUNNING HEAD

quantities, shapes and sizes on a single page) and captions – not to mention things like chapter and section headings.

It is possible to design a book in which every single page is laid out according to the whim of the designer, on no system except intuition. It *may* look good; it will cost more and it will take many many more hours longer both to design and also to make up for printing; but it is not the way to learn how to design books, and is a system to be practised only by experts.

The designer starts by studying his material. What are the ingredients in his mix? Can he separate the main text and the illustrations, so that the text is read straight through, and then the illustrations follow, to be looked at separately? Or must the main text be integrated with the illustrations – and what about the captions; are they long, or short, or can they be omitted entirely, or could they be relegated to the back, in a numbered list? How is the book intended to be used?

The book designer must here exercise his own creative function. The author is an expert in his own subject, whether it is carpentry, ornithology, marine archaeology, or whatever; but the designer's expertise lies in *communicating* (on behalf of the author), attractively and efficiently. Are the pictures the right pictures for the job? They may have to be used anyway, but the question is worth asking. If they are right, what exactly are they intended to convey, and do they need captions? Captions, their purpose, content and treatment, are discussed in Chapter 10.

A grid much in use today for large illustrated books: text set to normal page width (*c.* 24–30 picas), captions to narrow measure. Four choices of illustration width are shown (tinted areas).

The *Mrs Howard* is the only sketch model for a neoclassical monument that is illustrated; unfortunately there are no models of this kind by Banks or Flaxman in the collection. But the swing back to a naturalism which is, to some extent, linked with the romantic movement is exemplified by Sir Francis Chantrey's sketch (No. 50 and Fig. 7) for the monument to *Bishop Heber*. All allegory, whether Christian or pagan, has now disappeared. The bishop, a free-standing figure with no background, is shown kneeling as in life, wearing his episcopal robes. The handling is broad and firm, the conception direct and simple. The world of the eighteenth century, with its nostalgia for Antiquity, has gone, and the bishop belongs to a new age, eager to meet the challenge of the present.

VII Reliefs

The reliefs in the Museum's collection are, in three cases at least, extremely revealing. David Le Marchand's *Matthew Raper* (No. 1) is, admittedly, an unusual work, but the attempt at illusionism, the heavy curling folds of the cloak, and the draped curtain in the background link it directly with the baroque.

Rysbrack's model for the *Allegory of Charity* (No. 7) is a far more important piece. Made in 1746 for a chimney-piece at the Foundling Hospital, it comes from the decade when rococo influences were at their height in England. The setting is pastoral, as in many rococo paintings, the scene has charm rather than grandeur, and the relief is varied between high and low, in such a way that the surface is broken by little flecks of light and shade. Its handling is therefore very close to Rysbrack's figures of *Rubens* and *Van Dyck* (Nos. 8 and 9), and far lighter than the firmly modelled head and deeply cut folds of the model of *Newton* (No. 5).

Thomas Banks's *Thetis and her Nymphs rising from the Sea to console Achilles for the loss of Patroclus* (No. 40) makes a most telling contrast to Rysbrack's *Charity*. The mood is not pastoral but heroic—Flaxman described the work as 'of the epic class'— and with the change of mood there is a complete change of handling. Banks was working in Rome when the relief was made in 1778, some thirty years later than the *Charity*, and the new ideals of neoclassicism were in the air. One important tenet of the new movement was the importance of contours. Banks's figures,

therefore, even when the relief is low, rise sharply from the ground. There is no blurring of the edges, and except for the indication of waves in the lower part of the relief, none of the pictorial quality which gives the *Charity* much of its charm. The modelling is smooth and rather hard, and there is an obvious recognition of the importance of the nude. Many of these characteristics are taken from antique art, but the building of the design on linear rhythms, and the exaggerated gestures of the figures do not come from Antiquity. The first is due to the talent of Banks, and the second, in all probability, to his friendship with Fuseli.

The reliefs after Flaxman for the Covent Garden frieze (Nos. 45 and 46) are also examples of neoclassical art, but though the subjects are dramatic, they have none of the tense agony of Banks. Except for the mounds on which certain characters are seated, there is no indication of a setting, and the figures are silhouetted against a plain ground. The subjects need reading before they can be understood, for to Flaxman content as well as handling was of importance, and their learned quality is very far indeed from the easy intention of the *Allegory of Charity*, which is obvious at the first glance. The contours are again sharp, though less so than in the Banks, and while Flaxman's talent for linear design is evident in every figure, this is slightly less apparent in the design of the whole. But above all it is clear that Flaxman's inspiration comes from a different source from that of Banks. Two years before he designed these works, he had reported on the condition of the Elgin Marbles, shown for the first time in London, and to his eternal credit had advised against restoration. At many points— the chariots and horses and the slow procession of Muses—the Parthenon frieze would seem to have been in his mind. If so, this is the earliest example of its impact on English sculpture.

VIII Summary and Conclusion

It will have become clear that English sculpture after about 1720 presents a late baroque style, though often much modified by classical influence. From about 1740 to 1770 a more rococo manner is dominant, though the older style still persists beside it. In the 1770s the first examples of neoclassical sculpture appear, though again older styles continue. Neoclassicism remains the correct style until well into the nineteenth century, but from

20

21

extremely like Mr. Pope, more like than any sculptor has done I think'. John Flaxman, whose father was employed as a modeller by Roubiliac, and who almost certainly made casts for him, remembered late in life that his father saw Pope sitting in an armchair, while Roubiliac worked on the bust.[3] And Sir Joshua Reynolds passed on to Edmond Malone the sculptor's own account of the sitter: 'Roubiliac the statuary, who made a bust of him from life, observed that his countenance was that of a person who had been much afflicted with headache, and that he should have known the fact from the contracted appearance of the skin between his eyebrows, though he had not been otherwise apprised of it'.[4]

Roubiliac had indeed created an unforgettable portrait of a man who had suffered much throughout his life; but he had seen and conveyed that, though Pope may have had a bitter tongue, he had also the endurance and the fine discrimination to become the greatest poet of his age.

[3] Winsatt, *op. cit.*, p. 229. It is not impossible that some of the existing plasters are the work of the elder Flaxman.   [4] J. Prior, *Life of Edmond Malone*, 1860, pp. 428–29.

No. 22

Louis-François ROUBILIAC
1705?-62

JONATHAN TYERS
(d. 1767)
About 1738

Bust in terracotta
H. (including base)
2 ft 4 in. (71·1 cm.)
A.94—1927

Tyers is shown clean-shaven and full-face, wearing a soft cap. His shirt is open at the neck, and loose drapery covers his shoulders.

Jonathan Tyers contributed much to the life of eighteenth-century London, for in 1728 he leased land at Vauxhall, where in 1732 he opened the famous Vauxhall Gardens, with a *ridotto al fresco*, providing orchestral concerts, and after 1745 vocal music as well.

He was a friend of Hogarth's, the supper boxes were decorated by Francis Hayman (some parts of these decorations being in the Museum), and he gave Roubiliac his first important commission (see No. 20). A drawing by Thomas Rowlandson showing the gardens rather later in the century is also in the Museum (P.13—1967).

The bust, which appears to have been owned at one time by Tyers' descendants,[1] in all probability dates from the time when he was employing Roubiliac, and therefore forms a group with the busts of Handel (terracotta, Foundling Hospital; marble, Windsor Castle) and Hogarth (terracotta, National Portrait Gallery). It is careful and competent in modelling, a convincing portrait of a shrewd businessman, and a good example of the sculptor's busts in informal dress, though it has not the superb quality of his later work in this manner. The marble, which is less lively in quality, is in the City Art Gallery, Birmingham.

[1] K. A. Esdaile, *Louis François Roubiliac*, 1928, p. 41.

82

Two openings from Margaret Whinney's *English Sculpture 1720–1830*, Victoria and Albert Museum, London 1971 (reduced from 245 mm deep). Designed by Ruari McLean for HMSO. The book consists of text, footnotes and plates (mostly full page), with details of attribution, size, etc., for each plate. Printed throughout on art paper, the non-symmetrical layout of facing text pages is not affected by see-through. Set in Bembo (details in Bembo Bold).

134

Once the grid has been designed, in pencil, and tested against all the different features of the book, it must be drawn accurately on white paper, with at least an inch of white margin all round (for writing instructions and showing 'bleeds' – see below – if bleeds are used throughout, the bleed rule will probably be incorporated in the drawing). The book title and trimmed page size in millimetres or inches should be shown at the top; and as many copies made of the grid as will be needed in production. The designer must retain one copy, and at least one copy should go to the printer with the setting instructions.

If the book is profusely illustrated and page-by-page layouts need to be made, the designer must ask the printer or publisher to supply printed copies of the grid: it is usually wise to ask for $2\frac{1}{2}$ times the number of pages the book makes, i.e. if the book makes 200 pages, ask for 250 double-spread layout sheets, in case a mistake is made and the whole book has to be redone. The printed layout sheets should be printed in grey or blue (preferable to black, since the grid lines are simply for the designer, and the effect of layouts is easier to judge if they are not prominent), with at least one inch white margin all round, on white paper that is both strong enough for pasting up and some rubbing out, and transparent enough for occasional tracing. White bank paper is ideal.

Examples of different grids are illustrated here; and for Tschichold's definitive grid for King Penguin covers, see p. 86 of *Jan Tschichold, Typographer* (London 1975). See also Alan Bartram's article 'The grid; an aid or an end?' in *Penrose Annual*, 63 (1970), in which an expert designer points out the danger of grids becoming stultifying straitjackets: 'I think designs where the grid is dominant are too near in spirit for comfort to the increasing standardisation, impersonalism and conformity which is the negative side of life today . . . Modern design doesn't *have* to be ruthlessly regimented and anonymous.' He has an important point; but, as always, you have to learn *how* to use grids, before you can afford to discard them.

An instructive example of an illustrated book in which a grid has *not* been used is Eric de Maré's *The Nautical Style*, mentioned above. It is full of visual excitements; the author's own superb photographs are mixed with other photos, old engravings and drawings by John Piper and Gordon Cullen. In my opinion it is a classic example of a book that would have benefited from a grid; and the captions set in italics, sometimes over 20 lines long, to all sorts of measures, are less easy to read than they should have been. But look at it and make up your own mind; it would be an excellent exercise to try to redesign it on a grid, and see what you find.

The printed layout sheets mentioned above are used for making a page-by-page paste-up of corrected galleys and proofs of the illustrations. When the paste-up is complete, the book can be seen as a whole, discussed with the author and publisher, and alterations and adjustments can be made easily

Felix Brunner, *A Handbook of Graphic Reproduction Processes*, Tiranti, London 1962 (reduced from 203 mm deep). Designed by Felix Brunner. A Swiss book with parallel texts in English, German and French. The Swiss have specialized in multi-lingual layout. The grid adopted here is especially suitable when there are many illustrations both large and small. The folios have been set in the back margins, presumably because the designer wanted very narrow outer margins, where there would not have been enough room.

before the sheets go to the printer for final make-up. In an offset-litho book, the next stage is ozalid page proofs, which are necessary to see that the designer's instructions have been carried out. These proofs are made from the paste-up of film, before printing plates are made, so corrections are still possible, though expensive. It is vital to check the ozalid page proofs meticulously, to see that every item is present (e.g. every line of every caption, in its corrected form); and these page proofs must be preserved, as they are a proof of what the designer and publisher have passed for press. It is not unknown for items to come unstuck from the film assembly and disappear before plate-making; if the ozalid page proofs were correct, and the printed pages wrong, the designer is exonerated.

TREATMENT OF ILLUSTRATIONS

Many interesting problems concerning the design of illustrated books are outside the proper scope of a manual of typography. Here, we will deal with books in which text and pictures are in close relationship.

In all such books, the main design problem is to create a harmonious relationship between text and pictures, so that the book feels and looks like an ordered unity, not a hotch-potch, and so that the functional relationships between text, captions and illustrations are clearly defined and easily understood.

In a conventional reading-book with a few plates, the plates may be printed on the same paper as the text, or on a different paper. The two papers should either look the same, or look noticeably and intentionally different. If both papers are white, but one is cartridge and the other is coated ('art'), care should be taken to ensure that the colour of both papers is identical. Two papers nearly but not quite the same nearly always look like a mistake. One way of avoiding the problem, when coated paper is essential for printing the plates, is to print the entire book on coated paper; but this may be aesthetically unpleasing. Coated or 'art' paper is shiny, brittle, unsympathetic to the touch and the eye, heavy and expensive. An alternative is to use 'matt art', which is less unpleasing to look at; but it is not so easily available, and is sometimes much less easy to print on.

If a book consists of a number of text pages (which are all the same shape) and the pages include a number of squared-up illustrations, all different shapes, the unity of the book is immediately threatened. The illustrations should all have the same width as the type area (unless they 'bleed' off the page; 'bleeding' is discussed below) and align with the top of the text (or with the top of the running heads, depending on how they are arranged); if they can also, with captions, make the same depth as the text, so much the better. If not, the captions should either all go beneath the plates, separated by the same gap, or at the foot of the type area; if they (or the plates without captions) exceed the correct depth of text pages, the unity of the book is again threatened.

If a book is designed with wide foredge margins, and it is strongly desirable to make an illustration wider than the type measure, it can be taken into the margin, provided it is conspicuously wider than the text; but if it is done more than once, the larger illustrations should be all the same width. This may diminish the apparent unity of the book but is usually preferable to the other way of making landscape illustrations bigger (discussed above), which is to place them long ways on the page, forcing the reader to turn the book in his hand to look at them. 'Turned' illustrations are almost as annoying as finding a page of text printed upside down.

When a designer has to design a book with many illustrations, he must first of all understand the purpose of the

Two consecutive openings from Hugh Honour's *The European Vision of America*, Cleveland Museum of Art, 1975 (reduced from 222 mm deep). Designed by Merald Wrolstad. The conventional three-column grid of this exhibition catalogue is used for biographies and lengthy captions, set in 9 on 11 pt Sabon × 13 picas, ragged right, and references in 8 on 9 pt Sabon. Introductions to sections (not shown) are set to 27 picas. There are no folios except on the 27-pica pages and the indices at the back, but every caption is numbered and nearly always begins on the same page as its illustration. The grid allows maximum flexibility in sizing the very varied illustrations, of which there are 339 on 400 pages: they do not necessarily follow column widths.

book and its illustrations, which may mean reading the text and discussing the book with the author, editor, art editor or publisher. He must also look carefully at the illustrations provided. Are they complete? Are they what they are supposed to be, and correctly identified, including showing 'top' when this is not obvious? Have necessary permissions been obtained, and what acknowledgments must be printed? Are they suitable for reproduction? (Are they clean, undamaged, good prints or whatever? Retouching photographs for spots, dirty marks, tears, etc., can be very expensive.) All these questions are perhaps not the designer's job, and should be the publisher's responsibility, but the designer may be the person best qualified to answer them.

When satisfied on these points, the designer must understand the relative importance of the illustrations, and decide which should be large, which small, and so on. Should the illustrations be in chronological order, or any other order? If they are reproductions of works of art, should they all be to the same scale? It is normally undesirable to make a small object look bigger than something else when it is actually smaller, and this may be more important when the differences are small – e.g. if the illustrations show a collection of snuff boxes. This is a point which the author or editor may have to decide.

If the illustrations include colour transparencies, it is important to be absolutely certain that they are the correct way round and not back to front. The emulsion side (which can be seen when the transparency is held obliquely to the light) should be on the reverse *unless it is a copy*.

When marking up photographs or transparencies for reproduction, the instructions should ideally be marked on

Jan van Kessel the Elder
Flemish, 1626–1679.
Van Kessel was born in Antwerp, the son of a portrait painter, Hieronymus van Kessel, and, through his mother, grandson of Jan Breughel the Elder. After being trained under the genre painter Simon de Vos and possibly his uncle Jan Breughel the Younger, he became a master of the Antwerp painters' guild in 1644-45. He was mainly a meticulously accurate painter of flowers, insects, and animals. But his work is usually decorative in intention and often relieved by touches of fantasy, e.g. his use of snakes and caterpillars wriggling to form the letters of his name. He often depicted exotic flora and fauna, sometimes combining them with fabulous beasts.

Jan van Kessel the Elder
109 *America*
Oil on copper. Signed and dated: *Jan van Kessel fecit 1666.* 19⅜ x 26⅞ inches (48.3 x 67.3 cm.). Provenance: Probably in the Düsseldorf Gallery ca. 1716; from 1780 in the Mannheim Gallery, with which it was transferred to the collection of the Elector of Bavaria in Munich, 1799.
Munich, Bayerische Staatsgemäldesammlungen.
(Exhibited in Washington only.)

This painting is inscribed on its original frame *Parahba on Brasil*, but seems to have been conceived as an evocation of a seventeenth-century *Wunderkammer*, or collection of natural and artificial curiosities. It forms part of a series of paintings in which each of the four continents is represented by a panel of

this size surrounded by sixteen small landscapes crowded with birds, beasts, and reptiles associated with the region. The American landscapes thus include such birds as the macaw, turkey, and toucan, monstrous bats, snakes, monkeys, and alligators. But they are joined by many Old World beasts—elephants, giraffes, zebras, and, for good measure, a unicorn charging across the pampas near Buenos Aires. In the central panel, exhibited here, a personification of America is seated on the floor beside a group of gold weights as emblems of mineral riches. On the wall there are paintings of Tapuya Indians, including a female cannibal with a human foot sticking out of her basket, derived from paintings by Albert Eckhout (see colour transparencies, gallery 5). Most of the wild-life is American and derived from

recent books on natural history, notably that by Piso and Marcgrave [↑8] and perhaps also J. E. Nieremberglus: *Historia Naturae*, Antwerp, 1635—armadillo, agouti, ant-eater, iguana, cassowary, toucan, several types of fish, and some outsize butterflies and beetles. But some elements in the painting come from the "other" Indies—the figures dancing through the door, the statues of Brahmins, the painted scenes of suttee, and the Japanese armour in the corner are all Far Eastern, partly or largely derived from J. H. van Linschoten: *Itinerario Voyage ofte Schip vaert naar Oost ofte Portugaels Indien 1579-1592*, Amsterdam, 1596. Thus, while each item is represented with the fidelity demanded of naturalists of the time, the effect is one of fantasy and generalised exoticism.
The inventory of the possessions of an Antwerp silversmith, Jan Gillis, drawn up in 1681 mentions a set of *Continents* painted by van Kessel in collaboration with Erasmus Quellinus (1607–1678). It cannot be established whether this is identical with the set now in Munich. Several other small landscapes by van Kessel very similar to those in the Munich group are in the Prado, Madrid, and it is known to have painted at least one other set of the central panels as well. But it seems probable that Quellinus, who is known to have collaborated with van Kessel on other occasions, was responsible for the human figures in the panel exhibited.

Literature: F. J. van Branden: *Geschiedenis der Antwerpsche Schilderschool*, Antwerp, 1883, p. 1120; K. Zoege von Manteuffel in *Monatshefte für Kunstwissenschaft*, XIV (1921), p. 41; E. Greindl: *Les peintres flamands de nature morte au XVIIᵉ siècle*, Paris-Brussels, 1956, p. 148; E. Köllmann, K.-A. Wirth et al. in *Reallexikon zur deutschen Kunstgeschichte*, vol. v, Stuttgart, 1967, cols. 1141, 1163; Ulla Krempel: *Jan van Kessel d.Ä. 1626-1679—die vier Erdteile* exhibition catalogue, Alte Pinakothek, Munich, 1973.

110 *Covered Cup*
Germany (Augsburg). Carved rhinoceros horn with a silver gilt mount. ca. 1660-1668. Marked on the mount with the Augsburg city hall-mark and HL in monogram for the unidentified goldsmith. Height 22⅞ inches (58 cm.). Provenance: Acquired for the Kunstkammer of the Elector of Saxony, 1668.
Dresden, Grünes Gewölbe.

In a collection of the type called a *Kunstkammer* or *Wunderkammer*, such an object as a carved rhinoceros horn had a double significance: as a curiosity of nature and as an example of ingenious artistry. The piece exhibited here—from one of the largest and most impressive of all *Kunstkammer*, that of the Electors of Saxony in Dresden—was given still stronger appeal by the exotic subject-matter with which it was decorated. The horn is carved in the form of two embracing American Indians with feather skirts and head-dresses serving as the stem of the cup, which is ornamented with *richly* dressed personifications of the four continents. The anonymous Augsburg goldsmith responsible for the mount embossed the base with a rhinoceros (derived from Dürer's famous woodcut) and an elephant battling with a crocodile and dragon. But he crowned the work with a European figure of Eros, perhaps intending to suggest that love rules mankind in all four parts of the world, thus transforming the object into a Baroque *concetto* of a type popular with poets and artists.

Literature: M. Rosenberg: *Der Goldschmiede Merkzeichen*, Frankfurt-am-Main, 1922, vol. I, p. 138; J. L. Sponsel: *Das Grüne Gewölbe zu Dresden*, Leipzig, 1932, vol. IV, p. 154; Sylvia Rathke-Köhl: *Geschichte des Augsburger Goldschmiedegewerbes*, Augsburg, 1964, pp. 101, 165; E. Köllmann, K.-A. Wirth et al. in *Reallexikon zur deutschen Kunstgeschichte*, vol. v, col. 1283.

an overlay. Photographs can be irretrievably damaged by writing on the back with pencil, ball-point or pen, or by using paperclips. With transparencies, the easiest thing is often to put each one in a separate envelope, with its identification and instructions written on the front of the envelope *before* the transparency is inserted. Transparencies should in any case always be kept in cellophane bags to protect them from the acids in people's hands and scratching.

For sizing, it is essential to use a wheel which gives percentages, since process cameras are set by percentages and not by measurements. When measurements are given, they are usually now required in millimetres or centimetres. Money can be saved by using as few percentages as possible: i.e. if it can be organized that all the illustrations are S/S (same size) or, say 25 per cent reductions, the camera operator's time will be much less than if he has to alter the setting of the camera for every illustration.

When marking illustrations for process block-making (i.e., for letterpress printing), and several squared-up photographs (for example) are to be grouped close to each other, an exact diagram should be made showing the plan, so that the metal blocks can be mounted by the blockmaker to make one plate. Blocks have flanges of about ⅛ in. (3.4 mm) so that if a caption or number is required to be set close to a block, the blockmaker must be told this and can cut the flange. The printer will have to send the block back to the blockmaker if this has not been done when the block was originally made.

Half-tone illustrations in a book are usually 'squared up' – the illustration area is required to be perfectly square or rectangular, in harmony with the type area. The blockmaker

Printing 1770–1970

five or more persons and only 0·2 per cent one thousand or over.[7] Nevertheless, large firms have been responsible for a considerable proportion of the total production of the printing industry: the four largest printers in London accounted for over a third of the total output of London printers in the 1850s,[8] and just over a century later firms with one thousand employees or over, though representing only 1·4 per cent of the total number of firms in the country, accounted for 22 per cent of net output.[9] Apart from a few specialist printers, such as newspaper and periodical houses, most large firms of the nineteenth century installed greater quantities of exactly the same kind of equipment as the small printer; and this situation has not changed significantly this century. The small printer has, of course, always been slower in taking up new ideas for want of sufficient capital, but, allowing for this time lag, the methods he has used for composing type and printing have been much the same as those employed by the larger firms. The small printer has survived because so many jobs in printing are related to the scale of human needs and the relatively stable size of social groups; and while the increased capacity of a large printing works allows more ambitious jobs to be undertaken more efficiently, the small printer can often undertake small jobs just as well and, because his overheads are less, very much more economically.

Until the second half of the nineteenth century hardly any printers worked in premises specially built for the purpose. Before then the most typical printing works was the private house, with its floors shored up to take the extra weight of tons of metal and equipment. Expansion was normally effected by buying up neighbouring property and adding wings and outhouses, so that the plan of the original building was usually adapted beyond recognition. Judging from contemporary descriptions, the conditions in such houses were chaotic and appallingly squalid, and men were crammed together in badly lit rooms with little ventilation in summer and no source of warmth in winter. Stocked with reams of paper and quantities of oil and turpentine, and with the naked candle the usual form of illumination, such printing houses were a great fire risk, and many ended up in flames. Charles Manby Smith, who worked for a time in one of the largest of the London firms (probably Hansard's), described the premises as little better than a ruin in the 1830s, and claimed that though money had been spent on repairs not even the oldest workman could remember a single sixpence being spent for the purpose of cleanliness or sanitary precaution:

'The ceilings were black as printers' ink with the candle-smoke of two or three generations, and the walls, save where they were polished to a greasy brown by the friction of the shoulder, were of the same colour. The wind and the rain were patched out from the clattering casements and the rotting window-frames by inch-thick layers of brown paper and paste. Type of all descriptions, old as the building itself, or shining new from the foundry, was abundant as gravel in a gravel-pit, and seemed about as much cared for. Pots, pans, dishes, and cooking-utensils ground the face of it as it lay upon the men's bulks, and the heels of the busy crowd, as they tracked their sinuous path through the piles of forms stacked together in every available space, razed the corners of the pages nearest the ground.'[10]

Such conditions may not have been absolutely typical, but they were not exceptional, and the unsanitary nature of the printing trade in general is supported by the incidence of pulmonary disease amongst printers. A Royal Commission, quoted by the London Society of Compositors in 1866, recorded that the death rate of printers was 47 per cent higher than that of the community at large, and that 70 per cent of the deaths could be ascribed to some form of chest disease.[11]

[7] British Federation of Master Printers, *Economic study of the printing industry* (1965), p.25

[8] Alford (1964), *op. cit.*, p.107

[9] Census of Production, 1958. Quoted British Federation of Master Printers, *Economic study of the printing industry* (1965), p.25

[10] C.M.Smith, *The working man's way in the world*, 3rd issue (London, 1857), with preface and notes by Ellic Howe (London, Printing Historical Society, 1967), pp.242–3

[11] E.Howe, *The London compositor; documents relating to wages, working conditions, and customs of the London printing trade 1785–1900* (London, Bibliographical Society, 1947), p.270

8

The information explosion

4 The principal composing room of the Temple Printing Office, built for James Moyes in 1825. Wood-engraving by Samuel Williams from *Specimens of the types commonly used in the Temple Printing Office*, 1826.

5 A printer's workshop of the 1820s or 1830s. Wood-engraving by Thomas Kelly. *St Bride Printing Library.*

One of the first large premises known to have been constructed in the nineteenth century specially for printing was the Temple Printing Office, built in Bouverie Street for James Moyes in 1825 after his previous premises had been destroyed by fire. The illustration of the principal composing room [4] certainly presents a very different picture from that painted by Charles Manby Smith, but it should be pointed out that Moyes's building was designed as a model establishment. Probably more typical is the printing works used by Thomas Kelly as the basis for his wood-engraving of the 1820s or 1830s [5], which shows both composing and printing being practised in the same room. Though the room is well lit and comparatively spacious, there are indications of real activity and of the chaos described by Smith; and this

illustration certainly has a ring of truth about it that others lack. Towards the end of the nineteenth century factories began to be specially built as printing works as London firms moved into the provinces, and since then the industry as a whole has changed drastically; but the small printer, working in conditions not so very different from those described by Smith, survived for many years [6] and is not unknown even today.

6 A composing room in the Great Hall of 'Colston's House', Small Street, Bristol. Photographed before 1868. *Reproduced by courtesy of Reece Winstone Esq.*

The printer's lot in the nineteenth century may not have been any worse than that of the average industrial worker, and was a good deal easier than that of some, but this should not disguise the fact that the printer worked long hours under conditions of considerable strain. During the first half of the century a twelve-hour day was not exceptional; what is more, a printer could be called upon to work from six in the morning until ten at night, and in some houses had to be prepared to work for as long as two whole days without a break for sleep in order to meet a deadline for some Parliamentary printing or other urgent work. Regular employment was not easy to find in the printing trade in this period, and labour was only taken on when it was needed. Apprenticeship lasted seven years, after which the successful boy became a journeyman printer and earned full rates of pay. There was no limit, as there is today, to the number of apprentices a master printer could employ, so that many preferred to exploit cheap boy labour. Consequently, as soon as an apprentice became a journeyman he found it more difficult to find work, and some printers even travelled to the continent to earn a living at their chosen trade.

Nevertheless, there were compensations in the work of the printer. The compositor in particular would have had every chance to meet authors and clients, some of them of great distinction, and may even have been able to discuss problems and requirements around the printing frame. Because of the nature of the work, the printing trade attracted some of the most intelligent boys and provided as good a means of self-education as any occupation for

9

Printing 1770–1970

those who wished to take advantage of the opportunities it offered. In addition, the trade had evolved over the centuries its own mysterious customs which helped to create a strong corporate unity amongst printers. Each printing house had its own organisation, known as the Chapel, to which all journeymen printers belonged. The chapels functioned in a disciplinary capacity to ensure that work ran smoothly on the shop floor, for printing is a trade in which departure from a stringent code of conduct can lead to chaos; but they were also benevolent and social bodies, and their complex and imaginative rules gave plenty of opportunity to break the tedium of work by making some procedure or punishment an excuse for quenching the thirst with a pot of beer. The chapels also gave corporate voice to grievances, and it was largely through their initiative that the printing trade became one of the first to secure wage agreements. In the course of the nineteenth century some of the functions of the chapels were taken over by the unions, the first of which was founded in 1801, shortly after the Combination Acts had legislated against trade societies. Numerous unions associated with the printing and allied trades were formed after the repeal of the Combination Acts in 1824/5, and towards the end of the nineteenth century they moved towards a nation-wide federation which was eventually founded in 1902 and called the Printing and Kindred Trades Federation. Well before this, however, the unions had successfully negotiated for better rates of pay and working conditions. As a result of their efforts the weekly hours of the printer were gradually reduced until the eight-hour day became the norm by the end of the nineteenth century.

The proliferation of printing houses and the growth of existing ones continued throughout the nineteenth century and brought about a steady increase in the quantity of work produced. The Census of Production for 1907 reveals that in terms of net output the printing and bookbinding trades stood in tenth position among all industries of the United Kingdom. It is difficult to give any reliable statistical record of the growth of the printing trade itself during the last two hundred years, as output for the early period is not known, but the general pattern is probably revealed by the growth of the dependent trades of book publishing and paper-making. The number of books published annually in the United Kingdom rose from an average of fewer than six hundred in the first quarter of the nineteenth century[12] to 32,393 in 1969. Paper production in the United Kingdom shows a similar rate of growth: 11,000 tons were produced in 1800, 100,000 tons in 1860, and 652,000 tons in 1900.[13] These figures provide some general indication of the growth of the printing industry and its impact on the community in the period as a whole. A more specific assessment of its growth in a particular period has been made by B. W. E. Alford, who estimates that the gross output of the letterpress printing industry of Great Britain doubled in the twenty years from 1831 to 1851, when it grew from £750,000 to £1,500,000.[14]

7 A billposter of the early nineteenth century. From an etching by John Miller in Griffin & Co.'s *Book of trades.*

Something of the influence of printing on the environment in the nineteenth century can be gleaned from studying contemporary prints, paintings, and photographs of London, many of which show posters displayed on every available piece of wall [8 – 10]. Billposting was one of the new trades of the nineteenth century, and illustrations of the billposter in sets of London characters or books of trades usually show him respectably setting about his work [7]. In fact, the billposter's job was really rather a disreputable one, and he often worked surreptitiously at night so as to be able to disfigure a private wall or paste over a competitor's advertisement. Sampson describes the billposter as 'a nuisance of the most intolerable kind',[15] and records that his peak period of activity was early on Sunday mornings, when he would aim to be early enough to avoid detection, but not so early as to run the risk of having his work disfigured by rival billposters.

[12] C.H.Timperley, *A dictionary of printers and printing* (London, 1839), p.901

[13] S.H.Steinberg, *Five hundred years of printing* (Harmondsworth, 1955), p.191

[14] Alford (1964), *op. cit.*, pp.96–7

[15] H.Sampson, *A history of advertising from the earliest times* (London, 1874), p.25

10

The information explosion

8 John Parry. London street scene, 1835. Water-colour painting. 760 × 1065 mm. *Alfred Dunhill Ltd, St James's.*

9 Alfred Concanen. 'A railway station in 1874'. Lithograph in five colours, printed by Stannard & Son. From H. Sampson, *A history of advertising from the earliest times*, 1874. Image 158 × 309 mm.

10 Poster-covered wall of the Alhambra Theatre, Leicester Square, 1899. Photograph. *Reproduced by kind permission of Aero Films and Aero Pictorial Ltd.*

11

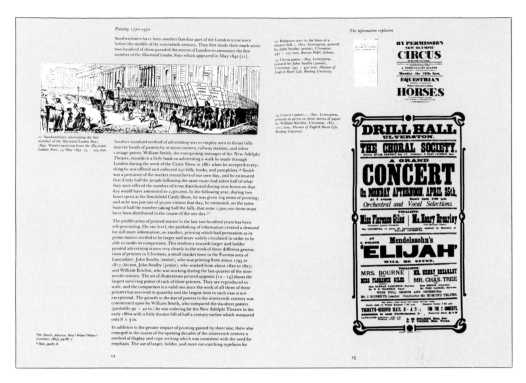

Three consecutive openings (pp. 8–13) from Michael Twyman's *Printing 1770–1970*, Eyre and Spottiswoode, London 1970 (A4: 297 × 210 mm). Designed by Michael Twyman. The basic grid consists of two columns, of 14 and 29 picas, repeated on every page asymmetrically. The narrow column contains long captions and long footnotes, as well as illustrations. The wide column is for the main text, and illustrations. All setting is ragged right. These three openings show how the designer, although making the illustrations virtually any size he wants, has preserved his grid. The book, which contains 294 pp. and 880 illustrations, is a notable example of controlled book design, as well as a fascinating visual record.

will 'square up' mechanically when so instructed, but the designer is responsible for giving this instruction and for the result. Some photographs, even of rectangular paintings, are out of true, and if squared up there may be an unacceptable loss. Judicious air-brushing or painting in of a shadow ('fudging') may restore this situation. One must also be prepared for modern paintings which are intentionally not squared up.

Illustrations may also be 'cut out'. The background can be painted out, or cut away, leaving the object. This can be effective, for instance with a human head, or whole figure; but there is a particular danger in doing this with sculpture, which is intended to be seen against a background. If the background is cut out, it means that the outline of the sculpture is in effect drawn, not by the sculptor, but by other craftsmen, and the work of art falsified, by a greater or lesser amount. When reproducing good photographs of sculpture, it is usually wiser to leave the photograph as it was intended and not reproduce it as a cut out, devoid of background and scale.

A background can also be painted in solid (not necessarily in black) and this may help to define an object with an indistinct outline, if it is necessary to emphasize it.

Colour and black-and-white proofs are submitted by blockmakers and platemakers and are capable of correction.

In double-column layouts, this sort of arrangement of illustrations should be avoided, since the eye tends to read on to the nearest, but wrong column. The interruption of the text is unnecessary, as blocks can be placed at the head or foot of the page.

Opposite: two consecutive openings (pp. 12–15) from Elgar and Maillard's *Picasso*, 3rd edn, Thames and Hudson, London 1960 (reduced from 210 mm deep). Designed by Marcel Jacno. This book contains two separate texts: one, describing the artist's works, is set in 11 on 14 pt Garamond × 25 picas; the second text, a biography, is set in 10 on 12 pt Garamond italic × 11½ picas. The captions are set in 9 pt Garamond small caps, roman and italic to varying measures (i.e. no grid observed). There are no running heads, and on three consecutive openings the designer has chosen to omit folios. An interesting solution, and incidentally, a superb picture book in a small format.

In colour printing, it must be emphasized that if reproduction is being made from transparencies, fidelity to the transparency is all that can be asked for: to compare a colour proof with an original which plate- or blockmaker has not seen is unfair. Transparencies should be checked first, and if necessary rephotographed, and used for reproduction only when it is agreed that the transparency is acceptable as the original.

It must be remembered that any printed photographic reproduction of a work of art in colour, even in the actual size of the original, can only be an approximation. If the original is in flat colours, a true facsimile *may* be possible, but if it is in tone, and must be reproduced by the four-colour process using dots, the result is a kind of optical illusion – the surprising thing is how well it can sometimes be made to work.

Any alteration in size is an added distortion; to reproduce a large painting in a postcard size can never be more than a reminder, and a 'perfect' result is an impossibility.

The placing of illustrations on the page depends, for a start, on whether the illustrations can be treated as a sort of catalogue, for reference (when they can be arranged in columns, and their impact on each other, or the page as a

ES-SERVEIX-BEURE-Y-MENJAR-A-TOTES-HORES

PERE ROMEU - 4 GATS

CARRER B MONTESION.

POSTER FOR 'ELS QUATRE GATS' (THE FOUR CATS), BARCELONA, 1902.
Foreground, Picasso. Left to right: Pere Romeu, Rocarol, Fontbona, Angel F. de Soto, Sabartés.

which meant nothing to him. "Neither Malaga, nor bulls, nor friends; just nothing at all." What else could he expect? But on the contrary, for Pablo Barcelona was a springboard from which he could set out to conquer the world. He already felt himself raised to sublime heights, for in 1896 when he was hardly fifteen, he was admitted to the Lonja school, having completed

in a single day the task set for the entrance examination, for which a month was normally allowed. Making up his mind to encourage his son to the utmost, Don José soon afterwards hired a studio in the Calle de la Plata. This was Picasso's first studio of his own. It was there that the young artist painted Science and Charity, a canvas for which his father worked

12

dancing-girls, and women leaning against bars, show a tendency to analyse poverty and vice which he could have inherited from Ribera and Goya. In the works most directly inspired by Toulouse-Lautrec we are less conscious of the haughty pathos, the scornful elegance or bitter, sparkling irony of his master, than of Picasso's own resigned melancholy, an incurable sadness, an unchangeable sense of solitude. Picasso had painted portraits, landscapes and flower-pieces in his childhood, but now he stopped trying to paint man's outward environment and took man himself as his theme. By man, he meant Picasso himself, his own impulses and problems, his own inner conflicts, his own loves and hates. When he was twenty he saw

out both the composition and the title. This work portrays a figure on a sick-bed being attended by a doctor and a nun. Don José himself insisted on posing for the doctor, who sits in the foreground beside the bed, taking his patient's pulse. This canvas was awarded an honourable mention at the Madrid Fine Arts Exhibition in 1897.

October 1897—During the vacation there must have been much discussion in the family about Pablo's future, for at the beginning of term his Uncle Salvador's advice was followed and the boy was sent to continue his studies in Madrid. Repeating the same academic performance which had enabled him to enter the Lonja, he had himself accepted at short notice by the Royal Academy of San Fernando. But Picasso was not long in being disgusted with the official teaching and stopped attending his classes. When he fell ill at the end of the winter he decided to return to Barcelona, which he did in

THE ARTIST'S FATHER. BARCELONA, 1898. CONTÉ, 11¾″ × 9½″.

life in a gloomy and disconsolate light. But thanks to a kind of hereditary fatalism he accepted it as it was, with all its shortcomings and evils. It was only later that he was gripped by the urge to cry out in protest. Whereas most artists begin their careers in anger or revolt—witness Rouault or Ensor—but end in wisdom and serenity, Picasso gradually passed from acceptance to refusal. As he grew older he gave vent to his individualism in works of anger, revenge and loud denunciation. With years and increased experience he became only more unbridled and explosive in his protests. By the time he was world-famous and praised right and left, deluged with wealth and honours, and when he was in a position to gather in the

PICASSO AND CASAGEMAS. 1900. INDIAN INK.

June 1898, and from there went to Horta de San Juan (Horta de Ebro) together with his friend Pallarés, at whose home he was able to rest and build up his threatened health. While he was there he shared the rough, simple life of the peasants, and for him this period was in a sense an apprenticeship to existence. Long afterwards, speaking of those eight months spent in the country, he said, "I learnt everything I know in Pallarés's village."

In April 1899, on his return to Barcelona, Picasso went to live and work at the home of one of his friends at 1 Calle de los Escudilleros Blancos. The Catalan city gave him the environment his exuberant youth required. Less conservative than Madrid, Barcelona was then the centre of what amounted to an artistic renaissance. The young were received with open arms and any new idea was sure of an immediate response. Whether in the magazine Joventut or the review

Pel y Ploma (Fur and Feather) it was taken for granted that all the various currents of European thought were to be welcomed. Nietzsche and Schopenhauer, Germanic mythology and Wagner, were given the same attention as Maeterlinck, Ruskin, Verhaeren and Ibsen. In painting, Böcklin and the English pre-Raphaelites were in equal favour with the French Impressionists, news of whose works had been brought back from Paris by Ramón Casas, then a fashionable draughtsman. Miguel Utrillo was in the process of rediscovering medieval Catalan art and the painting of El Greco, while the famous 'Modern-Style' architect, Gaudí, was designing the Grüell Park. Picasso used to go to the 'Four Cats', which combined a bar with a café-concert, and which at that time was the favourite meeting-place of the young intellectuals of the city. The 'Four Cats' were none other than the founders of the establishment, an imitation of the 'Chat Noir' in Paris: these were Pere Romeu, Ramón Casas, Santiago Rusiñol and Miguel Utrillo. Here Picasso made friends with Angel and Mateo Fernandez de Soto, the poet Jaime Sabartés, the painters Carlos Casagemas, Sebastian Junyer, Nonell, Opisso, Canals, the writer Ramón Reventós, the sculptor Julio Gonzalez and many others, drawing their portraits from life as and when he happened to meet them. All these portraits were exhibited in the small

PICASSO, SELF-PORTRAIT. MADRID, 1901. CONTÉ. Published in Arte Joven.

whole, need not be taken into account), or whether they must be treated as individuals. It is undesirable to lay down a set of rules, as every book must be considered on its own (even if it is in series), since its illustrations may be quite different in character from any other book. But a few 'rules of thumb' are helpful to remember – to be used as suggestions, not as laws. If two pictures are placed one above the other, they should be either identical in width, or conspicuously different. If they are unavoidably of nearly the same width, they should not be aligned on one side, but placed full out to left and right respectively, so that comparison is not obvious.

Normally, pictures which 'look' strongly in one direction or another (e.g. because a face or series of faces is looking in one direction or because there are strong lines of perspective) should 'look' into the book and not out of it – e.g. a face looking right should be on a left-hand page, and vice-versa. When two or more photographs appear on the same page, the picture with the most distant horizon should be at the top of the page, furthest away from the reader's eyes, and the picture with the closest foreground should be at the foot of the page.

When colour and black-and-white illustrations occur in the same book, juxtapositions must be even more carefully considered than usual: colour plates may look better facing pages with text than pages with heavy black-and-white illustrations.

The printing of colour is always a considerable factor in production costs. Colour plates are usually printed on one sheet, if this is possible, which is then cut up into four-page sections and the colour plates wrapped round or inserted into the centres of sections. Alternatively, if colour pages are required at closer intervals than 8 or 16 pages, they will be printed on the same sheet as text pages, but probably on one side of the sheet only, because it is more economic to print in four colours on one side than on both sides of the sheet. In any case, the designer must make a page plan to show exactly where the colour will or can be placed, and this must be made in agreement with the printer and binder, whose estimates of costs may be based on the plan. If a wrapped-round or inserted colour plate is bled off all round, the caption for it will normally have to be printed on the facing page, which will be an entirely different sheet. It must then be ascertained that such facing pages can accommodate captions, and do not themselves bleed off all round, or pose other problems.

Book design sometimes fails because the author and editor have not decided whether they want a textbook with pictures, or a picturebook with text. An example of a picturebook with two different texts running through it is shown on p. 143. If a book is intended to be principally text, with illustrations playing a helpful but secondary role, its function may be spoiled by having long captions.

Press Cuttings: a Topical
Sketch compiled from the
editorial and correspond-
ence columns of the Daily
Papers by Bernard Shaw, as per-
formed by the Civic and Dramatic
Guild at the Royal Court Theatre,
London, on the 9th July 1909.

Constable and Company
Ltd. London: 1913.

A bold title-page design in 30
and 24 pt Caslon Old Face (slightly
reduced). This was published as a
paperback at one shilling and the
same design (without the publisher's
name and date) was repeated on the
front on a blue-grey handmade or
mould-made laid paper. Bernard
Shaw was using nearly ragged-right
typography from 1898.

Illustrations which run off the edge of a page are said to 'bleed'. But this requires a larger sheet of paper than the printer would otherwise have needed. The sheet is held on the machine by a gripper which must be outside the printed area. Therefore a bleed on a gripper edge requires an extra inch or so of paper, which, after printing, is trimmed off to produce the bleed.

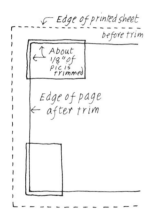

'BLEEDS'

One way to enlarge illustrations is to 'bleed' them, i.e. to extend them so that they are trimmed off the page on one, two or all three sides. This technique is far too often used thoughtlessly and spoils the look of a book, but it can also be valuable visually, if used with discretion.

The first consideration to remember is the practical one that 'bleeding' requires a larger sheet of paper than printing without bleeding, so it cannot be adopted unless paper in the larger required size is available. The cost factor must also be remembered: bleeding in a long-run large book may add *thousands of pounds* to the paper costs.

Secondly, 'bleeding' should not be used for illustrations in a book unless there is a real, recognizable advantage to be gained. The best way to decide this is to look at the books on your own shelves and analyse all the examples of bleeding you can find. It depends very much on the nature of the illustrations: the size gained is often no advantage, and many pictures need a white margin, and look bigger if they have it than if they don't. It must also be remembered that if a work of art is trimmed, it is no longer the complete work of art intended by the artist, and becomes technically a 'detail': it is a solecism to bleed reproductions of paintings in a serious art-book without reminding readers that they are in fact incomplete (the artist's signature often being lost in this way). When the photographs supplied are of paintings in *frames*, the small amount lost when frames (and the shadows of frames) are trimmed is usually of no significance.

Portraits, in which the main interest is focused on the face, and also many photographs, can be made more dramatic by enlargement and bleeding. But think very carefully before deciding to bleed, and do not over-work the trick until it becomes boring. And do not trim anything off a photograph without considering its composition. If a photograph is a work of art, as many are, its value can be destroyed by thoughtless trimming; and the photographer may have stipulated that the work must be reproduced untrimmed, or not at all.

The normal parts of a book which, if present, require consideration from the designer are: prelims; main text; illustrations; captions; appendices; bibliography; index; end-papers; case; jacket.

PRELIMS

Prelims traditionally include:
i   Half-title, or 'bastard' title
ii   Blank or frontispiece, or list of other books by the same author
iii Title-page (or ii & iii double title-page)
iv   Verso of title (credits, imprint, copyright, ISBN, etc.)
v   Dedication
vi   Acknowledgments
vii Preface (or foreword, usually not written by the author)
viii Continuation of Preface, or blank
ix   Contents
x   List of illustrations
Possible additional items: list of abbreviations; errata
1   First page of text

These are often condensed today to:
Imprint
Contents
List of illustrations
Preface (including acknowledgments)
Main text

All these items are traditional components of the preliminary pages of a book, but they are also functional; if not functional, they should not be there. The designer should always question the purpose and usefulness of every item and see if any better solution can be offered.

i *Half-title*   The historical reason for this page is that until the middle of the nineteenth century books were published unbound, and first offered for sale by booksellers in temporary paper wrappers. The half-title was therefore a protection for the title-page: it also gave the opportunity on its verso for material, e.g. an illustration, to face the title, or for the title to run across two pages.

It can carry information not given elsewhere, e.g. the number of a book in a series. Usually, it states (perhaps in a shortened version) only the title of the book, and possibly the author.

ii *Blank, or frontispiece illustration* (which may be printed on different paper from text and tipped in).

iii *Title-page*   The title-page states, in words, the actual title (and sub-title, if there is one) of the book and the name of the author and publisher, and sometimes also the number of illustrations, but it should do more than that. From the designer's point of view, it is the most important page in the book: it sets the style. It is the page which opens communication with the reader. In the words of an American

Previous page: nineteenth-century drawings of sixteenth-century initial letters (enlarged).

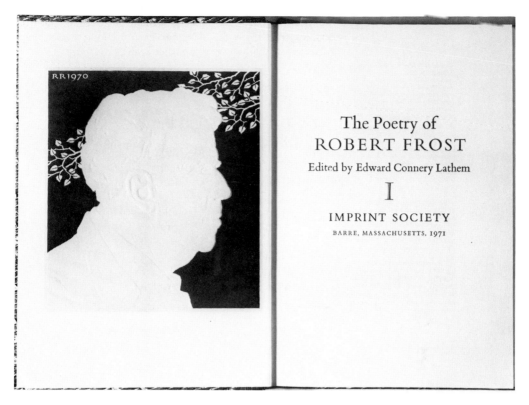

The Poetry of
ROBERT FROST
Edited by Edward Connery Lathem

I

IMPRINT SOCIETY
BARRE, MASSACHUSETTS, 1971

Title-page opening of vol. 1 of *The Poetry of Robert Frost*, Imprint Society, Barre, Mass., 1971 (reduced from 237 mm deep). Designed by Rudolph Ruzicka. The display lines are set in Monotype Bembo, the text in Ruzicka's Linotype Fairfield. The frontispiece portrait of Frost, drawn by Ruzicka and embossed, was printed in blue by the Meriden Gravure Company; the title-page in black and blue, and the text, were printed by the Stinehour Press.

designer: 'Here is the one chance the usual commercial book gets to make a little melodious noise; to play a few bars of incidental music while the curtain rises; to get the audience into a sympathetic frame of mind. . . . Some hint of welcome on the title-page, then – some touch a little less frigid than your bank report. Border designs do not accomplish it; borders do not seem to fit into the modern book. Pictures, perhaps; little devices; a nosegay. But usually the so desirable warmth has to be devised out of type.'*

If the book is one of a series in uniform style, such as a Penguin or Everyman, or one of the Gollancz novels of the 1930s designed by Stanley Morison, the typography cannot say anything about that particular book; but if a distinctive and distinguished style for the series has been achieved, it will say: 'This is a title in a distinctive and distinguished series and is worth your attention'.

If illustrations play a large part in the book, the title-page opening should, or may, express this visually. If any form of decoration is used inside the book, e.g. for chapter openings, one would expect this to be repeated or echoed on the title-page.

*From W. A. Dwiggins, *MSS by WAD*, New York, The Typophiles, 1947, 'The Structure of a Book' (written in 1927): a short essay that is both enjoyable and instructive. W.A.D.'s dismissal of borders should not be taken too seriously. Plenty of modern books have been enhanced by imaginative use of borders, e.g. Chatto & Windus's Zodiac Press title-pages, and many of the Edinburgh University Press books designed by George Mackie.

UR:

THE FIRST PHASES

By

LEONARD WOOLLEY

The KING PENGUIN *Books*
PUBLISHED BY PENGUIN BOOKS LIMITED
LONDON *and* NEW YORK
1946

A King Penguin title-page before
Jan Tschichold took over the design
of the series. The prominence of the
unimportant word 'By' is perhaps
the first thing to catch the eye. As a
minor detail, one wonders why, of
three words in the imprint in Bembo
italic, two are letterspaced and the
other is not.

A BOOK OF SCRIPTS
by Alfred Fairbank

Penguin Books

A King Penguin title-page designed in 1949 by Jan Tschichold, with a tautness lacking in the page opposite, although set in the same types. The use of Roman caps with italic lower-case is an appropriate historical touch in a book on this subject.

A PROSPECT OF

𝔚𝔞𝔩𝔢𝔰

—

A SERIES OF WATER-COLOURS
BY KENNETH ROWNTREE
AND AN ESSAY BY
GWYN JONES

PENGUIN BOOKS

LONDON

Title-page for King Penguin no. 43, 1948 (reduced), designed by Jan Tschichold, exploiting the decorative quality of one word in black letter.

Whatever the style of the book, the title-page should give a foretaste of it. If the book consists of plain text, the title-page should at least be in harmony with it. The title itself should not exceed in width the width of the type area, and will normally be narrower. The title-page need not be the same depth as the text, and is often made a pica or two shorter at head and foot. If a border is used (whether typographical or drawn, but regular) it should almost always have the same outside dimensions as the type area; and the margins round the type matter inside the border should be either definitely wider or definitely narrower than the page margins outside the border.

It should also be remembered that the title-page is where librarians and cataloguers, as well as readers, look for the basic information they need to identify the book, so it *must* show the correct title, the author or principal editor, the

Misericords

MEDIEVAL LIFE IN ENGLISH WOODCARVING

BY

M. D. ANDERSON

PENGUIN BOOKS

Title-page for King Penguin no. 72, 1954 (reduced), designed by Jan Tschichold: the word 'Misericords' is a reduced version of the title on the cover, designed by Berthold Wolpe, who also drew the crown.

illustrator if any, and the publisher. It should also include the date of publication (necessary to establish whether the book is the most recent edition), but in some cases publishers are shy about this and put the date less conspicuously on the verso, or occasionally omit it altogether.

iv *The title-page verso* carries a miscellaneous amount of necessary but unglamorous information and is often neglected by designers – perhaps because it is sometimes not compiled until the very last moment and is never shown to the designer.

It should carry the date of publication (if this is not on the title-page), and if it is not a first edition, it should carry the date of all editions and impressions in the form shown in British Standard 4719 (1971).

It carries the publisher's and printer's imprints, still a legal requirement in Britain, and this means the names and *addresses*

*Among the exempted items are price lists, catalogues and advertisements of goods and property for sale. A summary of the law is published by and available from The British Printing Industries Federation, 11 Bedford Row, London WC1.

in words.* Names and addresses of co-publishers in other countries are optional unless they have been stipulated by the publisher.

The title-page verso usually carries the ISBN number (International Standard Book Numbers are the librarian's positive identification of a book, and are allocated by, and obtained from, The International Book Numbering Agency, 12 Dyott Street, London WC1A 1DF) and British Library and Library of Congress cataloguing data, now often included in international editions.

The copyright owner's notice, including a date, goes on this page, with such other legal copyright warnings as the publisher wishes to add.

Credits to the designer and other contributors and suppliers (e.g. of paper, or binding) may be included here, and also general acknowledgments, unless it is felt that these require, as they often do, a special page.

The large number of words often make this a full page. It is usually set in a small size of type, probably that used for footnotes, and requires skill to make it look coherent and attractive. Look for good examples to copy.

v *Dedication*   This deserves a right-hand page to itself, but sometimes it has to be squeezed in elsewhere, perhaps on the half-title or the verso of the title-page. It may take the form of a drawing or engraving.

vi *Acknowledgments*   These may be short or long, but must not be forgotten. They should be the author's and publisher's acknowledgments to people who have helped in the writing of the text; there may also be a list of sources, etc. used in collecting the illustrations, or the loan of material.

vii, viii *Preface or Foreword*   If this is short, and not part of the book (i.e. if it is not written by the author), it may be placed before the Contents (but see below). If it is written by the author, it can probably be considered to be part of the book, and should immediately precede the first chapter. It should normally be set in the same style and type as the text.

ix *Contents*   (Some consider that the contents page is so important that it should always follow the title-page, as the next right-hand page, where it is easier to find.) The contents page usually shows only the chapter titles, with their page references. The titles *must* be checked against the text, with which they must be identical in wording, spelling, capitalization and punctuation; if not, the designer must ask the publisher or author which is right, or take the decisions himself, to see that the titles are the same as given in the text itself.

If chapters have sub-headings and divisions, the decision must be taken whether to include these on the contents page. If chapters do not have sub-heads, but are long and/or complicated, it may be helpful to include summaries. If the

Proof of a title-page showing Jan
Tschichold's meticulous spacing
corrections. The figures indicate
points in or out. This was the fifth
of eight proofs before Tschichold
was satisfied, reproduced in P. Luidl
(ed.), *Jan Tschichold*, Munich 1976.

Some Passages
in the Life of

MR. ADAM BLAIR

Minister of the Gospel
at Cross-Meikle

—••E)(3••—

BY J. G. LOCKHART

with an Introduction by David Craig

EDINBURGH

Chapter

3

—••E)(3••—

. Nobody, after that day, ever heard Mr Blair mention
his wife's name. A little picture of her in crayon, which

usefulness of the book to the reader is increased by their inclusion, they should appear here.

x *List of illustrations*   This is necessary if it helps the reader. It depends on the kind of book and the kind of illustration. If illustrations are by different artists, this may be the best place to give this information. If plates are not numbered and not folio'd, as sometimes happens, then a list of plates is needed to show the purchaser or reader of the book whether the book has the correct number of plates or not, and to indicate their position in the book. The list of illustrations is sometimes placed at the back of the book.

Additional items: list of abbreviations   Some texts require a list of abbreviations, or symbols, or other special information required to understand the text, e.g. repeating foreign words and phrases. This could go at the back of the book, but if so, the fact that it is at the back of the book should be indicated in the Contents. *Errata* Prelims are always printed last, so that if mistakes are found in the text after it has been printed, they can be corrected in a list of *errata* (mistakes) in the prelims. If they are not discovered until after the prelims have been printed, and are important enough, a special slip or page has to be printed and pasted in, which is cheaper than reprinting the book.

MAIN TEXT

The text page

Given a book or booklet to design, the typographer must start by designing the page, the basic unit from which the whole concept will be evolved. A reading of the text will show what kind of book it is, and from this will come a mental picture of how it should look in print – bearing in mind the guidance already asked for, and received, from the publisher. The typographic design is worked out in pencil layouts which will, when finalized, form the basis for instructions to the printer. It may not be necessary to read the whole book, but it is usually necessary to look at every page of the copy for setting, in order to find out if there are any problems that require special instructions: e.g. quotations, in prose or verse or in foreign languages, mathematical or other formulae, tables, diagrams, sub-headings, dialogue, footnotes and so on.

In designing the basic page, one has to take into consideration the length of the text and an acceptable length for the printed book: some texts have to be padded out, some condensed. The typographer must know how to make a cast-off (see Chapter 8) and this task becomes difficult if the text has not been typed uniformly throughout: many publishers rightly insist that manuscripts from their authors must be correctly typed to the publisher's specification. There are also the usual considerations of printer and typefaces available.

Opposite: title-page and chapter opening from J. G. Lockhart's *Adam Blair*, Edinburgh University Press, 1963 (reduced from 172 mm deep). Designed by George Mackie. Union Pearl, the typeface used for the word 'Chapter', is the oldest surviving decorated type, dating from about 1690: a twentieth-century designer's happy use of old materials for the reprint of a text that first appeared in 1822.

Texte de Pierre Gascar
Photographies d'André Martin
Collection "Le génie du lieu"
Delpire Éditeur

CHAMBORD

Backing up

'Backing up' means that the lines of type on one side of a page fall in the same position as, or 'back up', the lines on the other side. In the old days of heavy impression from metal type, this was very important, since legibility was much impaired by the impression coming through from the other side of the sheet between the lines one was reading. Nowadays it is still important if there is any 'show-through' in the paper, which, if the lines do not back up correctly, is just as harmful to legibility.

Whatever leading is adopted, it must be adhered to throughout the book and when space is added between items, e.g. before and after a quote, it must be in units of the 'type + leading' in use (i.e. if the text is set in 12 pt, 3 pt leaded, or '12 on 15 pt', then extra space must be added in units of 15 pts, otherwise the lines of type on the reverse side of the page will not 'back up'). It might also be a problem if the system of 'asymmetric' openings' is being used, e.g. if all pages, both left and right, have a narrow left-hand margin and a wide right-hand margin, so that the type areas do not back up.

Show-through may also be a problem on title-pages (which often have a lot of white space) when printing occurs on the verso. Very black, heavy, illustrations create similar difficulties. Pages of particular visual importance should, therefore, not have any printing on their versos, if this can be avoided. An ingenious designer's solution to this problem can be seen on the prelim pages of *Lynton Lamb, Illustrator*, by G. Mackie (London 1979).

Running heads

The purpose of running heads is to help the reader find a place in the book conveniently; in reference books or textbooks, a more accurate and detailed form of sign-posting in the running heads than usual may need to be devised. It must also be remembered that running heads may identify a page that has become detached from a book. And running heads also provide a decorative element in the design of a pair of pages. The folios may be incorporated in them, or placed at the side or foot of the pages. Running heads need not be at the top of the page: they can be set in *outside* margins or at the foot.

Will the book need running heads on every page? Normally, the title of the book is on every left-hand page and the chapter title, abbreviated if necessary, on the right, but the typographer must think what will be most helpful to the reader.

Running heads are usually best set in small caps, letterspaced, or in italic: roman upper and lower case might look too much like a chapter heading or part of the text. Italic caps may sometimes be used, but as Oliver Simon shows well in his *Introduction to Typography* (London 1963), most italic caps were not designed for setting in words: their irregular

Opposite: three consecutive openings from *Chambord*, published by Delpire, Switzerland, 1962 (reduced from 230 mm deep). This was the first of a series of books entitled 'Le génie du lieu', seeking to express the essential character of places (in this case, a royal palace on the Loire) by means of pictures and text. The arrangement is entirely unconventional; the book opens with a series of photographic doublespreads, some in colour. Shown here are the seventh, eighth and ninth openings, the last being in colour. There are no ordinary prelims except the title-page shown centre; the first page of text is on the tenth opening. The designers and producers of the book achieved a remarkable effect, for the reader feels he knows the palace, has been there and that its complicated towers and chimneys are familiar to him.

slope (especially in Bell, Caslon, Garamond, Walbaum) makes a distracting pattern. Baskerville, Perpetua, Times and deliberately designed 'sloped romans' are better in this respect. Baskerville italic, however, as designed by John Baskerville, has, in Simon's words, 'Seven dandified capital letters, in the J K N Q T Y and Z, which border on being swash letters' and do not, in the original version, have alternatives. Words set in italic caps including those letters might look queer.

Running heads should be separated from the first line of text by white space, not less than 6 points and not more than a blank line of the text size. A rule, plain or thick/thin, can sometimes be used with good effect, and an example is illustrated on p. 164.

In some books which do not have chapter titles, or where space is at a premium, e.g. cheap paperbacks, or when a very simple page is required (e.g. ill. p. 165), running heads may be omitted altogether. Books have also been published with no folios at all on the pages; it is then impossible to tell if a leaf or section is missing, or to give a page reference.

Folios

There are many choices with folios and the designer must, as usual, observe with a critical eye all the ways of using them that he can find. The following elementary points should be borne in mind:
(1) If folios are set in the 'gutter', or back of the page, as opposed to the outer edge, they are of diminished use, since the book has to be opened right out to find them.
(2) If the text contains figures, the folios must be placed far enough away from the text, or be in a different size or face, or otherwise differentiated, to avoid confusion.
(3) Folios can be 'lining' or 'non-lining'. They should, normally, be in the same face and same type as the text, unless there is a good reason for being different.
(4) In estimating costs, folios are charged as a whole line, and are also reckoned as defining one edge of the type area.

Quotations

The essential requirement in dealing with quotations is to signal clearly what is quote and what is author's text. Short quotations, of a few words or sentences, are enclosed in quotes. For a longer quotation, especially if it goes over a page, it will often be better to set it in a different size, either larger or smaller than the text, but its effect on cost must be ascertained and approved. Otherwise, indenting could be used, on one or both sides of the page; leave a blank line of space, at least, before and after the quote. To make the change to a quotation absolutely clear, an indent of from $1\frac{1}{2}$ to 3 picas on the left may be needed: or two picas at each side.

To set quoted matter in italic raises the question of the legibility of the italic available in the length of passages to be set.

'Benighted'

shone but wanly, casting the greyest of faint
shadows from the fretted spire over the tombs
of a Frenchman, Jules Raoul Dubois, and the
Virgin on his left hand.

> *Here sleeps a Frenchman: Would I could*
> *Grave in his language on this wood*
> *His many virtues, grace and wit!*
> *But then who'd read what I had writ?*
> *Nay, when the tongues of Babel cease,*
> *One word were all sufficient—Peace!*

Thick English grasses waved softly over him beyond the faint moonlight, and covered as deeply
the grave of one left nameless:

> *Blessed Mary, pity me,*
> *Who was a Virgin too, like Thee;*
> *But had, please God, no little son*
> *To shower a lifetime's sorrows on.*

Just a message out of nothingness, for the words
summoned no picture, scarcely even the shadow
of a human being, into the imagination. Not so
those over which the last of our twenty-one
battled feebly against the moon:

[61]

A page from Walter de la Mare's
Ding Dong Bell, Faber and Faber,
London 1936 (reduced from
177 × 116 mm), showing quoted
verse, set in Arrighi Italic to contrast
with the text, which is set in Centaur
and considerably more leaded.

The treatment of quotes will always depend on the nature,
importance and frequency of the quoted passages. Poems
quoted need special attention (see below). In books in which
the quoted verse is an important feature (cf. *Ding Dong Bell*,
above) to set it in italic will make it stand out strongly and
decoratively. Look at as many books containing quotes as
you can find, and decide what treatments are most successful.

Justified and unjustified setting

As has been said earlier, continuous text *must* be set with close
and regular spacing between words, not irregular and wide
spacing that calls attention to itself and is an obstruction to
smooth reading. In setting with ten or more words to the line
this is not difficult, but it becomes progressively more
difficult the shorter the measure. Erratic word-spacing and
annoying word-breaking should be controllable by specification to the printer. It can also be avoided by unjustified
setting: the instruction can be 'set flush left, ragged right,
even close word-spacing, no word-breaks', or 'as few word-
breaks as possible'.

If word-breaking at the ends of lines is forbidden, the 'raggedness' will increase, particularly if the text contains long words; and slightly less copy will fit in a given number of lines than if word-breaking is permitted. But if word-breaking is permitted, it will be at the compositor's discretion, and author's corrections will be incurred if you disagree with his word-breaks or there are too many of them. In most cases it is better to avoid half-measures and stipulate 'no word-breaks'. What is certain is that ragged right setting gives more even composition. Most people (accustomed anyway to ragged right in typed and handwritten letters) do not notice whether printed matter is justified or unjustified. In all narrow measure setting it is to be preferred; in multi-column pages, e.g. in magazines or newspapers, 4 mm space minimum, or a vertical rule, will be required between columns. A preference for ragged right setting, even in normal measures, was arrived at in a study of the design and appearance of Open University printing undertaken by a group of fourth-year typography students at Reading University. Their report was of such interest that it was edited and published by the Open University under the title *Open University Texts: criticisms & alternatives* in 1975.

Footnotes

Footnotes are normally set two sizes smaller than the text, but should have the same leading; i.e. 11/12 pt text would have 9/10 pt footnotes. A different amount of leading in footnotes will tend to make them look a different colour from the text.

Footnotes must be separated from the text by space, which may vary, but should probably be not less than 6 points. A rule should not be used except if, for some unavoidable reason, a footnote is set either in the same size as the text or a size indistinguishable from it, when a short rule (not longer than 2 or 3 picas) can be placed to range left, between text and footnote. In short pages, e.g. at the end of a chapter, the footnote should be at the foot of the page, not close up to the last line of text.

Footnotes are an editorial problem, and a vexed one, before they become a typographical problem. It must first of all be said that footnotes should be avoided altogether, if possible. Very often they are an indication of sloppy or inefficient writing by the author. When needed, in works of scholarship, they are usually of two kinds: the kind that will be too obtrusive if incorporated in the text, but should appear on the text page because it may aid comprehension; and the kind that does not aid comprehension, but provides references which will be needed later. These can be placed at the back of the book, but must be so arranged that they can be easily found. If both kinds of note are used, they can be distinguished by having conventional symbols such as the asterisk (*) for the former, and superior figures for the latter. When footnotes are placed at the back of the book, it is not enough to group them in chapters: the page reference *must* be given, on the footnote pages, to facilitate backwards and forwards references.

Chapter openings

The treatment of chapter openings makes an important contribution to the design of a book. Normally a chapter should begin on a new page, right or left, and the break be emphasized by a drop of two or more lines: this drop, if used, must be consistent throughout the book, and should also be followed for all the prelim titles. The style and amount of decoration put in to the chapter opening by the designer must depend on the book and the general effect being aimed at. The designer may have a better idea than the author on what is right for the book. The word 'chapter', for example, is often added by the author when it is in fact quite unnecessary and pompous: a plain number (arabic numbers are intrinsically beautiful shapes) may do all that is required, whether with or without a title. When chapter titles are in the form of sentences, authors are again often pompous and always inconsistent in their use of caps. There is a convention that headings in upper and lower case (in any form of printing, not only books) should have either every word or every noun beginning with a cap – presumably to give added emphasis or importance to the heading. The prominence appropriate to the heading should be given by the typography, not by the use of caps. If caps are used, they must at least be consistent throughout the publication. The argument against the use of caps in this way is that it gives an unnatural and spotty effect to the sentence, and prevents caps being used as they are intended, to signal that a word is a proper name, a title and so on. The best rule is *never* to use capitals to begin lower-case words except when they are necessary: e.g. Act of Parliament, not act of parliament; Labour Day celebrations, not labour day Celebrations. In some cases, e.g. Reports and Accounts, and for other terms in financial documents, the correct use of capitals is not easy to decide: but a decision must be reached (and consistently applied), a list of words for capitalization prepared, and the copy sub-edited carefully to conform with it, before going to the printer, otherwise potentially heavy author's corrections will be incurred. The basic rule remains that capitals should be used *only* when they indicate a special meaning.

Drop initials are another way of signalling a new chapter. Whatever their size and shape, they must fit correctly, and every good book on typography (e.g. Oliver Simon's *Introduction to Typography*) shows examples of how they should and should not be used. The first word, or words, after an initial, is usually set in caps or small caps. Designers will make their own collections of decorated initial letters, and books showing them, but they should not neglect the opportunity of drawing their own: if a new book deserves decorated initials, why not give it new ones?

Factotum initials are decorated shapes, usually square, with a blank space in the middle into which any initial may be dropped. Initials printed in a second colour, or even several colours, like medieval manuscripts, can be especially attractive.

The setting of plays

The chief necessity in designing the typography for a play is to signal clearly (a) the act and scene one is reading; (b) the name of the speaker; (c) the stage directions, which must be clearly differentiated from the text of the play itself.

Bernard Shaw is the classic example of an author who realized the importance of typography, and who, having designed the printing and layout of his plays himself from the beginning and found an excellent solution, made sure that they were printed by the same printer (R. & R. Clark, in Edinburgh) in the same style for ever afterwards. (An entertaining and well-illustrated account of this association is in James Shand's article 'Author and Printer' in *Alphabet and Image*, 8 (December 1948).) The Penguin Shakespeares, both as originally designed by Edward Young and as later redesigned by Jan Tschichold, are also excellent examples of play design.

In plays do not abbreviate the speakers' names into absurd monosyllables such as HAM, MAC and HEN.

Opening from *The Poems of John Donne*, edited by H. J. C. Grierson, Oxford University Press, London 1929 (reduced from 182 mm deep). Running heads and folios inside fine rules, two-line initials, and footnotes. No broken lines.

294   *Divine Poems.*   *Divine Poems.*   295

III.

O Might those sighes and teares returne againe
  Into my breast and eyes, which I have spent,
That I might in this holy discontent
Mourne with some fruit, as I have mourn'd in vaine;
In mine Idolatry what showres of raine
Mine eyes did waste? what griefs my heart did rent?
That sufferance was my sinne; now I repent;
'Cause I did suffer I must suffer paine.
Th'hydroptique drunkard, and night-scouting thiefe,
The itchy Lecher, and selfe tickling proud
Have the remembrance of past joyes, for reliefe
Of comming ills. To (poore) me is allow'd
No ease; for, long, yet vehement griefe hath beene
Th'effect and cause, the punishment and sinne.

IV.

O H my blacke Soule! now thou art summoned
  By sicknesse, deaths herald, and champion;
Thou art like a pilgrim, which abroad hath done
Treason, and durst not turne to whence hee is fled,
Or like a thiefe, which till deaths doome be read,
Wisheth himselfe delivered from prison;
But damn'd and hal'd to execution,
Wisheth that still he might be imprisoned.
Yet grace, if thou repent, thou canst not lacke;
But who shall give thee that grace to beginne?
Oh make thy selfe with holy mourning blacke,
And red with blushing, as thou art with sinne;
Or wash thee in Christs blood, which hath this might
That being red, it dyes red soules to white.

V.

I Am a little world made cunningly
  Of Elements, and an Angelike spright,
But black sinne hath betraid to endlesse night
My worlds both parts, and (oh) both parts must die.
You which beyond that heaven which was most high
Have found new sphears, and of new lands can write,
Powre new seas in mine eyes, that so I might
Drowne my world with my weeping earnestly,
Or wash it, if it must be drown'd no more:
But oh it must be burnt! alas the fire
Of lust and envie have burnt it heretofore,
And made it fouler; Let their flames retire,
And burne me ô Lord, with a fiery zeale
Of thee and thy house, which doth in eating heale.

VI.

T His is my playes last scene, here heavens appoint
  My pilgrimages last mile; and my race
Idly, yet quickly runne, hath this last pace,
My spans last inch, my minutes latest point,
And gluttonous death, will instantly unjoynt
My body, and soule, and I shall sleepe a space,
But my'ever-waking part shall see that face,
Whose feare already shakes my every joynt:
Then, as my soule, to'heaven her first seate, takes flight,
And earth-borne body, in the earth shall dwell,
So, fall my sinnes, that all may have their right,
To where they'are bred, and would presse me, to hell.
Impute me righteous, thus purg'd of evill,
For thus I leave the world, the flesh, the devill.

III. 1635-69 and one MS. group: omitted 1633 and some MSS.
7 sinne; now I Ed.: sinne, now I one MS.: sinne I now 1635-69
IV. 1635-69: II. 1633 and some MSS.: V. other MSS.

V. 1635-69: omitted 1633 and some MSS.: VII. other MSS.
6 lands MSS.: land 1635-69   11 have MSS.: hath one MS.: om.
1635-69   12 their] those one MS.   13 Lord] God one MS.
VI. 1635-69 and some MSS.: III. 1633 and other MSS.   7 Or
presently, I know not, see that Face, all MSS.   14 the devill.] and
devill. all MSS.

V.   VII.

Mid-summer is to spring as one to ten.   5
He says the early petal-fall is past,
When pear and cherry bloom went down in showers
On sunny days a moment overcast;
And comes that other fall we name the fall.
He says the highway dust is over all.   10
The bird would cease and be as other birds
But that he knows in singing not to sing.
The question that he frames in all but words
Is what to make of a diminished thing.

BOND AND FREE

Love has earth to which she clings
With hills and circling arms about—
Wall within wall to shut fear out.
But Thought has need of no such things,
For Thought has a pair of dauntless wings.   5

On snow and sand and turf, I see
Where Love has left a printed trace
With straining in the world's embrace.
And such is Love and glad to be.
But Thought has shaken his ankles free.   10

Thought cleaves the interstellar gloom
And sits in Sirius' disc all night,
Till day makes him retrace his flight,
With smell of burning on every plume,
Back past the sun to an earthly room.   15

His gains in heaven are what they are.
Yet some say Love by being thrall
And simply staying possesses all

120

In several beauty that Thought fares far
To find fused in another star.   20

BIRCHES

When I see birches bend to left and right
Across the lines of straighter darker trees,
I like to think some boy's been swinging them.
But swinging doesn't bend them down to stay
As ice storms do. Often you must have seen them   5
Loaded with ice a sunny winter morning
After a rain. They click upon themselves
As the breeze rises, and turn many-colored
As the stir cracks and crazes their enamel.
Soon the sun's warmth makes them shed crystal shells   10
Shattering and avalanching on the snow crust—
Such heaps of broken glass to sweep away
You'd think the inner dome of heaven had fallen.
They are dragged to the withered bracken by the load,
And they seem not to break; though once they are bowed
So low for long, they never right themselves:
You may see their trunks arching in the woods
Years afterwards, trailing their leaves on the ground
Like girls on hands and knees that throw their hair
Before them over their heads to dry in the sun.   20
But I was going to say when Truth broke in
With all her matter of fact about the ice storm,
I should prefer to have some boy bend them
As he went out and in to fetch the cows—
Some boy too far from town to learn baseball,   25
Whose only play was what he found himself,
Summer or winter, and could play alone.

121

Opening from *The Poetry of Robert Frost*, vol. 1, the Imprint Society, Barre, Mass., 1971 (reduced from 237 mm deep). Designed by Rudolph Ruzicka and set in his own typeface Linotype Fairfield. No running heads (see also p. 149).

The setting of poetry

Poetry above all things wants to be allowed to speak for itself, and should – usually – be set as plainly as possible so far as its own text is concerned. A type size must be chosen that allows, if it is possible, even the longest lines to be set without breaking. If lines have to be broken, they should be broken according to sense, which means every break should be individually marked.

The type size must be chosen not only to have as few turned-over lines as possible, but, in conjunction with the page size, to avoid too many poems going over on to a second page by just a line or so. If a poem is complete on two pages, it is desirable to have it as a visual entity on two facing pages.

Poems should normally be centred on the measure, and they should be centred visually, not mechanically on the longest line.

Where poems do not have titles or numbers, and cannot be printed one to a page, but must follow on, it is essential to signal the beginning of a new poem by adequate space, rule or some sort of motif, such as a typographical ornament.

In an ordinary book of poems, every poem should begin on a new page, but in a tightly packed anthology this will not be possible. When poems are mostly short, and are set one to a page, they may be leaded much more than usual, but this may

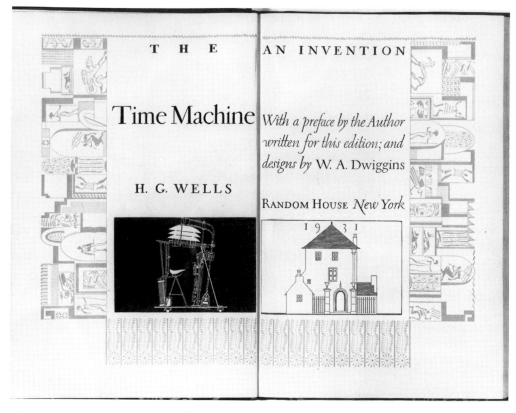

Title-page opening, the next-right
hand page and a text opening from
H. G. Wells' *The Time Machine*,
Random House, New York 1931
(reduced from 231 mm deep).
Designed and illustrated by W. A.
Dwiggins (who himself also wrote
space fiction), it is one of the most
interesting and extraordinary
examples of book design of the
twentieth century. The title-page
was printed in four colours; the
illustrations were stencilled in
colours and the decorations made up
from Dwiggins' own monochrome
stencil designs. The style is highly
idiosyncratic and unconventional
but, in my opinion, wholly
successful and appropriate for Wells'
imaginative text.

32

energy in security; it takes to art and to eroticism, and then come languor and decay.

Even this artistic impetus would at last die away—had almost died in the Time I saw. To adorn themselves with flowers, to dance, to sing in the sunlight; so much was left of the artistic spirit, and no more. Even that would fade in the end into a contented inactivity. We are kept keen on the grindstone of pain and necessity, and, it seemed to me, that here was that hateful grindstone broken at last!

As I stood there in the gathering dark I thought that in this simple explanation I had mastered the problem of the world—mastered the whole secret of these delicious people. Possibly the checks they had devised for the increase of population had succeeded too well, and their numbers had rather diminished than kept stationary. That would account for the abandoned ruins. Very simple was my explanation, and plausible enough—as most wrong theories are!

As I stood there musing over this too perfect triumph of man, the full moon, yellow and gibbous, came up out of an overflow of silver light in the northeast. The bright little figures ceased to move about below, a noiseless owl flitted by, and I shivered with the chill of the night. I determined to descend and find where I could sleep.

I looked for the building I knew. Then my eye travelled along to the figure of the White Sphinx upon the pedestal of

33

bronze, growing distinct as the light of the rising moon grew brighter. I could see the silver birch against it. There was the tangle of rhododendron bushes, black in the pale light, and there was the little lawn. I looked at the lawn again. A queer doubt chilled my complacency. "No," said I stoutly to myself, "that was not the lawn."

But it *was* the lawn. For the white leprous face of the sphinx was towards it. Can you imagine what I felt as this conviction came home to me? But you cannot. The Time Machine was gone!

At once, like a lash across the face, came the possibility of losing my own age, of being left helpless in this strange new world. The bare thought of it was an actual physical sensation. I could feel it grip me at the throat and stop my breathing. In another moment I was in a passion of fear and running with great leaping strides down the slope. Once I fell headlong and cut my face; I lost no time in stanching the blood, but jumped up and ran on, with a warm trickle down my cheek and chin. All the time I ran I was saying to myself, "They have moved it a little, pushed it under the bushes out of the way." Nevertheless, I ran with all my might. All the time, with the certainty that sometimes comes with excessive dread, I knew that such assurance was folly, knew instinctively that the machine was removed out of my reach. My breath came with pain. I suppose I covered the whole distance from the hill crest to the little lawn, two miles, perhaps, in ten minutes. And I am not a young man. I cursed aloud, as I ran, at my confident folly in leaving the machine, wasting good breath thereby. I cried aloud, and none answered. Not a creature seemed to be stirring in that moonlit world.

When I reached the lawn my worst fears were realised. Not a trace of the thing was to be seen. I felt faint and cold when I faced the empty space among the black tangle of bushes. I ran round it furiously, as if the thing might be hidden in a corner, and then stopped abruptly, with my hands clutching my hair. Above me towered the sphinx, upon the bronze pedestal, white, shining, leprous, in the light of the rising moon. It seemed to smile in mockery of my dismay.

I might have consoled myself by imagining the little people had put the mechanism in some shelter for me, had I not felt

---

lengthen a book unacceptably if many of the poems are long. Some wise and amusing remarks on the design of anthologies, and on the printing of verse in general, can be found in Beatrice Warde's *The Crystal Goblet* (London 1955).

Sir Francis Meynell's remark (already mentioned) that poetry should be set in italic, because poetry should be read slowly, need not be taken too seriously, but it is worth pondering. An example of poetry set in italic is shown on p. 161.

CAPTIONS

The first thing to decide about captions is, what part do they play in the book? How much information should they supply, starting from the question, are they needed at all? And if they are needed, will it not be better to keep them as short as possible? Are the captions that have been provided the most effective for the job? The designer has every right to ask this question, and, if he is not satisfied, he must say so, and show how he thinks they may be improved. Quite often, he will have to write them himself anyway, if he is choosing and laying out the illustrations, since the way the captions are written may depend on how the pictures are placed.

Copy for captions should always be prepared for the printer as carefully as the main text, and typed clearly on separate paper. Consistency of style (capitalization, punctuation, etc.) is as important here as elsewhere.

Do the captions require references? For instance, the source of the illustration, the name of the photographer or artist, the proof of the illustration's authenticity or validity, the place (e.g. museum) where the original can be studied, the size of the original, and whether it is a detail or part only of something bigger, e.g. a painting? If these details are necessary, is it really necessary to include them in the caption, or could they be placed somewhere else, to be looked up when needed? It can be argued that if all the information that might conceivably be needed is included together, the result, when printed, is so cluttered, and therefore so visually unattractive, that it puts the reader off, and the whole exercise is rendered abortive. This may be due to poor typographic design, or it may be poor editorial thinking: both are the book designer's responsibility. He must also decide, with captions, whether they are for *reading*, or for consultation: there could be a difference in typographic treatment. If for reading, they must follow the normal guide-lines for readability; if for consultation, they might need to be more prominent (larger, or bolder) but could also be in a more exotic, but less easily readable, typeface.

Captions are normally set in a different size or weight or kind of type from the text, so that they cannot be confused with the text; and should be separated from text by adequate space or, if necessary, by a thin rule.

If the illustrations are half-tones, bold type may harmonize better with the blackness of the pictures than a roman face. Bold type, if properly used, can be legible, but may make the captions too prominent, especially if they are long. It depends what effect is required. If you are thinking of using italic, as a good visual contrast with the text in roman, remember that many italics are intrinsically less easy to read than roman, so that if the captions are long – say, of two lines or more – you may be decreasing readability. Of course, it depends on the italic and how it is used (see Chapters 3 and 5).

It is obviously a saving of time and trouble at several different stages if captions can all be set in the same type to the same measure. This usually looks better, too. If directions like 'above left', 'above right' and so on have to be used, they *must* be consistent, and the correct instructions should be worked out before the captions are sent for setting, otherwise author's correction charges will be incurred.

When captions are not set directly under, or beside, their pictures, the best way to link them is by numbering both captions and pictures. These two sets of numbers should be identical (in type, size, and weight) and not confusable with the folio numbers. They will be more easily picked up by the reader if set in bold. If they are set in the same size and weight of type as the captions themselves, they must be separated from the first word of the caption by either a full point or a space of not less than one em of the type size.

If pictures are numbered, they must be numbered consecutively from the beginning to the end of the book, so that an unambiguous and concise reference can be given for any illustration at any time.

When captions are set to very short measures (10 picas or less), it is usually better to set them ragged right without word-breaks (even if the main text is justified) to avoid irregular and excessive word spacing.

If the illustrations are all of different sizes, and the captions are identificatory (e.g. in a book about painting, giving name of artist and title), there may be a strong argument for placing the captions underneath the pictures and it may not be feasible to set all captions to the same measure.

Probably, all captions should be set flush with the left-hand side of the picture and should certainly not extend beyond the right-hand edge of the picture. When captions make more than one line, it may be better to have two – or three – equal lines rather than one very long and one very short line. There is no rule about these choices: the main considerations are the appearance of the page (coupled with function) and the practicalities of the make-up. In a long book or periodical, the way the captions are set and placed may make a considerable difference to costs, and this should be discussed with the printer.

When pictures bleed on all sides, a caption if required has to be printed on the facing, preceding or following page, or overprinted on or reversed out of the picture. A caption more than one opening away from its picture is annoying to the reader.

The design of illustrated pages including captions is one of the typographer's most challenging tasks. It starts with the writing of the captions. The captions must be right, their relationship with the illustrations must be crystal clear, and they must not be allowed to spoil the effect of handsome pictures.

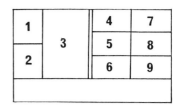

1 *Palazzo Dario seen from Palazzo Corner della Ca' Grande.*
2 *Late fifteenth-century spiral staircase and loggias at the Palazzo Contarini del Bovolo.*
3 *Palazzo da Mosto (centre); the lower two floors are Veneto-Byzantine.*
4 *Palazzo Corner-Spinelli, built between 1490 and 1510.*
5 *Courtyard and external staircase of Ca' d'Oro.*
6 *Rich fourteenth-century tracery of Palazzo Arian.*
7 *Palazzo Sagredo seen from the fish-market.*
8 *Palazzo Belloni-Battagia (left), the Venetian granary (centre) and the Fondaco dei Turchi (right).*
9 *Palazzo Contarini degli Scrigni seen from Palazzo Falier.*

Opposite page (above) *Living-area.* **(Below left)** *View from office to living-area.* **(Below right)** *Looking from living-area to office.* **This page (above)** *Entrance hall.* **(Right, top)** *Bedroom.* **(Centre)** *Kitchen and bathroom.* **(Below)** *Plan showing 'before' and 'after'.*

Two methods of captioning illustrations, from one issue of a contemporary British magazine. The diagram method is usually clear. The lower method tends to present a puzzle in decipherment, at the expense of interest in the material.

APPENDICES

Appendices are supplementary matter, of any kind, that the author does not wish to include in his text but wants to have in the book. Appendices should follow the typographical style of the text as closely as possible, but may, of course, be set in a smaller size of type and in double column if necessary to save space. It is important to signal clearly on every page that they are appendices and *not* text.

Normally, the first appendix should appear on a right-hand page, with its title treated as (and ranging with) the chapter titles; and subsequent appendices each starting on a new page.

BIBLIOGRAPHY

A serious bibliography at the back of a scholarly book should contain the following minimum information: name of author, title of book, and place and date of publication. The name of the publisher is desirable, but modern co-publishing in various countries simultaneously often makes this too complicated to be feasible. The fullest guidance on this problem is probably that given in the *MLA Handbook for Writers of Research Papers, Theses, and Dissertations* (New York 1977) (obtainable in the UK and Europe from Kraus-Thomson Organisation, FL–9491 Nedeln, Lichtenstein). The order should always be: name of author(s) or editor(s), preferably surname first (for ease of reference when you are searching for the author's name in a list); book title in upper-and lower-case italic correctly capitalized, *not* in quotes (this is important because the italic shows that those words are the *book's title*; the title of an article, or chapter, in a book or periodical is set in roman, in quotes); number of volumes, if more than one, and the number of the particular volume to which reference is made, if that is needed; name and city of publisher (in an English publication, 'London' is assumed and often omitted, but if it is not London, the place should be stated); year of publication. Each of these items is usually followed by a comma; brackets for the publisher and year are unnecessary.

For a reference to a periodical the order should be: name of author(s), title of article in roman in quotes, name of periodical in italic upper and lower case, identification of issue in simplest form, e.g. volume number followed by date (in brackets) (some periodicals are undated: an approximate date should be given, if known, in brackets after 'n.d.' – 'no date'); page or pages of the periodical to which reference is made.

The correct names of periodicals can usually be found in: *World List of Scientific Periodicals*, 3 vols. (London 1964) and the updated *British Union Catalogue of Periodicals* (British Library). See also British Standard 1629:1976, *Recommendations for Bibliographical References*.

The more important thing is that the system used in any one work should be consistent in that work, and that it should be a system that is most appropriate to that work.

INDEX

An index is an extremely important part of any serious book. It is easier to design than to compile. The first design requirement is, of course, clarity. An index is usually set, like footnotes, two sizes smaller than the text, but very often has to be fitted into a given number of pages which complete the last section in the book, and which cannot be increased except at considerable extra expense. So the index has to be set in whatever size the available space will accommodate: into two, three or four columns if necessary. It should – if possible – begin on a recto.

The typography depends on the construction of the index. Typographers should therefore know something about how an index works and how it may be made; they may even have to make one themselves, from time to time, and will find that it requires a degree of imaginative skill that is not unlike typography.

In a good index, a word is not followed by a long string of undifferentiated page references, if it is possible to identify them, or at least print the main one in bold. The use of bold and italic, and even a different face and indenting, may all be needed to make a complicated index useful. Each new letter of the alphabet should be indicated by a space, and a cap, which may be treated as a decorative feature.

A good index should be preceded by an introductory note, explaining the indexing decisions made, and drawing attention to any matter excluded from the index, and to the system of alphabetization chosen.

For further information on indexes, see *Making an Index* by G. V. Carey (one of Cambridge University Press's invaluable 'Authors' and Printers' Guides'), and British Standard 3700: 1988, *The Preparation of indexes to books, periodicals and other publications*. You can also consult, or join, the Society of Indexers, 16 Green Road, Birchington, Kent CT7 9JZ (Secretary, Mrs Claire Troughton).

END-PAPERS

End-papers are not strictly a typographical problem, but they are an important element in the design of a book which it will often fall to a typographer to specify. It is a pity to neglect the opportunity to do something attractive rather than have plain white paper; even a coloured cartridge would usually be preferable to plain white and costs very little more. End-papers should be chosen to match, or contrast with, the outside cover of the job.

On a large, expensive and ambitious book, a specially designed end-paper should be a very small extra item, well worth considering. Sometimes, it could also be used as a binding design: in any case, it must be planned as part of the book as a whole object, produced not by accident but by design.

CASE*

Since the flowering, in this century, of the jacket, as a work of art or design to sell the book, the binding case has been sadly neglected. It is of course a matter of money: why, say publishers, spend a penny more than necessary on the case, when it is never seen?

*'Binding' is a loose term, meaning the cover of a book. 'Case' is a technical term, meaning a hard cover that is fixed to a book by adhesive, not by sewing. This is the normal mass-production method: by the traditional hand methods, the binding is held to the book by sewing.

The case *is* seen, and sometimes very quickly, when the jacket is removed. For a book collector, the jacket is part of the book as originally published, and should therefore be preserved, but not on the book, where it will inevitably, if slowly, disintegrate. For the ordinary reader, the jacket is worth preserving only if he likes it, and if he does, it should again be removed, and either folded and kept in the back of the book, or mounted in a collection. Left on the book, the jacket will just get tatty. So the book, in all these instances, will end up on the shelves in its case, and show the world whether it was well designed or neglected.

It is not possible to lay down laws about case design: it is the designer's responsibility to create. The following points may be noted.

(1) We are talking, first and foremost, about *spines*. The spine *must* carry the title of the book, and, preferably, the names of author and publisher, so that it can be identified on a shelf. Too many spines, on expensive books produced by famous and reputable publishers, look squalid, perfunctory or accidental.

(2) Lettering to appear in gold on a cloth or cloth-substitute spine has to be impressed on it with heat, by a brass engraving of the lettering or by a 'chemac' block, made photographically from artwork or a reproduction proof. So the designer has to provide either drawn lettering or a 'repro pull'.

(3) Lettering on a book spine must read either across, or up and down. If it is to read across (the most natural way), words usually have to be broken, and this is normal on book spines. But very often, a typeface is too wide in 'set' to give a large enough size to be properly legible within the narrow width requirement: before the designer decides on vertical arrangement, the possibility of drawing the wording in condensed lettering should be considered. Often this is the best solution, but it is more trouble and expense.

(4) If it is decided to make a vertical design, the designer has to choose whether to run the wording down from the top or up from the foot. Both methods are practised, to the confusion of all who search along bookshelves! I have never understood the logic of running it up. The good reasons for running it *down* are (a) one expects to start reading from the top, which is where the title is on most books; (b) if the book is laid down on its back, front side uppermost, the spine lettering is the right way up for legibility. Of course, if a publisher has a house style, that must be followed.

(5) There is a third solution: to print the letters normally, but individually in a column, reading from the top. This can work, and the shorter the title, the better.

(6) The only thing that jacket and case design have in common is the spine. It is worth remembering that very often the same design – and therefore the same lettering or repro pull – will do for both, which may be a saving of both money and effort.

Experimental cover designs, by a
Royal College of Art student, for the
Lion and Unicorn Press edition of
H. V. Marot's translation of
Bodoni's preface to the *Manuale
Tipografico*. Leather or cloth spines,
with designs printed in various
colours on paper on boards, 1953.

(7) It must be remembered that gold or silver lettering on a dark cloth – or even a light cloth – is not the same as black type on white paper: the design is an affair of reflected light, like motorway signs.

(8) To make a distinctive, eye-catching design on the narrow width of a normal book spine, either the lettering must be big and run the whole length of the spine, or some other decorative element must be added, such as a drawing, an ornamental pattern, or a heraldic shield or symbol. The effect of gold blocking in gold on decent cloth or paper is nearly always handsome; it is one of the easiest and pleasantest of the designer's tasks.

(9) The design possibilities of decorating the front and back of the case are infinite; it is really a matter of expense. With the richly blocked cases of Victorian books in mind, let us, in the insecure but imaginative 1990s, see what we can do. Permanence is no longer a vital virtue, and paper-on-boards lasts longer than most people realize: here is a much-neglected opportunity for designers to make even cheap novels more attractive.

If a publisher cares about the appearance of his books, and wants to make them stand out from the ruck, the spine is the first part of the book that most people see, and deserves special attention.

Among instantly recognizable and attractive spines in the history of publishing, one thinks of – among others – William Pickering's purely typographical spines, often with printed paper labels, published in London in the 1840s and 1850s; T. N. Foulis's books published in Edinburgh at the beginning of the present century, with lettering by the French calligrapher George Auriol; Alfred Knopf's books in New York with colour-blocked stencil designs by W. A. Dwiggins; Jonathan Cape's books, made distinctive by neat typography and the Cape 'urn' symbol; Faber books with lettering by Berthold Wolpe; and cases designed for Chatto & Windus by Ian Parsons and Norah Smallwood.

JACKET

The purpose of the jacket today is not so much to protect as to *sell*. It is a special kind of poster.

A jacket design is usually commissioned and paid for by the publisher, so it is his privilege to say what kind of jacket he wants. No formula exists for successful jacket design and no one knows to what extent jackets sell books anyway: the title, the author's name, reviews, the ambience of the bookshop and the mood of the buyer must all contribute to a greater or lesser extent. If a publisher can define the market for a particular book (e.g. ex-members of the Eighth Army, or women golfers) and can guess what visual treatment of a jacket will move that group of people to buy, he can specify a design: otherwise, he would be well advised to commission a

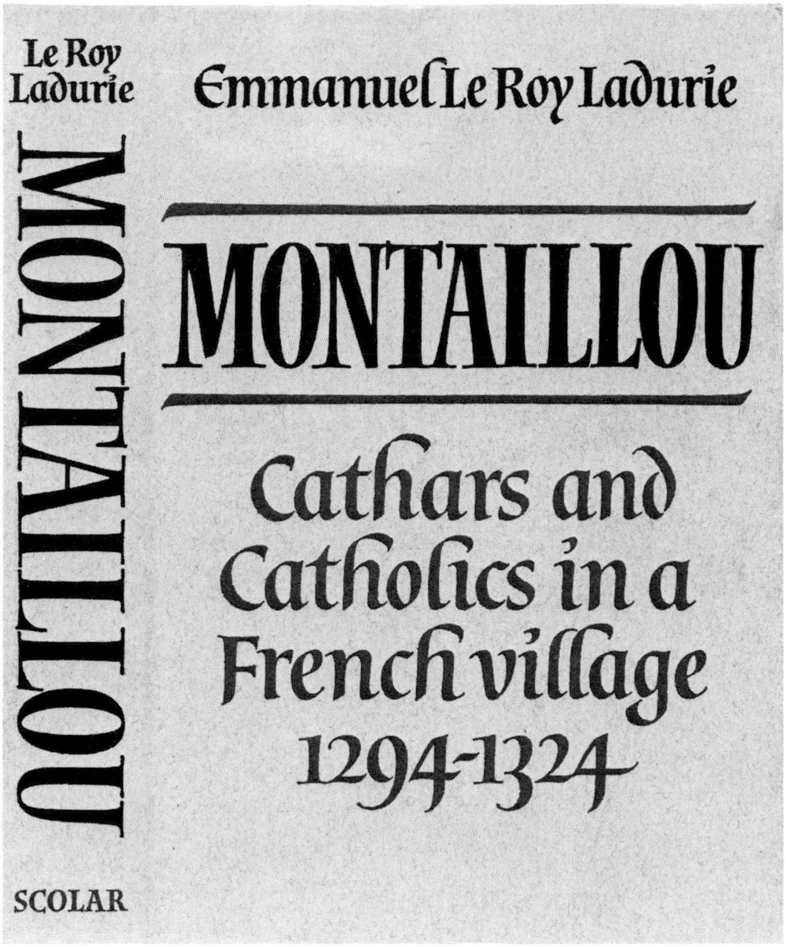

Le Roy
Ladurie   Emmanuel Le Roy Ladurie

MONTAILLOU

MONTAILLOU

Cathars and
Catholics in a
French village
1294-1324

SCOLAR

jacket design that pleases him, so that at least one person likes it.

If it is agreed that the basic purpose of the jacket is to make the book noticed among the competing books in a bookshop, that is something for a designer to tackle, within restraints of cost and 'taste', and the probable nature of the market for the book.

The design of the pictorial part of a jacket is outside the scope of this book, but a typographical or lettered jacket, or the lettering or type on a design or photograph, are the typographer's business.

Having decided whether the main impact of the design comes from the picture or the lettering – one or the other should have precedence, or they may cancel each other out – the designer must then consider priorities in the lettering; often, the author's name is a better selling factor than the title, and should be made more prominent. A long title is, of course, a bad title from a jacket designer's point of view; it would in that case be desirable to pick one or two words to

Jacket designed and lettered by Michael Harvey for E. le Roy Ladurie's *Montaillou*, Scolar Press, London 1978 (reduced from 240 mm deep). The original was printed in red, brown and black on a light-brown paper.

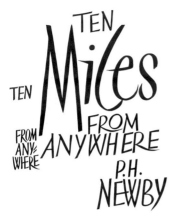

Characteristic lettering by Hans Tisdall from a jacket design for Jonathan Cape. Reduced from one of the colours used.

stand out. The normal rules of legibility and design in display will apply; the design must be judged from a distance of say fifteen or twenty feet, and the eye must 'comprehend' the design at a glance and not be confused by too many elements: more than three elements will be too many for such a small area as a book jacket. And if the important lettering (name of author, and/or book title) cannot be read at a distance of fifteen feet (or in a bookshop window, by a passer-by on the pavement) then the design cannot be much use, unless the image is so compelling that it lures the customer to come closer!

One way to design eye-catching jackets is to design something completely different from the current fashion, if one can decide what that is. When Penguin books were first launched in 1935, the orange-white-orange cover designs were in strong contrast to the largely pictorial full-colour jackets that were then prevalent in the bookshops. Some of the earliest successful 'typographer's designs' were the typographical jackets printed in red, mauve and black on daffodil yellow paper devised by Stanley Morison for Gollancz in the 1930s. From 1936, the publishing firm of Jonathan Cape made their books recognizable at a distance by having a large number of their jackets designed in a very personal calligraphy by Hans Tisdall (who had been taught in Germany by Anna Simons, who had herself been a pupil of Edward Johnston): whether the jackets sold the books might be difficult to decide, since they were good books anyway, but Cape's faith in Tisdall's brilliant graphic designs continued for years.

Two other outstanding series of jackets were the designs by Clifford and Rosemary Ellis for Collins New Naturalist Series (remarkable because over a period of twenty or more years they remained fresh and original against a background of ever more sophisticated graphics by new generations of designers) and the auto-lithographed jackets, all with hand-drawn lettering, by Barnett Freedman for Faber and Faber. And Duncan Grant and Vanessa Bell drew jackets for the Hogarth Press; and Nicholson for Heinemann . . .

Many books today are conceived and designed as 'packages'; i.e. the motive behind them is not the desire of an author to communicate his ideas, but the desire of a business man to make a large profit. Serious books – books that have something to say that is worth saying, beyond mere entertainment – normally sell only a few thousand copies, and cannot hope to make large profits, so that the costs of production, including design, must be kept as low as is prudent by the publisher. Books that may become 'bestsellers', however – whether by a bestselling author, or as a well-conceived package – require and deserve the highest design skills that can be bought, for they are competing in the world's markets with every other glamorous product intended to extract money from our pockets.

11 Jobbing typography

The principles of using type are the same, whether one is designing a book or a visiting card or a proclamation: nevertheless, a few hints on some specialized kinds of job are offered here.

If typography is a problem-solving activity, then the first requirement is to identify the problem and agree that it is best solved by typography. If the problem is people parking cars where you don't want them to, a physical obstruction that makes it impossible is a far better solution than a notice in words – which if it is in one language only may be understood only by those who can read that language. If Mr B. wants you to design him a visiting card, you have to find out why he wants it and how he will use it, and also what is the image of himself that is to be projected. On all typographical jobs of every kind, the words must be right, and getting the words right is often the most difficult part of the whole operation. If the typographer is given the words that the client says he wants, it does not remove from the former the responsibility of looking at them very critically: improvements can often be suggested.

Stanley Morison's redesign of the British Post Office Telegram form[1] is a classic example of the 'editorial' function of typography (see illustration in James Moran, *Stanley Morison*, London 1971, p. 121); indeed, forms in particular are a question of words first, typography second, and of both interacting on each other.

WORKING WITH CLIENTS

Earlier in this Manual I distinguished between the work of an artist and that of a typographer, in that the former need not necessarily work for a client, but the latter invariably does. It is perhaps appropriate to comment here on the typographer-client relationship, as frequent reference is made to it in this chapter – while remembering, of course, that the relationship exists, in one form or another, in every other operation discussed in this book, even if the 'client' is an employer.

Working with clients who become your friends is one of the most rewarding parts of a designer's life. It is also an important part of the work itself: a design job always involves two people, the client and the designer, and very often it requires a creative input from both parties: the concept of what is wanted comes from the client, the concept of how to do it from the designer. Two intelligent people working together can help push each further ahead than either could have achieved singly. The designer should always keep an open mind and be receptive to any suggestions or criticisms. It is only when your client wants to take over your own part of the job completely, and, for example, starts specifying the typefaces and type sizes, that you begin to be wary.

Previous page: design cut on linoleum by the author, 1937.

If you want to keep a client – and all designers have occasional experiences of clients they don't want to keep – do not argue with him, and, above all, do not prove that he is wrong. If you see clearly that he *is* wrong, try to arrange things so that he makes the discovery himself, even if it costs him money to learn what you have been trying to tell him. If you want to keep him as a client, let him learn for himself who was right and who was wrong, and never say 'I told you so!'

All designers have a double task: to do the designing, and then to get it accepted. Some designers are brilliant at design but hopeless at 'selling': they need a partner or an agent. Faced with a design problem, a creative designer may see six or twelve solutions; it requires another kind of talent to see which of those solutions is the right one in the circumstances. Not all designers have that extra talent.

Having your work turned down – whether by an individual or by a committee – is part of a designer's life, and you must learn to cope with it. The first rule – and it applies throughout life, not only in design – is 'Never fight a major battle over a minor issue.' The second is to see whether your client can provide a reason for rejection. A client is entitled to have whims and prejudices and is under no obligation to be rational: but neither has a designer any obligation to go on working indefinitely for such a client. There comes a moment when the designer has to decide if there is any point in continuing to work for a client with whom no understanding appears possible.

A client who can produce *reasons* for rejection is worth striving to please. The designer must also, of course, be prepared to explain his reasons for what he has done.

When a designer has completed a long, arduous and perhaps complicated job, it is annoying to have alterations asked for by the client or employer – especially if they seem niggling and unnecessary. No rules can be laid down about changing a design: designers survive by pleasing clients and employers, not by antagonizing them. However, one thing is never acceptable, and that is for anyone to change a design without the designer's knowledge or agreement. This is more likely to happen when the designer's client is a publisher, who has direct access to the printer. When it does happen, a parting of the ways is indicated, or a promise that it will never happen again! In serious cases, advice may have to be sought either from one's professional body, such as the Chartered Society of Designers, or from a lawyer. It is of particular importance if the printed work carries the designer's name, and the change is something of which the designer strongly disapproves.

Committees

A designer's heart sinks if he hears that his work has to be judged by a committee. It is always desirable for a designer to have a direct contact with his client, principal to principal. If his client turns out to be a committee, he must be prepared to

UNIVERSITY OF SOUTH FLORIDA

TAMPA · ST PETERSBURG · FORT MYERS

COLLEGE OF SOCIAL AND BEHAVIORAL SCIENCES
DEPARTMENT OF HISTORY
TAMPA, FLORIDA 33620

16 April 1977

813: 974-2807

My dear Ruari,

    You must have typed,or handwritten (I forget which),the envelope to your
last letter under the influence of Catriona's wedding breakfast,and no doubt with
your ninth glass of champagne lingering xxxxix sweetly on the tongue. As,in a
rational moment,you will be the first to acknowledge,there is no such town as
"Tampa St.Petersburg Sarasota Fort Myers". Those are the locations of the putative
four campuses of the university. Fort Myers is over a hundred miles from here,and
if your letter had gone there first I shouldn't have got it yet. Or very likely,
the US mails being what they are,got ■ it at all.

Someone who is not familiar with place names in South Florida *might* be excused for thinking, as did the present writer, that 'Tampa, St Petersburg, Fort Myers' was the main address of the university, instead of the location of the three campuses.

The letterhead also shows an example of a 'symbol' that is unsuitable for its purpose. None of the components in the drawing are clear.

face and talk to the committee. The situation when a committee's views are relayed to the designer by a third party is hardly ever acceptable.

DESIGNING STATIONERY: LETTERHEADS

Designing a letterhead is one of the commonest tasks typographers are given: it may look one of the simplest, but it can be one of the most difficult.

Private clients

Take first of all a private letterhead for a friend with, presumably, only one person to please. If it is for a husband and wife, there may be a good reason to have 'his' and 'her' own letterheadings (but it will be advisable for them to share the same envelope sizes). The options are in style, typeface, sheet size, kind and colour of paper (not forgetting matching envelopes), printing process, ink colour, and range of items.

The things that have to be settled first are the wording and the quantity. It is surprising how many people do not know either their correct address (and telephone number and postcode) or how many sheets they will need, and the designer should be prepared to give advice on both.

The following notes are a reminder of some of the considerations that will affect the decisions that must be taken.

Style What is your client's taste and life-style? Modern or old-fashioned? Daring or dignified? Colourful or severe?

Typeface Sans-serif, or seriffed, roman or italic? Or it could be hand-lettered, or letraset, and printed offset-litho. What printer will be used and what are his facilities? How much does the client want to spend?

| action   space |

a voluntary association of artists concerned with creative play, education and the visual arts

89C Fitzjohn's Avenue
London NW3

01-435 8368

Studios at Space Ltd
St Katharine's Dock E1
Rehearsals at London
New Arts Laboratory
1 Robert Street NW1

KING'S COLLEGE RESEARCH CENTRE
KING'S COLLEGE CAMBRIDGE ENGLAND CB2 1ST
TELEPHONE CAMBRIDGE (0223) 350411

Top: asymmetric letterhead (reduced from A4), designed and printed by Desmond Jeffery, in which every relationship (size of type, position, space) is most carefully considered. Courtesy St Bride Printing Library. *Above:* centred letterhead designed and printed by Sebastian Carter in 'Octavian' (a typeface designed by Will Carter and David Kindersley).

Sheet size and paper Are the letterheads principally for typed or handwritten letters? Does the client insist on envelopes exactly matching the stationery? Does he/she require either self-seal or window envelopes? Has the client got strong feelings on surface, colour and quality of paper? Will blank (or printed) continuation sheets be required? (If for typewriting, carbons and copy paper will be needed in correct sizes.)

Printing process This will normally depend on what printer is to be used, whether an illustration is to be used that could only be printed by litho, and consideration of quantity and cost.

Colour If white paper is chosen, a coloured ink does not cost more for the printing, and is usually more distinctive, personal and attractive, for a private letterhead, than black.

Range If a person's output of correspondence is large, two sizes of heading, perhaps A5 and A4, is often an economy, but this requires two envelope sizes. If the correspondence is global, envelopes printed with the sender's name and address are useful, for returning to sender when the addressee has moved. Postcards, gummed labels for parcels, and compliments slips, or gummed slips with name and address, are also to be considered.

Finally, *design*. There are no rules, except those of taste and practicality. A designer should from the very beginning make a collection of interesting letterheadings, both good and bad, in order to analyse *why* they are good or bad; and a collection of different examples is often useful to show a client, to help find out what he wants.

The principal skill in designing a typographical letterhead is in matching the size of the type to the words and the size of the paper. Too small may look mean, and be difficult to read (hard-to-read telephone numbers are a common mistake and profoundly irritating), and too big is usually clumsy.

Evenly letterspaced capitals (if there are not too many of them and they are not too big) are more formal, and for that reason often more suitable for letterheads, than upper and lower case. But it is a matter for the taste of the designer and the client.

Business clients

Many, if not all, of the considerations that apply to a private client apply also to a business, but on a larger scale. A letterhead, or more usually a stationery range, for a business must convey a great deal more information, and it is necessary to be aware of the legal requirements in the country in which the stationery originates: in Britain, for example, the registered office and company number of a limited company must be shown, as must the names of directors of any company registered under the Companies Act since 1916.*

*The full legal requirements are stated on p. 699 of the *Printing Industries Annual*, published by the British Printing Industries Federation, 11 Bedford Row, London WC1R 4DX.

Apart from the obligatory material, there is much other information that may or may not be included, and the designer should, from his previous experience, be able to advise on this. It can be assumed that all information about communication (addresses, telephones, telex, etc.) *must* be included; degrees and honours after directors' names are a matter of choice; professional qualifications are part of the information that professional firms (lawyers, accountants, doctors, etc.) will normally wish their clients to know. Getting the words right is the first prerequisite and not always easy.

The company may well want to include its symbol or trademark. Letterheadings are part of the company's image. If a company has associations with a particular colour this should be reflected in their range of stationery. This should be carried through everything, including such items as memorandum pads, even if they are purely for internal use.

Having assembled the correct 'copy', the designer must get his brief right, and he will usually have to compile this himself by asking the right questions. He must understand (in simple terms) the business of his client, the sort of people the correspondence will be addressed to, the exact purpose of each piece of stationery, and by what systems it may be processed: for instance, the kind of typewriters on which the letters will be typed will determine questions of interlinear spacing, and invoice forms may be prepared and 'typed' by the firm's computers.

What quantities and printing processes will be needed? Some firms want their stationery to be flamboyant, others require it to be discreet. Some firms want different qualities of paper and heading, for example expensive or expensive-looking paper for the managing director, a less expensive version for ordinary use, and a cheaper mass-produced version for publicity hand-outs or whatever, which may be printed in millions – but all with the same basic design.

Although there are always exceptions, the following rules are useful guides in designing business stationery.

Rationalization It is part of the designer's job to see that the design and production of printed stationery is rationalized: this means as few different sizes of both paper and envelopes as possible and that the paper can be easily folded to fit into the envelopes. The international A-system of paper sizes should now always be recommended unless there is a good reason against it. Most filing and other paper systems in Europe are now based on A5 and A4 and their use makes life simpler in many ways and at many levels.

Design An asymmetric design is nearly always more practical for complicated business letterheads than a centred design, since it can be altered more easily: in a centred design, all line lengths are critical, and an alteration to one line may mean altering the whole thing. The names of directors and partners are frequently changed and a design that does not allow for this is not functional.

Letterheads with more than one address need very careful treatment: it must be made clear to the recipient (who may not be familiar with the language in which the letter is written, and who may not even be 'intelligent' in his or her own language) to which address a reply should be sent. Telephones, telex, cable addresses and other information which are not part of the postal address should be clearly separated from it.

Window envelopes must be discussed, because if they are required, the design must conform. The use of window envelopes saves an extra typing and minimizes the chance of the wrong letter going to the wrong client.

The work of the typist should be considered: the design should enable all the heading information (date, reference numbers, etc.) to be typed in the one line if at all possible. In a big company, either roughs or printed proofs should be circulated for testing and approval by office staff as well as by the responsible director or manager.

Since typed letters have a straight edge of typing on the left, the design should take account of this. It is nearly always necessary that the typing should align with the left-hand edge of the heading, and if the typing should begin at an exact point which is not otherwise shown, a dot should be printed (very small, if possible in grey or colour) to guide the typist: a dot or dash which bleeds is also helpful to indicate folding points. *A letterhead should be designed to look good* not as a blank sheet but *as a typed letter*, and it is vital that it should be typed to conform with the design. It is normal to allow about 1 in. (or more) as a left-hand margin, so that, for example, the letter can be held in the fingers, or incorporated in a filing system, without obscuring part of the letter.

If the design is a centred one and the longest line is less than about $2\frac{1}{2}$ in. wide, the exact point at which the typing begins *may* not matter, but a centred letterheading with lines that nearly but not quite align with the typing may be irritating.

It is not desirable to give any narrow prescription for the actual design of letterheadings, because sheer originality is often what counts most; but a typographical letterhead (and it is really not practical to have a pictorial letterhead for, say, a firm of sober and respected lawyers or accountants with upwards of twenty partners and thirty branches in twenty countries) is subject to the same rules that apply to all typography: sensitivity in the choice and mixing of typefaces, in the relationships of type size and space, and the fineness of the impression – on a suitable paper.

Young designers must study, and collect examples of, the work of the masters – which are frequently reproduced in books and magazines – for example, Jan Tschichold, Max Caflisch, Herbert Spencer, and, indeed, anyone else whose work you admire. You should also have on your shelves, for reference – or at least study in a library – Herbert Spencer's *Design in Business Printing* (London 1952) and published collections of letterhead designs such as the two volumes of *Der Briefbogen in der Welt* ('An International Letterhead Review') published by J. W. Zanders, the German paper-makers, in 1958 and 1968.

Collections such as these show superb designs and absurdities; but let it not be forgotten that even absurdities – which obscure the sender's name and address and seem to resent the intrusion on the sheet of paper (sometimes dark brown) of anything so mundane as typing or writing – may achieve their true purpose of proclaiming that their owner is a smart fellow, and win a prize for the designer in a design competition. But when you've had your fun, try designing a letterhead with several hundred words on it. You don't often see those in the design anthologies.

It is always advisable to make at least one detailed finished pencil rough in the correct size, with the right margins all round. You can often learn a lot by making two or three such finished alternative roughs before submitting the best of them. A neat and detailed rough mounted on a black or coloured background will impress your client. He will be able to judge the final appearance of the letterheading best if you type a letter on it, and you can incorporate in the typing a few useful words of explanation. For instance:

'We have aligned the typing with the left-hand edge of the

heading above, and you will notice that the date is typed so that it precisely aligns with the first line of the address; the reference numbers align with the telex and telephone numbers at the right too.

'The letter has been typed with a minimum margin of $1\frac{1}{2}$ inches at right, the paragraphs are indented, and the ending of the letter is, once again, aligned at the left rather than centred.

'The line of type set along the bottom of your letterheading has an identical left-hand margin to the line of type at the top. There is a small full point printed top left which will show your secretarial staff the exact position to type the date, so that the letter has the correct margins at left.

'If you decide to use window envelopes we can print two small full points which will indicate the top and bottom limits for typing the name and address of the person to whom you are sending the letter.

'If you wish it, we can print two fine dashes at the extreme left edge of the paper which will indicate the precise position of the folding of this letter to fit a DL size envelope.'

OTHER STATIONERY

Invoice forms must be designed in conformity with the accounting system used by the client. They are frequently required to be numbered in triplicate or quadruplicate. Different computing systems have specialized spacing and other requirements. Some are printed on 'continuous' stationery.

Gummed address labels Many firms prefer to stick postage stamps on or frank the addressed labels before they are stuck on. This is an argument for printing the name and address of the sender at the *foot* of the label.

Since nearly all typing is in black, it will obviously be wrong (because confusing) to print the firm's name and address in black type on white paper close to where the address will be typed. A strip of background colour and perhaps reversed type will solve this problem.

Always include the phone number of sender, as well as the address, on gummed labels, as a convenience for recipients.

Compliment slips These are extremely useful and can accompany invoices, cheques, copies of letters, sales brochures, or information that has been requested, without having to waste time and money on dictating and typing a letter. They should have sufficient space for a note or lines of type if required, and include telephone numbers as well as address.

Visiting cards The conventional engraved or pseudo-engraved card is surely now a doubtful luxury. Most businesses are better served by typographical cards which can be reprinted (or ordered afresh) very quickly – and on which colour can be used freely, such as for a symbol or special wording.

Envelopes and window envelopes For window envelopes, see above. Letters sent overseas should carry the sender's name and address on the outside of the envelope, in case the letter cannot be delivered.

Information graphics includes timetables and lists of all kinds, teaching literature, wall-sheets for schools, clinics, information posters, guide-books and hotel information, instruction and information on consumer products, reports and many other things.

Again, the first problem is to analyse the job and to assemble and arrange the needed information in a lucid and logical order. The use of symbols, graphs and illustrations must always be borne in mind. In presenting a catalogue of information in as handy a format as possible (e.g. in travel guides), the skilful typography and use of symbols and maps in the annual *Good Food Guide*, published in London, and the *Guides Michelin* and *Guide Kléber*, from Paris, should be studied.

In any technical literature, particularly if it is addressed to laymen (e.g. the literature telling one how to use the things one buys, from medicines to mowers) the technical terms used *must* be explained, and illustrated if possible. Time and again one sees a beautiful, well-designed and expensive product accompanied by a shoddy-looking, ill-written and incoherent 'book of words'.

TABLES

Most tables are compiled with rules, ruled either by pen or pencil, or typed, because that is the easiest way for the compiler, particularly if the work is being done longhand.

If rules have a purpose, it is to separate columns of figures: in printing, this is better done by space. Rules should never be used in printing unless the function they perform cannot be performed in any other way. Omit them unless it can be shown that the table is made easier to read by including rules.

Rules set by hot-metal composing machines tend to look unsatisfactory in any case, because they are set as a series of short separate rules, which rarely join up properly. In hot metal, rules cannot cross each other, and if this is required, it has to be achieved either by drawing and making a line block, or by a second printing. In litho printing, rules are usually drawn anyway, and can be perfect.

Printing rules, words, figures, etc., in a second colour often has a pleasing decorative effect, and may even help communication. But the use of colour can be dangerous, especially in any matter concerning safety. The designer must bear in mind (a) colour blindness; (b) falsification of information if colours are printed out of register; (c) confusion of some colours seen in poor or coloured lights; (d) the nullifying of the effect if monochrome reproduction is ever likely.

Opposite: the table *above* (here reduced) was redesigned by Ruari McLean in the style shown *below* to give more information in less space. The complicated hand-setting of rules was avoided without loss of clarity. By courtesy of the Tobacco Research Institute, London.

186

TABLE 25 (b)

EXTENT OF INHALING IN 1961 ANALYSED BY TYPE OF PRODUCT SMOKED
WITHIN EACH AGE GROUP

	Age group					
	16–24	25–34	35–49	50–59	60+	All ages
	%	%	%	%	%	%
MEN						
Manufactured cigarette smokers						
Inhales deeply	29·0	34·0	34·4	37·6	23·4	32·2
Inhales moderately	50·7	49·8	45·2	32·2	32·9	43·1
Inhales slightly	12·4	8·8	10·4	12·4	11·2	10·9
Does not inhale	7·9	7·4	10·0	17·8	32·5	13·8
	100·0	100·0	100·0	100·0	100·0	100·0

Table 5.9.1 Extent of inhaling cigars by current (1965) and ex-manufactured-cigarette smokers analysed by the extent of inhaling of cigarette smoke when smoking manufactured cigarettes – Men

	CURRENT MANUFAC-TURED-CIGARETTE SMOKERS WHO INHALE CIGARETTE SMOKE					EX-MANUFACTURED-CIGARETTE SMOKERS WHO INHALED CIGARETTE SMOKE				
	Deeply	*Moderately*	*Slightly*	*Not at all*	Total	*Deeply*	*Moderately*	*Slightly*	*Not at all*	Total
Men	%	%	%	%	%	%	%	%	%	%
Cigar inhaling										
Inhales deeply	12·5	3·8	0·4	0·6	5·8	11·7	6·2	1·4	—	6·4
Inhales moderately	6·6	4·3	0·9	0·9	4·2	3·3	4·8	—	1·1	3·0
Inhales slightly	11·6	11·0	9·6	2·1	9·9	5·3	6·0	7·0	1·3	4·7
Does not inhale	28·7	39·3	48·9	56·5	39·3	22·2	25·4	29·4	37·3	27·3
Does not smoke cigars	40·6	41·6	40·2	39·9	40·8	57·5	57·6	62·2	60·3	58·6
Total	100·0	100·0	100·0	100·0	100·0	100·0	100·0	100·0	100·0	100·0

Table 1

High-intensity lasers

Laser Medium	Wave-length	Effi-ciency (%)	Peak power (W)	Pulse dura-tion	Laboratory
Nd : glass	1.06 μm	0·2	7×10^{11}	1·5 ns	Battelle, Columbus, USA
			4×10^{12}	230 ps	Lawrence Livermore, USA
			10^{12}	1 ns	KMS Fusion Inc. USA
			2×10^{12}	500 ps	Univ. Rochester USA
			5×10^{11}	2 ns	Lebedev, Moscow, USSR
CO_2	10·6 μm	3–5	5×10^{11}	1 ns	Los Alamos, USA
Iodine	1·31 μm	0·5	10^{11}	700 ps	Max-Planck-Inst. Garching, Germany
Hydrogen fluoride	2·7 μm	180 (elec-trical) 5 (che-mical)	10^{11}	35 ns	Los Alamos and Sandia, USA
Dye	605 nm	$<10^{-3}$	3×10^9	3 ps	Imperial College London
Xenon	173 nm	>2	4×10^8	20 ns	Los Alamos and Maxwell Labs. Inc. USA

91

Table 2 **Value of retail sales seasonally adjusted**

Index numbers of value of sales per week (current prices)   1971 = 10

(Sales in 1971 – £ million Final estimates)	All kinds of business (16 296)	Food shops (6 866)	Non-food shops Total (9 430)	Clothing and footwear shops (2 436)	Durable goods shops (1 897)	Other non-food shops [2] (5 097)
1971	100.0	100.0	100.0	100	100	100
1972	112.0	109.0	114.2	112	118	114
1973	126.9	123.0	129.8	128	136	128
1974	146.7	144.9	148.1	148	144	149
1975	174.4	175.0	174.0	171	168	178
1976	200.1	204.8	196.7	189	187	204
1977	228.0	234.7	223.1	216	206	233
1977						
1st qtr	216.4	223.8	211.0	204	192	222
2nd	222.0	230.4	215.8	204	202	227
3rd	234.2	239.4	230.4	224	213	240
4th	239.4	245.3	235.1	231	219	243
1978						
1st qtr	246.0	249.5	243.5	237	228	252
2nd	254.5	258.6	251.5	243	243	258
3rd	267.5	266.9	267.9	266	254	274
1977						
October	234.2	241.7	228.7	218	214	239
November	236.3	242.3	231.9	228	213	241
December [1]	246.0	250.6	242.7	244	227	248

Two clearly designed tables: *above*, from *Endeavour*, no. 122, May 1975; *below*, from *Trade & Industry*, 8 December 1978. In the latter example, the use of space, both horizontally and vertically, and the restrained use of bold type, is to be noted.

If reproduction without colour may happen, the designer can at least try to ensure that the information is not actually lost in such circumstances: for example, lettering printed in black or colour on a solid colour may disappear in reproduction, but should be legible if reversed out. When information is conveyed by lines, an alternative to different colours is variation in the lines, e.g. pecked, dotted, squares, etc.

If rules are being used, they should if possible be of one thickness only, and of never more than two. If two thicknesses of rule are being used, it is because there is an important distinction in meaning between them, and the difference should be distinctive, bearing in mind the printing process, which if poor may cause thin rules to thicken, and vice versa. Non-specialist readers will not notice a difference in rule thickness unless it is very obvious: e.g. (perhaps) $\frac{1}{2}$ pt (0.25 mm) and 2 pt (0.75 mm) if properly printed. This applies also to the use of bold type. In many fonts, even Times New Roman, the bold is not distinctive enough, especially in poor printing. Bold is better contrasted with a light version of a type, as in Univers Light. Double rules are of little value, and should be avoided.

Where tables consist of long vertical columns of figures, it is desirable to insert a space after every five lines of figures, for ease of reading.

In most composition systems, all figures have the same width, usually an en, so that it is easy to calculate how many figures will fit in a given length of line. But note the point made in Chapter 6, that in deciding column widths, the 'set' of the type must be taken into consideration.

In designing a complicated table, perhaps with fractions, superior figures, letters and words, it is important to design using only what is available on the die-case or font (otherwise the cost of composition will greatly increase) and this must be ascertained beforehand.

The design of the figures becomes an important factor in table setting. The designer must decide whether lining or non-lining figures should be used, and find out if they are available. The designer must also make sure that his client, who may be an expert with figures, approves of the way the designer wants the tables to look.

Tables, like illustrations, are often 'landscape' in shape, and the old problem will arise of whether to set them sideways so that the page has to be turned to read them. Since having to turn the page for some tables and not for others is a nuisance, it should be avoided if possible. It is surprising how often tables can be redesigned or divided so that they can be set to fit on a normal upright page.

It is obviously more economical to set all tables in a single work in the same size of type, and this will be the size in which the longest table can be made to fit. But to avoid setting a mass of tables in a size that is too small for convenient reading, it should be remembered that a table that is too long to fit on a page can be reduced photographically (or set across a double spread if it is very big, but this solution creates further problems of alignment) or, as an exception, set in smaller size. If the job is being printed lithographically, type can be photographed down to a very small size indeed and still be legible.

If the tables are included in a two- or multi-column setting, a problem arises affecting the continuity of the text. A table (or for that matter any illustration) should *never* be placed in the middle of a multi-column page, since it interferes with reading continuity. If the table or tables cannot be placed on a page by themselves, they should be placed at the head or foot of the page, and separated from the text by a considerable white space or a fine rule. If a table can be designed to single column width and can be placed above or below its relevant text, it may be better placed in its column, perhaps with a rule above and below, but the look and reading-continuity of the page as a whole must be considered.

Timetables, like every other typographical problem, require a strict analysis of exactly what information is required by whom, where and when. A good introduction to timetable design, but now rather out of date, is Christian Barman's article 'Timetable Typography' in *Typography*, 5 (1938). Timetables should be designed using the twenty-four hour clock, unless there is an extremely good reason for not doing so.

PROGRAMMES AND MENUS

In *In The Day's Work* (Cambridge, Mass., 1924) the Boston printer Daniel Berkeley Updike gives some advice, still valid more than fifty years later, on how a printer (or typographer) should handle his clients on questions of design. And on menus, he writes:

'One can only plan successfully these smaller pieces of work by considering minutely what they are meant to accomplish. Let us take a menu. What questions would be uppermost in one's mind in planning that? The first that would occur to me would be the hour of the meal and where it was to be served. Was it to be by day or night? If by day, by artificial light or not? The colour of the card and the size of type would be somewhat dependent on this. Was there any particular scheme of colour in the decorations of the table? Because my menu must either match or at least not be discordant with it. Was it to be a big table with ample room for each guest, or a small one? Was the menu to be laid on a napkin or to stand upright? That would dictate my choice of size; for a menu is an incident, not a feature, at a dinner, and should not be so large as to be in the way if laid down, nor so big as to knock over glasses and fall into one's plate if it is to stand. Decide all these little points in the light of "What is

South Wales —→ The North
Mondays to Saturdays

	Swansea	Cardiff Central	Newport	Pontypool	Abergavenny	Hereford	Leominster	Ludlow
		05 32	05 49	06 06	06 20	06 56g	07 12	07 25
C	05 44	→	→	→	→	→	→	→
	06 40	07 50	08 07	08 23	08 36	09 11	09 27	09 41
B								
A								
C	09 59	→	→	→	→	→	→	→
	09 43	11 30	11 46	12 04	12 17	12 50	13 06	13 19
H						13 42H	→	→
H						14 57H	→	→
C	12 25	→	→	→	→	→	→	→
K						15 23K	→	→
	13 43	15 10	15 24	15 42	15 55	16 27	16 43	16 56
J						17 12J	→	→
C	14 53	→	→	→	→	→	→	→
	15 43	17 10	17 27	17 44	17 57	18 29	18 45	18 58
	17 43	18 45	19 02	19 18	19 30	20 01a		
						20 15	20 31	20 44
F								
A	18 43A	20 05A	20 23A	20 39A	20 54A	21 27Ar	→	21 50A
C	18 57	→	→	→	→	→	→	→
A								
	19 43	22 25	23 02	23 19	23 31	00 01a		

London—→Reading—→Didcot—→Oxford
Mondays to Fridays

		Paddington depart	Reading arrive	Reading depart	Didcot arrive	Oxford arrive
				00 03	00 18	00 35N
				00 09N	00 42N	01 05N
		00 15M	01 00M	01 06M	01 26M	01 45M
		01 48	02 39			
				06 14	06 44	07 06
		05 12b	06 42	06 44	07 14	07 31
		05 42	07 02			
	125	06 40	07 07	07 07	07 21	
R	125	06 45	07 14	07 14	07 32	07 49
R		07 00	07 27	07 27	07 41	08 16
		07 00	07 27	07 49	08 19	08 41
R		07 30	08 01			
R	125	07 45	08 12	08 12	08 26	
R		07 55	08 29	08 29	08 49	09 05
R	125	08 15	08 37			
		08 15	08 37	08 44	09 14	09 36
R	125	08 20	08 43			
R		08 30	09 00			
R	125	08 47	09 14	09 14	09 28	10 13
		08 47	09 14	09 19	09 49	10 13
R		08 50	09 20	09 20	→	09 50
R		08 57C	09 27C			
		08 59	09 57	09 59	10 29	10 45
R		09 35	10 05			
R	125	09 45	10 12	10 12	10 26	10 45
R		09 55	10 25	10 25	→	10 57
R				10 36	→	11 06
R	125	10 15	10 37			
R	125	10 20	10 43			
		10 20	10 43	10 59	11 29	11 45
R		10 30	11 00			
R	125	10 45	11 12	11 12	11 26	11 45
R		10 50	11 21	11 21	→	11 53

Two admirable British Rail pocket timetable designs (actual size). Bold type indicates through trains, light type connecting services.

the thing used for? Where is it to be used? By whom is it to be used? What is the most suitable, practical, simple, orderly, and historical method of producing it?"'

And on music programmes, he observes: 'Here, again, you must know the hour; it must be printed on a single sheet of paper or upon a card; it must not have a printed border close to the margin; it must be in fairly large type. Why? Because the light makes a difference in the colour of paper and ink to be used; because a programme of more than one page rustles when turned over; because the ink may spoil light gloves if it is too near the edge and is much handled; and because all ages and kinds of eyes are to read it. If it is too long a concert for a programme on one page, then one can use a soft or unsized paper, so that it will not "rattle" when turned. And as to the style of the thing, "the world is all before you where to choose". What is the music to be played? Old or modern, French or English, sacred or secular, serious or gay? There are all sorts of sources to be consulted for the appropriate decorations for these varied classes of music.'

Inflation and the instability of prices in recent years has made it more and more difficult for businesses to publish price lists which remain valid for even a short time after they have been printed. As a result it has become common practice to print menus, for example, without prices, and to fill the prices in by hand as necessary. Complicated colour-printed catalogues are issued with separate pricelists which can be renewed as needed: these must therefore be dated and of course identified in some way with the catalogue to which they belong, in case they get separated from it.

Price lists are in one of those categories of printing in which any misprint may be disastrous. Typographers looking after price lists, with a responsibility for passing them for press, must always make sure that they have a passed proof *signed by the client*: because a price list with wrong prices in it is useless and could be rejected – the client refusing to pay for it – if it contains mistakes.

CALENDARS

The typographical design of a calendar depends on the distance at which it is to be read. Basically there are two kinds of calendar: ones to stand on the desk, which must therefore be neat and small, and which can be turned over with one hand if the other is holding a telephone; and others to be hung on a wall, which must be legible at a distance of say ten to fifteen feet at least.

Calendars can be designed in all sorts of ways, to show a week, a month, a quarter, or even a year at a time; many ingenious solutions have been found, and it is well worth making a collection of the most pleasing examples. If the calendar is seriously required as a calendar (not merely as a wall decoration) clarity in the figures is vital. A distinction

These borders, taken from a corner of Monotype ornament Broadsheet no. 3 (in *Monotype News Letter*, 54, March 1958) show some of the richness available to typographers that is today largely unexploited. These borders are mostly of nineteenth-century origin but are full of twentieth-century potential.

should be made in the figures for Sundays, e.g. by printing them in red, or in bold.

A calendar which is both useful and attractive enough to keep on one's wall for a year is a challenge for any designer's skill.

AMBIGUITY

The business of all designers, but especially typographers, is efficient and aesthetically satisfying communication. G. K. Chesterton's dictum that 'if a thing is worth doing, it is worth doing badly', is worth remembering for several reasons, one of them being the importance of analysing whether a thing is worth doing in the first place. When the matter to communicate is a public notice or for display on a public noticeboard, the problems for the typographic designer are acute indeed. The more important the message, the more important it is to find the right way to communicate it – *especially* if danger to life is involved. If the message is 'NO SMOKING because of danger from fire' then almost certainly this must be communicated pictorially with the use of red, a colour recognized internationally for expression of danger.

In a recent broadcast concerned with these problems, John Sparrow[1] quoted some good examples of typographic ambiguity; one was:

LOOSE STONES TRAVEL SLOWLY

He pointed out that the meaning would have been clearer if it had been presented in two lines as:

TRAVEL SLOWLY
LOOSE STONES

Similar observed ambiguities were PETROL SNACKS and PARKING TOILETS.

In short, and especially for 'warning' notices, the designer must always think if the message really needs words or could be better expressed pictorially or symbolically.

In longer messages – for instance the notices that tell people whether they qualify for, and how to register for, benefits – the words *must* be right before the typographer can turn them into type; the writing and the designing are the same problem. But even when the words are right, the typographer may make errors which are purely typographic: some examples are shown here.

4·1

Eg shop, shop with living
accommodation, office,
factory, sports ground etc

The omission of the full points,
normally permissible, here makes
one wonder if it is a misprint for
'egg shop'. (From an Inland
Revenue form about Rating.)

In 1975/76, 666,681 passengers
were carried on
the London to Glasgow
shuttle service.

During 1975/76,
British Airways Helicopters carried
80, 170 passengers on its service from
Penzance to the Isles of Scilly.

Two examples of typographical
ambiguity from the otherwise
admirably designed British Airways
Annual Report & Accounts 1975–76.
How many passengers were carried
on the London–Glasgow shuttle?
There should have been extra space
between 76 and 666 in the example
above, or, better still, the
juxtaposition of the two sets of
figures should have been avoided by
beginning the sentence with '666,
681'. In the lower example, the space
after the comma in 80, 170
(inconsistent with the spacing of
666, 681 above) does not help.

POSTERS

Pictorial posters, which at best carry fewest or no words, are outside the scope of this book. Typographical posters or wall-sheets are subject to the same rules and considerations that apply to all typography, modified by whatever special requirements exist for the particular job, the way and conditions in which it is displayed, the people it is aimed at and the distance at which it will be both seen and read. As in all 'display' typography, the number of 'groups' in the design should not exceed three or at most four, and the relationship between the groups, and the order in which they are read, should be absolutely clear and logical. A 'group' is something that is comprehended and understood (not necessarily read) at a single glance: it might be a symbol, a bold exclamation mark, a large capital letter, an illustration, or a paragraph, but it has to be a 'unity'.

If the poster is a long statement to be displayed and read (e.g. the announcement and details of a competition, or the Factories Act, or the details of course-enrolment for a university noticeboard) it should probably be treated as a normal reading page, enlarged to the size appropriate for the distance at which it is to be read. But to look coherent, headings should probably be set in extra bold upper and lower case, and all groups or sections should be clearly demarcated by generous use of white space.

A typographic poster (*c.* 1900) printed from wood letters: 'JAM POTS' is printed in red, the rest in blue (reduced from 425 × 342 mm). Simple and effective.

A poster designed by F. H. K. Henrion for an oil company in 1960.

12 Newspaper and magazine typography

'And the very first essential is to realise that design is part of journalism. Design is not decoration. It is communication.'

Harold Evans, *Newspaper Design* (London 1973), p. 1

The connection between writing and designing is even closer in newspapers and magazines than in books: the typographer in these fields cannot work in isolation, in an ivory tower. The pages of a newspaper are subject to total change up to within minutes of going to press. The processes of writing, editing and design may have to take place simultaneously, as the latest story comes in to the office by phone, wire or tape. A typographical style and master plan will have been laid down beforehand, but when it is put into practice, the words and the design have to be right first time; the presses cannot wait.

NEWSPAPER DESIGN

It is probably true that today London's newspapers are the best-designed, typographically speaking, in the world. *The Times* is considered by most typographers to be the world's best: but the *Financial Times*, *Daily Express*, *Evening News*, *Evening Standard*, and the two weeklies, *Sunday Times* and *Observer*, all maintain high standards. Whether any of them will still exist when this Manual is published, is anyone's guess. The future of national newspapers is in doubt all over the globe: the purveying of 'news' (which is only one of a newspaper's functions) is in several respects more interesting, more immediate and more dramatic on a TV screen. The greater part of all newspapers is given over to advertising (the revenue from which keeps them and magazines alive) and to features of comment, information and entertainment, which might just as well be found in magazines. If national newspapers succumb, at least in their present shapes and with the prime function of purveying the world's latest news, it may be a serious, even a tragic loss; but it is probable that local newspapers will continue to lead a healthy, useful and profitable existence for many years to come – and provide opportunities for typographers.

The design of newspapers and magazines is essentially related to the methods of composition and printing. London's national newspapers are all still set hot metal by Linotype and printed by rotary letterpress. Colour is at the moment not possible for news items because of the time factor, but is increasingly used for advertisements, which are pre-printed on one side of the paper by offset-litho in a different factory, and then have news printed on the other side of the sheet by letterpress, before being inserted into the complete paper.

A newspaper proprietor starting a new newspaper today, buying totally new equipment, would probably choose filmsetting, probably computer-aided and keyboarded by journalists, and offset-litho printing, if he could get the

Previous page: illustration from Joseph Crawhall, *Chap-book Chaplets*, 1876.

printing unions to co-operate: many newspapers in Europe and America (including most provincial British newspapers) are already being produced in this way. Apart from advantages in speed of composition and make-up, the quality of reproduction of photographs and drawings by litho is far superior to what can be achieved on newsprint by newspaper letterpress machines.

Although the principles of typography are basically the same in newspapers and in books, the purposes of news-papers, the methods of writing, editing, design and production, and the uses of newspapers, are all so different that it requires, not a chapter, but a Manual to itself, which has recently been provided by Harold Evans, the editor of the *Sunday Times* (see Further reading list).

Professional book typographers have been called in to design newspapers – Stanley Morison was the most notable, if not the first – but I think it is true that although the concept of a newspaper may be planned in isolation at a typographer's desk – or in his bath – it cannot become an effective reality until it is thrashed out in the newspaper office, under the pressures that exist there, in close collaboration between designers and journalists. In fact, good newspaper design (which doesn't have to happen, as in a book, once only, but has to happen daily, nightly or weekly) depends on designers becoming journalists, and journalists becoming designers. I myself experienced this in the offices of *The Observer*, when I was asked to help design, in 1960, the new 'Week-End Review'.

The Observer was the first of the British Sundays to divide itself into separate sections. For several months I designed, partly at home and partly in *The Observer's* office, the first page of the 'Week-End Review' section. On one occasion, the front page consisted of 21 poems called 'Symptoms of Love' by Robert Graves. I thought that if the poems were set in a conventional book face the page would look like something the readers would feel they had seen before, so I set the poems in a sans-serif, Monotype 215 (because Univers was not then available). To my astonishment, a senior book designer at Penguin Books wrote a pained letter to the editor, complaining that poems should never be set in sans . . .

I was then asked to redesign the whole paper. I could only have done this by leaving all other work and joining the staff, in fact by becoming a journalist – and a special kind of journalist at that, one whose week's busiest working time was Saturday and Saturday night. It wasn't practicable for me, but luckily just at that moment a journalist appeared who had made himself a designer, the first of a new breed. Clive Irving joined *The Observer* from the *Daily Express* and effectively redesigned *The Observer* before going on to the *Sunday Times*, accepting my suggestions, already made, to use Century Schoolbook as the main display face, the first time it was ever used editorially in a British newspaper.*

At the moment the future of national newspapers appears

*From a letter written at the time by Clive Irving to the author: 'The enticement-content of a headline depends, I think, eighty per cent on the wording and twenty per cent on the type.'

to be dim, but not that of local newspapers. They are still profitable, and badly needed: they perform functions in local and community life that cannot be performed by TV or anything else. But very many of them are badly designed – which means also that they are badly edited. The reporting of local news is too often 'parochial' in the worst sense; the real news, which is happening all the time, is badly reported (e.g. in an important coastal paper, catering for a seafaring community, three men were drowned in a boat accident, but it is impossible to find out what kind of boat, what sails were set, or the strength or direction of the wind or current). Such papers today are often printed by web-offset-litho, a process capable of giving superb quality of reproduction in both photographs and drawings: but the photographs are usually appalling and drawings are never used editorially. There is no sign, throughout the paper, of any art direction, of any appreciation that some things – many things – in daily life are beautiful; there is very little sign that some things in village, country and town life are interesting, apart from murder and rape. Yet everywhere there are thriving art schools and an abundant supply of young people who can draw – and are learning to design – with outstanding talent.

Colour is used only when it is paid for by advertisers, and if, because an advertiser has booked a page in colour, colour can be used editorially on the same side of the sheet, it will probably be misused: colour printing on newsprint by high-speed web-offset is not yet nearly as good or as predictable as monochrome printing, and subjects for it need to be chosen with care. Advertisers have more time to do this (although they do not always succeed) than editors; but it is no good designing a page with editorial colour for a small press in Neasden as if one had at one's disposal the colour-printing facilities of a Swiss photogravure plant. It must be obvious from experience that the human face is rarely a good subject for high-speed colour printing of dubious quality on poor paper: but simple subjects in close-up, in simple, strong colours, from large transparencies, have more hope.

For some reason, it is always assumed that 'colour printing' means 'four-colour process printing'. (The reason of course is that colour printing is usually paid for by advertisers, and advertisers cannot think of any other method of advertising in colour than colour photography, which can be printed only by the four-colour process.) But there is an alternative. It is simple. If the colour (i.e. four-colour process) printing available is poor, don't use colour photographs and don't use trichromatic process inks. Use drawings and one or two of the other less commonly used colours that are in the ink-makers' tins.

I know of only one occasion when this was done. An American designer, Arnold Varga, designed a series of full-page advertisements for a department store called Cox's, which consisted mostly of simple strong drawings and typography, white space, and simple, strong colours,

Opposite: one of Arnold Varga's series of advertisements for Cox's department store, in *The Daily News*, McKeesport, Pa., 3 July 1959 (reduced from 584 × 385 mm). The tongs were printed in black, the type in light blue and very slightly darker blue, on newsprint.

THE DAILY NEWS, McKEESPORT, PA., FRIDAY EVENING, JULY 3, 1959

COOL, MAN, COOL—THE BIG FASHION VALUES IN COX'S 3-STORE JULY CLEARANCE BEGINNING MONDAY, RIGHT AFTER A RED HOT FOURTH! AND BY THE WAY, DON'T BE A SQUARE. DRIVE SAFELY, BECAUSE WE WANT TO SEE YOU ON MONDAY (10 'TIL 9)

including subtler ones like greys and browns, used sometimes singly and sometimes together. The ads must have
been far cheaper to print than four-colour reproductions, and
were visually brilliant. They were printed in the McKeesport,
Pennsylvania, *Daily News* between 1956 and 1960, and
deserve an honoured place in any history of graphic design.
Some day, somebody will have this idea again, and it will also
be used to lift editorial pages. All it needs is a designer who is
a journalist – or vice versa – and a touch of brilliance.

MAGAZINE DESIGN

Many, if not most, of the pages in today's national
newspapers are in fact magazine pages: they are not 'news',
but for recreation and information. Many magazines (e.g.
Blackwoods and *London Magazine*) are essentially for serious
reading and therefore, from the designer's point of view, like
books.

Nearly all magazines depend, for commercial viability, on
advertising revenue: they are designed to interest a public
who have money to spend on clothes and cosmetics (*Vogue*,
Harper's & Queen), on houses, interior decoration, garden-
ing, food (*House & Garden, Good Housekeeping*), on cars (*Car,
Motor*), on wine (*Decanter*), on art and furniture (*Apollo, The
Connoisseur*), and so on. These glossy magazines with high
budgets (and, if unsuccessful, high losses) are dependent on
fashion, flair, brilliant art direction, all matters which are far
beyond the guidance on basic principles which is the
province of this book.

But many periodical publications, from parish magazines
upwards, or downwards, are produced on very low budgets
and constantly require a designer's guidance: they are one of
the jobs most often offered to young typographers. Whether
the work is adequately paid or, as often happens, completely
unpaid (because there is no money, but the typographer is a
Boy Scout, or a chess player, or whatever), they are usually
important in themselves (to their own public) and invaluable
to the young designer as a chance to exercise and prove his
skills.

A periodical, by definition, appears periodically. The first
design problem is therefore how to make use of this fact and
rationalize the design and production. From the customer's
point of view, there is normally a strong argument in favour
of a standard 'pattern': people who look at a magazine
regularly (whether they buy it, borrow it, or get it pushed
through their letterbox) want to recognize it as they do a
friend; they want the layout to be familiar.

The contributions that make up a magazine tend to come
from different sources, perhaps handwritten, certainly, if
typed, typed on different machines, in different styles and
with different amounts of skill and accuracy. They must first
of all be 'edited', i.e. given a fairly standard system of

spelling, punctuation and general style; given titles, sub-titles if used, by-lines and so on in the style of the publication, and generally prepared for the printer. The typographer has to devise a typographical treatment that is as simple as possible: the simplest is for every article to be set in the same typeface, same size, and to the same measure, similarly with the headings and by-lines. There is then no need to mark up every article individually. When galleys are received, the designer must then make an accurate page-by-page paste-up, incorporating whatever illustrations are used and marrying the editorial text with the advertisements. Sometimes one type size and measure is not enough: many magazines need to be organized as (a) main matter, in one size and in either single or double column; and (b) subsidiary matter (club news, book reviews, announcements) in a smaller size and in two or three columns. If all article titles can be given a standard typographical treatment, the designer should not need to mark them up individually.

The most economical way to manage a low-budget magazine is to send all copy for an issue to the printer, if necessary in instalments, with standard setting instructions, and make a page-by-page paste-up when everything has been set. If there are illustrations, the sizes can be decided when it is seen, at the paste-up stage, what space is available. The exact size of each illustration is drawn on the paste-up, captions are marked, and when blocks or plates have been made, the printer supplies complete page proofs. If illustrations can be made in a few standard sizes (e.g. single column, or double column), they can be so marked at the same time that copy is sent for setting – which will save time, but (unless an exact cast-off has been made for the article) at the paste-up stage there may be problems in making articles fit, especially if they should each begin at the top of a page. The problem is usually met by having a stock of 'fillers', i.e. short items (text or drawings) which can be used arbitrarily to fill empty spaces.

The questions that a designer needs to ask before designing a periodical are:

(1) Who is the publisher? Are there sales, business and advertising managers?

(2) Who is the editor?

(3) Does the periodical make a profit? Is it intended to make a profit, and is it possible for it to make a profit?

(4) What is the purpose of the publication? Who are its readers?

(5) What is the print run per issue, and how many issues are there per year?

(6) How is it sold? Are there bookstall sales, which would influence the cover design?

(7) What is the page size, number of pages, and other physical details, such as number of colour pages, advertisements, etc.?

(8) Who is the printer, what are the methods of composition, printing, etc., and what is the production schedule (i.e. how

Head of division

L. Lightman
K. G. H. Binning
I. H. Lightman

H. L. Cousins
B. A. Smouha
C. F. H. Morland
M. H. Peacock

W. R. Atkinson
D. M. Dell
W. R. G. Bell

D. C. Clark
J. H. Major ·

Head of division

J. F. J. Jardine
D. N. Royce
E. J. Field

G. Lanchin
S. Abramson

G. R. Sunderland
Miss M. J. Lackey
R. A. Browning
R. Williams

Letraset 'Cooper Black' figures given good use on information pages in the Government publication *Trade and Industry* (reduced by about 50 per cent from two different pages). Note the cutting in between the rules.

much time is available for the design and make-up of each issue; this will affect the possibilities of commissioning designs for lettering, illustrations, etc., at paste-up stage)?
All these questions will lead to other questions, depending on the nature of the magazine and its individual problems.

The design of a magazine is never simply a visual one: the words, especially the headings, article titles, sub-titles and so on, are part of the design, and must be right before the design can be right. Normally, one of the chief purposes of an article title is to tell the reader what the article is about, so that he can choose whether to read it or skip it. Article titles which are possibly witty but obscure in meaning are therefore to be avoided.

Magazines are not books, although the same basic principles of typography apply. A magazine designer is competing for the reader's attention with many other diversions: magazine pages should not, therefore (if possible), consist of unrelieved, solid columns of type. If illustrations are not used, solid type should be relieved, if possible, by paragraphs, by extra space between paragraphs, by crossheads, by initials, by any devices which are amusing, which will catch and please the reader's eye.

Designers should build up their own collections of pleasing magazine pages.

Cover of the *Sunday Times Magazine*, 30 December 1979 (reduced from 300 × 242 mm); art director Michael Rand; designer Clive Crook. A brilliant use of headlines from British and American newspapers to sum up the events of the previous decade.

Notes on the text

CHAPTER 1 (pp. 12–32)

1 D. Diringer, *The Alphabet*, 3rd edn, London 1968.
2 T. F. Carter, *The Invention of Printing in China*, 2nd edn, New York 1955, p. 31.
3 A. M. Hind, *An Introduction to the History of Woodcut*, vol. I, Boston and London 1935 (reprinted London 1963), p. 67.
4 C. P. Hargrave, *A History of Playing Cards*, 1930 (reprinted London 1966).
5 Hind 1935, op. cit.
6 See H. Lehmann-Haupt, *Gutenberg and the Master of the Playing Cards*, New Haven and London 1966.
7 See A. Ruppel, *Johannes Gutenberg, sein Leben und sein Werk*, Berlin 1947.
8 For an excellent illustrated account of the process see Paul Koch's article in *The Dolphin*, no. 1 (1933); see also *Fournier on Typefounding*, translated by Harry Carter, London 1930, and the photographs of punches, matrices, moulds etc. in *Printing and the Mind of Man*, London 1963.
9 The Monotype Corporation published the following table of recommended admixtures:

For
General low-
grade composition
with short runs

TIN 7, ANTIM 15, LEAD 78

Higher class work
with good length
runs

TIN 10, ANTIM 20, LEAD 70

Good news and
book, for long
runs and sharp
stereos. Free-
flowing

TIN, 12, ANTIM 18, LEAD 70

Large hard display
type, for long usage

TIN 12, ANTIM 24, LEAD 64

10 See C. H. Bloy, *A History of Printing Ink*, London 1967.
11 See H. P. Kraus, Catalogue 131, New York 1971, in which the Shuckburgh copy of the Gutenberg Bible is illustrated in colour and described. In 1978, this copy of Gutenberg's Bible came back to Mainz, at a cost of 3.7 million DM (approx-imately $2 million or £1 million); and Abe Lerner, *Fine Print*, San Francisco 1978.
12 See C. F. Bühler, *The Fifteenth Century Book*, Philadelphia and Oxford 1960.
13 A. F. Johnson, *Type Designs*, 3rd edn, London 1966.
14 Johnson 1966, op. cit.
15 For the history of italic, see A. F. Johnson, *Type Designs*, 3rd edn, Chs. 5 and 6.
16 An excellent facsimile with an introduction by James Mosley was published by the Eugrammia Press in 1965.
17 H. G. Carter, *Fournier on Typefounding*, 1930, p. xx.
18 Johnson 1966, op. cit., p.123.
19 Carter 1930, op. cit.
20 S. Morison, *A Tally of Types*, 2nd edn, Cambridge 1973. See also Allen Hutt, *Fournier, the Compleat Typographer*, London 1972, p. 76.

21 D. B. Updike, *Printing Types*, vol. II, Oxford 1922, p. 174.
22 Morison 1973, op. cit., p. 31.
23 R. McLean, *Victorian Book Design and Colour Printing*, 2nd edn, London 1972, p. 73.
24 McLean 1972, op. cit., p. 233.
25 O. Simon, *Printer and Playground*, London 1956.
26 J. Moran, *The Double Crown Club*, London 1974.

CHAPTER 3 (pp. 42–48)

1 S. P. E. Tract 23, *English Handwriting*, Oxford 1926.
2 P. Beaujon (B. Warde), *The Monotype Recorder*, vol. 32, no. 1 (1933).
3 In a speech in Edinburgh, 17 July 1933, printed in *The Monotype Recorder*, vol. 32, no. 3 (1933).
4 H. Spencer and Linda Reynolds, *The Study of Legibility*, Readability of Print Unit, Royal College of Art, London, n.d.
5 J. Kachergis, 'A Plea for Beauty', *Scholarly Publishing*, vol. 9, no. 1. (1977).

CHAPTER 4 (pp. 50–56)

1 *Encyclopaedia Britannica*, 14th edn, 1929.
2 *Dossier A–Z 73*, edited by Fernand Baudin, Association Typographique Internationale, 1973, p. 18.

CHAPTER 5 (pp. 58–78)

1 *La chose imprimée*, Paris 1977, p. 581.
2 G. K. Schauer, *Klassifikation: Bemühungen um eine Ordnung im Druckschriften-bestand*, Darmstadt 1975.

3 A. Nesbitt, *Lettering*, New York 1950.
4 Nesbitt 1950, op. cit.
5 P. M. Handover, 'Letters without Serifs', *Motif*, 6 (1961), p. 66.
6 *The Monotype Recorder*, vol. 41, no. 3 (1958), a special number devoted to Gill's work which is beautifully illustrated and essential reading. See also R. Harling, *The Letter Forms and Type Designs of Eric Gill*, Westerham 1976, with excellent illustrations.
7 K. Rowland, *A History of the Modern Movement*, New York 1973, p. 213.
8 See a reproduction of pages from it in H. Spencer's *Pioneers of Modern Typography*, London, 1969.
9 T. M. Cleland, *The Fine Art of Printing*, New York Public Library, n.d.
10 P. Gaskell, *A New Introduction to Bibliography*, Oxford 1972, p. 33.

11 Legros and Grant, *Typographical Printing Surfaces*, London 1916. See also W. Ovink, 'From Fournier to metric, and from lead to film', *Quaerendo*, Holland, vol. 9, no. 2 (1979), pp. 95–127.
12 *Typographic Dimensions*, leaflet p. 139/E/74 from 'Type Study Leaflets for Students', published by the Monotype Corporation.
13 Gaskell 1972, op. cit., p. 195.

CHAPTER 6 (pp. 80–92)

1 See *U & lc*, vol. 4, no. 3 (1977), pp. 54–56.

CHAPTER 7 (pp. 94–108)

1 *A Dictionary of Science*, Harmondsworth 1964.
2 R. H. Clapperton, *Paper and its Relation to Books*, London 1934, p. 55.
3 *The Dolphin*, no. 1 (New York 1933).

4 Dard Hunter, *Papermaking*, London 1957.
5 H. Williamson, *Methods of Book Design*, 2nd edn, London 1966, p. 297.

CHAPTER 8 (pp. 110–118)

1 Reproduced in full in R. McLean, *Jan Tschichold, Typographer*, London 1975.

CHAPTER 9 (pp. 120–146)

1 See H. de Balzac, *Droll Stories*, designed by W. A. Dwiggins, 3 vols., The Limited Editions Club, New York 1932.
2 I. Reiner, *Modern and Historical Typography*, St Gall 1946.

CHAPTER 11 (pp. 178–196)

1 Reprinted in *The Listener*, 5 July 1979, p. 15.

Appendix 1: list of suppliers

UK

STUDIO EQUIPMENT

British Thornton Ltd, P.O. Box 3, Wythenshawe, Manchester M22 4SS. 'Double Top' desks, 'Desra' system of furniture, work surfaces, etc., and some of the best-designed drawing instruments available.

Cowling and Wilcox Ltd, 26 Broadwick Street, London W1. Designers' and artists' equipment.

Geliot Whitman Ltd, 16A Herschell Road, London SE23 1EQ. Type gauges and studio equipment.

Langford & Hill Ltd, 38–40 Warwick Street, London W1R 5RB.

Letraset UK Ltd, 195/203 Waterloo Road, London SE1 8JA. Their catalogue includes the whole Letraset Graphic Arts System, Pantone products, Color-Key (the 3M process for producing colour images from black-and-white originals).

Lucas Furniture Systems, 616 Wick Lane, Old Ford, London E3 2JJ. Desks, chairs, screens and storage.

Magpie Furniture Ltd, Four Marks, Alton, Hants. Adjustable easels, seats and matching plan chests.

Mines & West, Downley, High Wycombe, Bucks HP13 5TX. 'Utopia' adjustable draughtsmen's chairs.

Rabone Chesterman, Whitmore Street, Birmingham B18 5BZ. Steel rulers.

Rotobord Ltd, Stanmore Industrial Estate, Bridgnorth, Shropshire. Rotary draughting machines and precision drawing equipment.

Rotring: write to Hartley, Reece & Co., Building no. 1, G.E.C. Estate, East Lane, Wembley, Middlesex HA9 7PY, for Rotring Catalogue of pens, drawing instruments, boards and other specialized design equipment.

Ryman Ltd, 126 Regent Street, London W1R 5FE. All office furniture and equipment.

TYPE SPECIMENS

Some are free; some have to be paid for, unless you are the purchaser of typesetting equipment, or a customer of the firm concerned.

The Monotype Corporation Ltd, Salfords, Redhill RH1 5JP publish a price list and catalogue of their publications. You will need their *Copy-fitting Tables for 'Monotype' and 'Monophoto' Faces*. See also their specimen sheets of special matrices (e.g. Crowns, Curves, Diamonds, Draughts, Engines and Waggons, Fish, Fists, Flags, and many others).

Linotype Ltd, Chelham House, Bath Road, Cheltenham, Glos. GL53 7LR, publish useful literature.

Many filmsetting companies produce invaluable specimens: e.g. Conway Group Graphics Ltd, 12–13 Molyneux Street, London, W1H 5HU, and Filmcomposition Ltd, 6–10 Valentine Place, London SE1 8QH.

Among many booksellers who specialize in fine books and printing are:

Bookworks, 'Gernon Elms', Letchworth Lane, Letchworth, Herts SG6 3NF.

Claude Cox, The White House, Kelsale, Saxmundham, Suffolk 1P17 2PQ;

Deval and Muir, Takeley, Bishop's Stortford, Herts;

Keith Hogg, 82 High Street, Tenterden, Kent TN30 7JJ;

Barry Mackay Rare Books, Kingstone House, Battlebarrow, Appelby-in-Westmoreland, Cumbria CA16 6XT;

Michael Taylor Rare Books, The Gables, 8 Nendham Lane, Harleston, Norfolk IT20 9DE.

PAPER

Suppliers aware of designers' needs for book and general printing papers

Grosvenor Chater & Co. Ltd, Bricknoll Park, Ashley Road, St Albans AL1 5UG.

G. F. Smith & Son (London) Ltd, 2 Leathermarket Street, London SE1 3ER.

Wiggins Teape Ltd, Gateway House, Basing View, Basingstoke RG21 2EE.

Fine papers

Falkiner Fine Papers Ltd, 76 Southampton Row, London WC1B 4AR.

T. N. Lawrence & Sons Ltd, 119 Clerkenwell Road, London EC1R 5BY.

Paperchase, 216 Tottenham Court Road, London W1.

Marbled Papers

The Basilisk Press Bookshop, 10 Adamson Road, London NW3 3HR.

The Cambray Bindery, 1 Bath Street, Cheltenham, Glos.

Compton Marbling, Lower Lawn Barns, Tisbury, Salisbury, Wilts SP3 6SG

Mitchell & Malik Ltd, 18 Cheshire Close, Salisbury, Wilts.

USA

GENERAL SUPPLIERS

Art Product News, P.O. Box 68356, Indianapolis, IN 46268.

Fine Art Materials Inc., 539 La Guardia Place, New York, N.Y. 10012.

Martin Instrument Co., 13450 Farmington Road, Livonia, Michigan 48150. Drawing desks, storage systems, drawing equipment, etc.

Rembrandt Graphic Arts, The Cave Farm, Rosemont, N.J. 08556.

PAPER

Andrews/Nelson/Whitehead, 31–10 48th Avenue, Long Island City, N.Y. 11101. Leading US supplier of fine

papers: stocks a wide range of domestic and imported European and Japanese handmade and machine-made papers.

Aiko, 714 North Wabash, Chicago, IL. Retail supplier of Japanese papers.

Yasutomo & Co., 24 California Street, San Francisco, CA 94111. Mainly wholesale supplier of fine papers.

Zellerbach Paper Co., 245 South Spruce Avenue, South San Francisco, CA 94080. Supplies fine papers to the western United States and the Pacific Islands. West coast dealer for A/N/W.

BOOKS ON TYPOGRAPHY

Herman Cohen, Walnut Tree Hill Road, Sandy Hook, Connecticut 06482. A bookseller who specializes in typography.

AUSTRALIA

Oswald-Sealy (overseas) Pty Ltd, 4 George Place, Artarmon, N.S.W. 2064. Wholesale importer and distributor of artists' materials, willing to inform artists of nearest retail stockist.

Appendix 2: British Standards Institution

The work of the British Standards Institution is wide-ranging and important throughout industry. Some knowledge of its activities, and those of similar bodies in other countries, with whom BSI collaborates, is necessary for every designer.

For publishers, BSI produces various documents recommending rationalization (on an international basis) in the presentation of standard

kinds of information, e.g. bibliographies, and showing how it should be done. To find the same kinds of information, in the same order, and expressed in the same, or similar, terminology, is an obvious help for both writers and readers.

In printing, there is a need for standardization in terminology, paper sizes and specifications, proof-correcting symbols and

usage, the specifying of colour, the application of the metric system to all printing measurements, and many other things. A number of recent standards deal with the preparation of copy destined to be put on microfilm.

BSI publish 'Sectional Lists' of British Standards, listing what is available in a given field. The two most applicable to readers of this book are: SL22 (*Printing and Stationery, paper and board*) and SL35 (*Documentation including UDC [Universal Decimal Classification]. Standards for the editor, publisher, librarian and information scientist*). The Sectional Lists give the number, title and price group of each publication listed, including any amendments issued since the original publication.

Full details (including

abstracts and prices) of all BSI publications are given in the *British Standards Yearbook*, which is complete to September of the preceding calendar year, and in *BSI News*, a monthly which provides information on all standards and amendments issued in the current year. The yearbook may be purchased from the sales department of BSI, but *BSI News* is available only to subscribing members;

enquiries concerning the advantages of subscribing membership (which brings, among other things, a substantial discount on the price of publications) are welcomed and should be made to Membership Services, BSI, Linford Wood, Milton Keynes MK14 6LE. Any other queries should be addressed to Customer Information, BSI, at the same address.

Glossary of filmsetting terms

(With grateful acknowledgments to *Glossary of Computer Typesetting Terms*, published by Seybold Publications Inc., and *Collins Dictionary of the English Language*, 1979.)

BINARY NOTATION OR SYSTEM A number system having a base of two, numbers being expressed by combinations of the digits 0 and 1, useful in computing, since 0 and 1 can be represented electrically as *off* and *on*. In a binary system (to a base of two) counting proceeds as follows: 0=0; 1=1; 10=2; 11=3; 100=4; 101=5, 110=6; 111=7.

CRT Cathode Ray Tube.

DIGITAL AND ANALOG Data expressed in binary notation is 'digital'; a 'digitized' typeface is drawn by steps on a grid. An analog computer performs arithmetical operations by using some variable physical quantity, such as voltage, to represent numbers. A light bulb may be on or off, and this would be a digital fact. But it could be brighter or dimmer, and this could be an analog fact.

FILMSETTER Machine for composing words on film.

H & J Hyphenation and justification. The division of words by the insertion of hyphens in order to justify lines (=make them of equal length) or avoid too ragged an appearance in unjustified setting. Words may be broken between syllables but not between all syllables. Rules for acceptable hyphenation have been established by various style manuals. In wide measures it may be possible to avoid hyphenation altogether. In all computerized setting, the rules for hyphenation must be written into the program.

HARDWARE Physical equipment used in a computer system.

LINE FEED The amount of advance between lines in a filmsetter, equivalent to 'leading' in hot-metal composition.

OCR Optical Character Recognition, i.e. the

conversion of graphic character images (usually typewritten in special characters) into electronically-coded data for subsequent processing. OCR sometimes stands for Optical Code (not Character) Recognition, where the image read consists of a bar diagram, or some combination of vertical lines, often accompanied, in the case of Datatype, by a human-readable character.

ON-LINE Equipment or device that is directly connected to and controlled by the central processing unit of a computer, by electronic signals and without recourse to an intervening medium such as paper tape.

PHOTOSETTER/ PHOTOTYPESETTER See FILMSETTER

SOFTWARE Computer programs.

VDT Visual Display Terminal.

VDU Visual Display Unit.

Further reading

INTRODUCTION

From the endless spate of books on design, the following by distinguished practitioners are recommended: none of them are 'How to do it' books.

Carter, S. *Twentieth Century type designers*, London 1987.
Fletcher, A. *Graphic Design: Visual Comparisons*, London 1963.
Gerstner, K. *The New Graphic Art*, Switzerland 1959.
Glaser, M. *Graphic Design*, New York 1973.
Hofmann, A. *Graphic Design Manual*, London 1965.
Rand, P. *Thoughts on Design*, New York 1947.
Ruder, E. *Typographie. Un Manuel de Création*, Switzerland 1967.
Scarfe, L. *Alphabets: an introductory treatise on written and printed letter forms*, London 1954.
Tracy, W. *Letters of Credit, a view of type design*, London 1986.

1 HISTORICAL OUTLINE

No definitive or good general history of printing exists. Try: H. G. Aldis, *The Printed Book*, 3rd edn, Cambridge 1951; and S. H. Steinberg, *Five Hundred Years of Printing*, London 1959, and Harmondsworth.
  Six well illustrated surveys are:
Art of the Printed Book, 1455–1955, New York 1973.
Blumenthal, J. *The Printed Book in America*, Boston 1977.
A History of the Printed Book, The Dolphin, vol. 3, New York 1938.
Levarie, N. *The Art & History of Books*, New York 1968.
Lewis, J. *Anatomy of Printing*, London 1970.
Morison, S. *The Typographic Book 1450–1935*, London 1963.

For an illustrated account of the history of the book in the East as well as the West, see H. D. L. Vervliet (ed.), *The Book through 5000 Years*, London 1972.

The history of illuminated manuscripts

D'Ancona, P. and Aeschlimann, E. *The Art of Illumination*, London 1969.
The Faber Library of Illuminated Manuscripts (numerous titles).
Harthan, J. *Books of Hours*, London and New York 1977.
Pächt, O. *The Master of Mary of Burgundy*, London 1948.
Les Très Riches Heures de Duc de Berry and other volumes of reproductions in colour of famous manuscripts, published by Thames and Hudson, London, and George Braziller, New York.

Miscellaneous

Heritage of the Graphic Arts, New York 1972. The text of twenty-two of the talks by various authors organized by Dr R. Leslie in New York, containing information and some portrait photographs not easily available elsewhere.
Morison, S. *The Art of the Printer*, London 1925.
Wilson, A. *The Making of the Nuremberg Chronicle*, Amsterdam 1976.

2 STUDIO AND EQUIPMENT

Editorial style and preparation of copy

Cambridge Authors' and Printers' Guides, a series published by Cambridge University Press.
Copy preparation and proof correction, BS 5261, parts 1 & 2, British Standards Institution 1975–6.
Dowding, G. *Finer Points in the Spacing and Arrangement of Type*, London 1966.
Fowler, H. W. (rev. Sir Ernest Gowers) *A Dictionary of Modern English Usage*, 2nd edn, Oxford 1965.
Gowers, Sir E. (rev. Sir Bruce Fraser) *The Complete Plain Words*, London 1973.
Hart, H. *Rules for Compositors and Readers at the University Press, Oxford*, 38th edn, Oxford 1978.
Hewitt, R. A. *Style for Print and Proof Correcting* London 1957.
Jacob, H. *Printed English*, London 1950.
Jarrett, J. *Printing style for Authors, Compositors, and Readers*, London 1960.
Rees, H. *Rules of Printed English*, London 1970.
Trebble, H. A. and Vallins, G. H. *An ABC of English Usage*, London 1936.

Miscellaneous reference works

Biggs, J. R. *Basic Typography*, London 1968.

Collins Dictionary of the English Language, 1979. The first new English Dictionary for many years.

Concise Oxford Dictionary, 6th edn, Oxford 1976, and other Oxford reference books, e.g. *The Oxford Paperback Dictionary*.

Der Grosse Duden (Picture dictionary of the German language), Harrap, London.

Fachwörterbuch des Buchwesens (Dictionary of Book Printing and Publishing terms, in German, English and French). Dr N. Stoytscheff, Darmstadt.

Garland, K. *Graphics, Design and Printing Terms*, London 1989.

Gibbs-Smith, C. H. *Copyright law concerning works of art, photographs and the written and spoken word*, Museums Association Information Sheet no. 7, from the Museums Association, 87 Charlotte St, London W1P 2BX.

Hostettler, R. *The Printer's Terms*, 4th edn, London 1963.

Jaspert, Berry & Johnson (eds.) *The Encyclopaedia of Type Faces*, 4th edn, London 1970.

Lettera 1, 2, 3, 4, Arthur Niggli Ltd, Switzerland (published in USA by Hastings House, New York). Valuable source-books giving whole alphabets of types and lettering for reproduction.

Lewis, J. *Typography: Design and Practice*, London 1977.

Periodicals

For typographic, printing and design periodicals, see the magazine racks in St Brides Printing Library, Bride Lane, London EC4. The following periodicals are to be recommended:

UK

The Designer, SIAD, 12 Carlton House Terrace, London SW1Y 5AH.

Typographic, Circulation Manager, Ed Cleary, 61 Water Lane, London SW2

USA

Visible Language (quarterly), Box 1972 CMA, Cleveland, Ohio 44106.

Fine Print, PO Box 7741, San Francisco, California 94120.

CA (Communication Arts), Coyne & Blanchard, Inc., 410 Sherman Avenue, Palo Alte, California.

U & lc. Free from U & lc. Subscription Dept., 2 Hammarskjold Plaza, New York, NY 10017. Published by International Typeface Corporation (ITC) who also publish an invaluable range of type specimen booklets.

Print, 355 Lexington Avenue, New York, NY 10017.

CANADA

Scholarly Publishing (quarterly), University of Toronto Press, Toronto, Canada M5S 146.

SWITZERLAND

Graphis

TM (Typografische Monatsblätter), Zollikofer AG, Furstenlandstrasse 122, 9001 St Gallen.

3 LEGIBILITY

Research into the legibility of print is voluminous. The best explanation and justification of research that matters is Herbert Spencer's *The Visible Word*, Lund Humphries, in association with the Royal College of Art, London 1969; it includes a bibliography of 464 items, so be warned. See also H. Spencer and Linda Reynolds, *The Study of Legibility*, Royal College of Art, London n.d.; Bror Zachrisson, *Studies in the Legibility of Printed Text*, Stockholm 1965; J. Hartley and P. Burnhill, *Textbook Design: a Practical Guide*, Unesco, May 1976; J. Hartley and P. Burnhill, *Programmed Learning and Educational Technology*, special issue of *The Journal of Aplet*, vol. 12, no. 2,

'Typographical Research', March 1975; and various numbers of *The Journal of Typographic Research* (renamed *Visible Language*), Cleveland, Ohio, e.g. Jeremy J. Foster, 'Locating Legibility Research: a Guide for the Graphic Designer', *Visible Language*, vol. XII, no. 2, Spring 1978. An excellent commonsense view of legibility and research, as particularly related to newspapers, is given in Book Two of Harold Evans, *Editing and Design*, London 1974.

Non-verbal communication

An introduction to this subject is James Hartley and Peter Burnhill, *Textbook Design* (simple guidelines for the production of primary school textbooks), Unesco: Division of Methods, Materials and Techniques, May 1976. From its bibliography we can also mention:

Davies, I. K. *The Management of Learning*, London and New York 1971.

Pictorial Representation, Edinburgh 1967.

Edwards, J. A. and Twyman, M. *Graphic Communication through Isotype*, University of Reading, Dept of Typography, 1975.

Wheatley, D. M. and Unwin, A. W. *The Algorithm Writer's Guide*, London 1972.

Programmed Learning and Educational Technology, vol. 12, no. 2, quoted above, gives a list of institutions in the UK currently engaged in various aspects of typographical research, and supplies contact names and addresses. The institutions named are:

College of Librarianship, University of Wales; Dept of Applied Psychology, University of Aston; Dept of Psychology, Brunel University; Dept of Psychology, University College London; Dept of Psychology, University of Keel; Dept of Typography,

University of Reading;
Institute of Science and
Technology, University of
Wales; Isotype Institute Ltd,
London; Loughborough
University of Technology;
Manchester Polytechnic;
MRC Applied Psychology
Unit, Cambridge; RAF
Institute of Aviation;
Readability of Print Unit,
Royal College of Art,
London; Textual
Communication Research
Unit, Institute of Educational
Technology, Open University.

4 LETTERING AND
CALLIGRAPHY

General

Ballinger, R. A. *Lettering Art
in Modern Use.* New York
1952. A fascinating
pictorial survey, with
commentary and some
instruction.
Baudin, F. and Dreyfus, J.
Dossier A–Z 73.
L'Association
Typographique
Internationale, 1973.
Dwiggins, W. A. 'The
Shapes of Roman Letters',
item IV in *MSS by WAD*,
New York, The
Typophiles, 1947.
Goudy, F. W. *The Capitals
from the Trajan Column,*
New York 1936.
*The Alphabet and
Elements of Lettering,*
New York 1963.
Gray, N. *Lettering on
Buildings,* London 1960.
Lettering as Drawing,
London 1971.
Massin *Letter and Image,*
London 1970.
Reiner, I. and H. *Lettering in
Book Art,* Zollikofer, St
Gall, Switzerland, 1948.
Steinberg, S. *The Labyrinth,*
London 1960.
The New World, London
1965.
Zapf, H. *About Alphabets.
Some Marginal Notes on
Type Design,* New York,
The Typophiles, 1960.
Excellent illustrations of
Zapf's working drawings.

Historical

Fairbank, A. and Wolpe, B.

Renaissance Handwriting,
London 1960.
Harvard, S. *Ornamental
Initials: the Woodcut Initials
of Christopher Plantin,* New
York, the American
Friends of the Plantin-
Moretus Museum, 1974.
Ogg, O. *The 26 Letters,* New
York 1964.
Marzoli, C. *Calligraphy
1535–1885,* Milan, La
Bibliofila, 1962. A
superbly edited and
illustrated catalogue of a
collection of writing-
books, with an
introduction by Stanley
Morison.
Wardrop, J. *The Script of
Humanism,* Oxford 1963.

Instructional

Chappell, W. *The Anatomy of
Lettering,* New York 1935.
Fairbank, A. *A Handwriting
Manual,* London.
A Book of Scripts, London
1949.
Harvey, M. *Lettering Design,*
London 1975.
Johnston, E. *Writing and
Illuminating, and Lettering,*
London (21st impression)
1945.
Thompson, T. *The Script
Letter: its Form,
Construction and
Application,* New York
1965.
*The Journal of the Society for
Italic Handwriting.*
Membership Secretary:
D. F. Fell, 29 Coval Road,
East Sheen, London
SW14.

Anthologies and Catalogues

Degering, H. *Lettering,* 3rd
edn, London 1954.
The Portland Art
Association *Calligraphy:
The Golden Age & its
Modern Revival,* Portland,
Oregon, 1958.
Sotheby & Co. *A Fine
Collection of Calligraphic
Books and Manuscripts,*
London 1972.
Tschichold, J. *Schatzkammer
der Schreibkunst,* Basel 1945.
*Two Thousand Years of
Calligraphy,* Baltimore,
Maryland, 1965.

Monographs on individual artists

Dreyfus, J. *The Work of Jan
van Krimpen,* Haarlem
1952.
Hellwag, F. *Johannes Boehland,*
Berlin, Heintze &
Blanckertz, n.d.
Hölscher, E. *Anna Simons,*
Berlin, Heintze &
Blanckertz, n.d.
*Der Schrift- und Buchkünstler
Emil Rudolf Weiss,* Berlin,
Heintze & Blanckertz, n.d.
Rudolf von Larisch, Berlin,
Heintze & Blanckertz, n.d.
Lange, W. H. *Rudolf Koch, a
German Writing-Master,*
Berlin, Heintze &
Blanckertz, n.d.
Otto Hupp, Berlin, Heintze
& Blanckertz, n.d.
'Max Caflisch', article in *Der
Druckspiegel,* December
1957.
*Pen and Graver. Alphabets &
Pages of Calligraphy by
Hermann Zapf.* New York
1952.
Simons, A. *Edward Johnston
and English Lettering,*
Berlin, Heintze &
Blanckertz, n.d.
E. R. *Weiss.* Special number
of *Die zeitgemässe Schrift,*
Berlin, Heintze &
Blanckertz, October 1935.

5 LETTERS FOR PRINTING

The history of type design is
both important and
fascinating, and is easily
available in many books. One
of the most readable accounts
is still the Boston printer
D. B. Updike's two-volume
*Printing Types, their History,
Forms and Use,* first published
in 1922 and still available in a
revised edition from Oxford
University Press. It is a long
work, originally a series of
lectures, but profusely
illustrated and rewarding.
The best short account is
A. F. Johnson, *Type Designs,*
3rd edn, André Deutsch,
London 1966.
Both these are essential
reading for typographers.
Harry Carter's *A View of
Early Typography up to about
1600,* Oxford 1969, contains
the best recent account of
early typefounding and

printing practice, and early type design, with excellent illustrations; and Philip Gaskell's *A New Introduction to Bibliography*, Oxford 1972, while much wider in scope, contains first-rate summaries of every aspect of early book production, and is also very well illustrated.

General

Goudy, F. W. *Typologia, studies in Type Design & Type Making*, Berkeley 1940.
Zapf, H., *About Alphabets, some Marginal Notes on Type Design*, Typophile Chap Books XXXVII, New York 1960.

General: the Modern Movement

Rowland, K. *A History of the Modern Movement*, New York 1973.
Spencer, H. *Pioneers of Modern Typography*, London 1969.
McLean, R. *Jan Tschichold, Typographer*, London 1974.
Damase, J. *Revolution Typographique depuis Stéphane Mallarmé*. Galerie Motte, Geneva, Switzerland, 1966.
Hirschfeld-Mack, L. *The Bauhaus* (Foreword by Walter Gropius), London 1963.

Nomenclature

Thorp, J. 'Towards a nomenclature for letter forms', *The Monotype Recorder*, no. 240 (1931), and no. 246 (1932).
Gaskell, P. 'A nomenclature for the Letter-forms of Roman Type', *The Library*, 5th series, Vol. XXIX, no. 1, (1974), pp. 42–49.
BS 2961:1967. British Standards Institution 1967.
Hostettler, R. *The Printer's Terms*, 4th edn, London 1963.

Roman types

See also James Mosley, 'English Vernacular', *Motif*, 11 (1963); and James Mosley, 'Trajan Revived', and Berthold

Wolpe, 'Caslon Architectural', *Alphabet*, vol. 1 (1962).

Sans-serif

Updike says nothing, and Johnson very little about sans-serif types. See *The Monotype Recorder*, vol. 41, no. 3 (1958), special number on Eric Gill
Handover, P. M. 'Letters without Serifs', *Motif*, 6 (1961).
Harling, R. *The Letter Forms and Type Designs of Eric Gill*, Westerham 1976.
Megaw, D. 'Twentieth-century sans-serifs', *Typography*, 7 (1938).
For special information on Univers, see *Monotype Newsletter*, 80 (Dec. 1966).

Egyptians (Slab serif)

McLean, R. 'An Examination of Egyptians', *Alphabet & Image*, 1 (1946).
Handover, P. M. 'Black Serif', *Motif*, 12 (1964).

Script

Hutchings, R. S. *A Manual of Script Typefaces*, London and New York 1965.

Fat Face

Johnson, A. F. 'Fat Faces: their history, forms and use', *Alphabet and Image*, 5 (1947).

Ampersands

Goudy, F. W. 'Ands & Ampersands', *Typography*, 3 (1937).
Standard, P. 'The Ampersand – Sign of Continuity', *Signature*, 8 (1938).
Tschichold, J. *Formenwandlungen der Et-Zeichen* ('The development of the Ampersand'), Frankfurt-am-Main 1953.

6 METHODS OF COMPOSITION

McPherson, Michael *Electronic Textsetting, the Impact of Revolutions in Composition on Typography and Type Design*. This was

produced in 1979 as a graduate thesis in the Graphic Design Department of the Rhode Island School of Design, and I am grateful to the author for allowing me to see it. It contains excellent illustrations and a bibliography and will hopefully be published in the near future.

Seybold, J. W. *Fundamentals of Modern Photocomposition*, Seybold Publications, Inc., no. 21, 28128 Pacific Coast Highway, Malibu, California 90265, USA.

7 PAPER

British Standards Institution. Sectional List of British Standards SL22, *Printing and Stationery, Paper and Board.*
Clapperton, R. H. *Modern Papermaking*, 3rd edn, Oxford 1952.
Haemmerle, A. *Buntpapier* ('Decorated Paper'), Munich 1961.
Hunter, D. *Papermaking through Eighteen Centuries*, New York 1930. *Papermaking. The History and Technique of an Ancient Craft*, 3rd edn, London 1957. *My life in Paper.*
Overton, J. *A Bibliography of Paper and Paper-making*, Cambridge University Press, for the National Book League, 1955.
Paper, its Making, Merchanting and Usage. The Paper Merchants Text Book, The National Association of Paper Merchants, London 1965. Revised edition, 1978.
Paper and Board Manufacture. A General Account of its History, Processes and Applications, Technical Division, British Paper and Board Industry Federation, London 1978. I have drawn heavily on both editions of this book for the technical information in this chapter and am very grateful to the Federation for permission to do so.

Paper Making. A General Account of its History, Processes and Applications, Technical Section of the British Paper & Board Makers' Association (Inc.), London 1965.

8 CAST-OFF AND LAYOUT

For useful guidance on layouts, copy preparation and production, see: David J. Plumb, *Design & Print Production Workbook*, Workbook Publications, 1978, Springfield Road, Teddington, Middlesex, TW11 9AP.

Craig, J. *Designing with Type*, New York 1971. *Production for the Graphic Designer*, New York 1974.
Tschichold, J. *Typographische Entwurfstechnik* ('How to draw layouts'), Stuttgart 1932. (English translation by R. McLean not yet published.)
For detailed guidance on style and copy preparation see the valuable articles on 'Putting on the style' in Monotype *Newsletters* 71–80 and 88, Monotype Corporation, October 1961 – February 1971; and the authorities mentioned for Chapter 2.

9 BOOK DESIGN

Bennett, P. A. (ed.) *Postscripts on Dwiggins*, 2 vols., Typophile Chap Book no. 25, New York 1960.
Hochuli, J. *Detail in Typography* (transl. R. McLean), Agfa Compugraphic 1987.
Hochuli, J. *Designing Books* (transl. R. McLean), Agfa Compugraphic 1990.
Morison, S. *First Principles of Typography*, Cambridge 1950.
Osley, A. S. (ed.) *Calligraphy and Palaeography*, London 1965.

Penrose Annual, 63, London 1970 (articles: Nicolas Jenkins, 'Redesign Book Design' and Alan Bartram, 'The Grid: an aid or an end?').
Reiner, I, *Modern and Historical Typography*, St Gall, Switzerland, 1946.
Williamson, H. *Methods of Book Design*, 3rd edn, London 1983.
Tschichold, J. *Asymmetric Typography* (transl. R. McLean), London and Toronto 1967.

10 THE PARTS OF A BOOK

Alphabet & Image, 8, London 1948.
British Standard 3700: 1976, *The Preparation of Indexes to Books, Periodicals and Other Publications*.
Carey, G. V. *Making an Index*, Cambridge 1951.
Dwiggins, W. A. *MSS by WAD*, New York 1947.
Evans, H. *Editing and Design*, Book Two, *Handling Newspaper Text*, London 1974. See particularly the discussion and illustrations of unjustified setting, pp. 54–60.
Macdonald-Ross, M. and Waller, R. *Open University Texts: Criticisms and alternatives*, The Open University, 1975.
MLA Handbook for Writers of Research Papers, Theses and Dissertations, New York 1977.
Newdigate, B. *The Art of the Book*, London 1938.
Simon, O. *Introduction to Typography*, London 1963.
Tschichold, J. *Designing Books*, New York 1951.
Warde, B. *The Crystal Goblet*, London 1955.
Williamson, H. *Methods of Book Design*, 3rd edn, London 1983.
Wilson, A. *The Design of Books*, New York and London 1967.

11 JOBBING TYPOGRAPHY

Barman, C. 'Timetable Typography', *Typography*, 5 (1938).
British Standard DD52: 1977 *Recommendations for the Presentation of Tables, Graphs, and Charts*, 'Draft for Development', with many useful ideas, from British Standards Institution.
Der Briefbogen in der Welt, J. W. Zanders, 1958 and 1968. No text but collections of interesting letter headings from designers in many countries.
Design of Forms in Government Departments, 3rd edn, HMSO, London 1972.
Lewis, R. A. and Herdeg, W. 'Annual Reports', *Graphis* (1971).
Moran, J. *Stanley Morison*, London 1971.
Spencer, H. *Design in Business Printing*, London 1952.
Updike, D. B. *In the Day's Work*, Cambridge, Mass., 1924.

12 NEWSPAPER AND MAGAZINE TYPOGRAPHY

Newspaper design

Arnold, E. C. *Modern Newspaper Design*, New York 1969.
Evans, H. *Editing and Design*, Heinemann, London: Book 1, *Newsman's English* (1973); Book 2, *Handling Newspaper Text* (1974); Book 3, *News Headlines*; Book 4, *Pictures on a page* (1978); Book 5, *Newspaper Design* (1973).
Hutt, A. *Newspaper Design*, 2nd edn, London 1967.

Magazine design

Hurlburt, A. *Publication Design*, New York 1971.
McLean, R. *Magazine Design*, London 1969.

Index